For John

Writers' Letters

Jane Austen to Chinua Achebe

Michael Bird
Orlando Bird

FRANCES
LINCOLN

Contents

5 'Everything is going badly' when troubles come

6 'Herewith a story' literary business

7 'Like an old war horse' voice of experience

8 'That's all' leave taking

Introduction

You don't have to be a great writer to be a great letter-writer, but it helps. Lord Byron loved letters – 'the only device', he said, 'for combining solitude with good company'. As a practitioner, he was a natural: chatty, charming, opinionated, outrageous (and, it must be said, fairly pleased with himself about all this). In April 1821, he writes to his friend and publisher, John Murray ('Moray'), from Ravenna, north-east Italy, where he's been shacked up with Countess Teresa Guiccioli. Life is good: the poems are coming along nicely, and he's finding plenty of time to drink, hunt and serve as an honorary *capo* in the Carbonari, a rebel group attempting to overturn Austrian rule. But there is something else on his mind. John Keats – whose poetry he'd been gleefully rude about – is dead. And the word from Byron's friend, Percy Bysshe Shelley, is that he was killed by a bad review. Can it be true?

Byron goes on to consider the quality of Keats's work ('spoilt by Cockneyfying and Suburbing') and the emerging literary form of the hatchet job ('I know by experience that a savage review is Hemlock to a suckling author'). He indulges in some casual self-mythologizing (his response to bad press, he claims, was to drink 'three bottles of claret') and even shows a little contrition (he edits himself to say that he's 'very sorry', rather than just 'sorry', to hear about the death of his rival). Today, this short letter conjures up particular moments in both English literature and Italian politics, while still striking an intimate, confiding note: you almost sense Byron leaning in as he gossips, throws down assertions, checks himself, appeals for his friend's opinion. Two hundred years later, the letter, as a literary form, has undoubtedly seen better days – but the best ones remain as fresh as ever.

This book contains ninety-four letters by as many writers – novelists, poets, essayists, playwrights. The earliest, composed in 1499, comes from the Dutch humanist Erasmus, who is trying to persuade Prince Henry of England (the future Henry VIII) that his gift to him – a poem – is worth more than the 'jewels and gold' offered by less inspired but more solvent visitors. One of the most recent, also dealing with literary business, is by Angela Carter, who's submitting a new story to Bill Buford, the editor of *Granta* magazine, and wants to alert him to the 'obsession with wolf children' running through her work. Elsewhere, we travel to Elizabethan London and 1980s Lagos, via Chile and China, Austria and Australia. We have ranged widely, though some of our choices *en route* were made for us by byzantine questions of copyright. The upside of this was that we had to dig deeper, which led us to letters by writers who should be much better known today. There's Gabriela Mistral, the first Latin-American winner of the Nobel Prize in Literature – or Akiko Yosano, one of the boldest and most inventive Japanese poets of the twentieth century, but little-read in the West. We hope that some of these letters will mark the beginning of your acquaintance with their authors.

Just about all the big moments in life are here. The radical writer Mary Wollstonecraft tells her husband, William Godwin, that she wishes she 'had a novel' to help her pass the time as she goes into labour. The bibulous American poet John Berryman, in a rare moment of domestic calm, is having a second shot at fatherhood ('The baby is up on all fours, seeking what she may devour'). Anton Chekhov writes to an old friend, reminiscing about the past and making plans for the future, even as his battle with tuberculosis reaches endgame.

Letters are primarily about the stuff of day-to-day life, and even the greatest writers have to deal with that. And so, in one of literary history's most enduring themes, we also have Paul Verlaine – celebrated poet, physical wreck – reminding Gustave Kahn, editor of *La Vogue* magazine, that he still hasn't been paid for a poem published a year ago ('O do it without delay!'). Jane Austen writes to her sister, Cassandra, giving a snapshot of middle-class Regency life – coach journeys, roast fowl, trips to the theatre – spiked with occasional asides about the tedious men she has to spend time with. Alfred Tennyson, who once claimed he'd rather 'kill a pig' than write a letter, clearly sometimes made exceptions: in these pages, we find him complaining to the journalist William Cox Bennett – about all the letters people have been sending him since he became poet laureate in 1850.

Besides their subject matter, does it make any difference that these are letters by writers? In short: yes. One reason for this is that all writing, however baldly utilitarian, is a performance, and writers know this better than anyone else. They are never truly off-duty. We've all at some point received a dauntingly funny, sharp, well-observed message – probably an email rather than a letter – and agonized over how to respond, even felt some competitive urge to go one better. Writers feel this pressure all the time. This may be what Samuel Johnson – that voluble colossus of eighteenth-century literature, living through a golden age of letter-writing – was alluding to when he confessed that 'I find myself very unwilling to take up a pen only to tell my friends that I am well'. He contended that 'a short letter to a distant friend is, in my opinion, an insult like that of a slight bow or cursory salutation.' Several centuries later, Samuel Beckett, an admirer of Johnson, expresses a similar anxiety (one that he more or less trademarked) when he replies to Harold Pinter, who has recently sent him a copy of his new play *The Homecoming*: 'Wish I could tell you better how I feel about it ... But too tired and stupid and have been waiting too long to be less so.'

Then there's the fact that to talk about the history of the letter is to talk about the history of literature: the two have been entwined for millennia. The ancient Romans had epistolary poems – Horace's *Epistles*, Ovid's *Heroides*. Nearly all of Shakespeare's plays contain letters. In the eighteenth century, the letter was instrumental in the development of the novel, allowing works like Fanny Burney's *Evelina* (1778) to place a fresh emphasis on the inner, subjective lives of their characters. (Nothing in Burney's novel, however, compares with the extraordinary, harrowing letter she writes to her sister in 1812, describing the experience of undergoing a mastectomy without anaesthetic.)

Unlike musicians or painters or actors, when writers write letters they are engaging with *their* tradition.

As a category, 'literary correspondence' sounds vague, up there with 'literary fiction' or 'intelligent dance music'. But how else to describe James Joyce's 'apology' to his patron, Harriet Shaw Weaver, in 1922? He is supposed to be finishing *Ulysses*; she knows that he's been spending her money on all-night benders with the artist–writer Wyndham Lewis and Robert McAlmon (a boozy dilettante of the kind often found crashing around on the fringes of literary life in the early twentieth century). Joyce, rather than just saying sorry, writes four pages, at once accepting and denying the charge, abasing himself ('My head is full of pebbles'), and questioning Weaver's interpretation of events. By turns delightful, bewildering and enraging, it is, in its way, a work of art – a virtuosic exercise in navigating multiple perspectives (like *Ulysses*, in fact). Which isn't to say that Joyce, for all his loquacious charm, deserves to be let off the hook.

In other letters, it's in a single phrase – some flash of perception, some finely tuned cadence – that you detect the hand of a writer. Charlotte Brontë, working as a teacher in Brussels, rages to her brother, Branwell, about the oppressively even-tempered Belgians: 'Nobody ever gets into a passion here – such a thing is not known – the phlegm that thickens their blood is too gluey to boil.' In some of his correspondence, Philip Larkin reached a pitch of tedium unrivalled in English literature ('The pegs that were put in the wall in April are rusting: I've never known anything like it,' he once whined to his mother at the age of thirty-four). But in the letter to his girlfriend Monica Jones included here, he gives a quiet, luminous, hazy beauty to an everyday summer scene: 'The weather was hot and splendid, & the riverside deserted except for a horse-drawn barge … I saw something I imagined to be a magpie, heard waterrats clopping in & out of the shallows.'

In bookshops and libraries, such correspondence is often shelved alongside literary biography – 'entertaining and nice to have around', in Barbara Everett's phrase, but entirely separate from the work. Yet even the most vigilant patrollers of the art–life divide must concede that the two things are different. Biographies, while offering the facts of a writer's life – and, fair enough, a bit of juicy speculation – have been written by someone else. Letters are the real thing. Of course, they don't provide the key to a writer's work – what does? – but they can widen or sharpen or usefully complicate our understanding of where it came from.

Some give an insight into the writing process. A young Charles Dickens, juggling too many commitments as a journalist and fledgling author, scribbles a note to his fiancée Catherine Hogarth, the daughter of his boss at the *Evening Chronicle*. He can't see her tonight: 'You know I have told you that my composition is peculiar; I can never write with effect … until I have got my steam up, or in other words until I have become so excited with my subject that I can't leave off.' On one level, this is just a high-flown excuse for letting Catherine down, but these manic bursts of energy were a recurring feature of Dickens's working rhythm, and you feel them in the ebb and flow of his prose. Elsewhere, the voice of the letters anticipates the literary voice. In 1946, Norman Mailer writes to his doting mother and father from occupied Japan, where he has been serving as an army cook since the end of the Second World War. He blusters away about his plans for 'the novel' (which would turn out to be *The Naked and the Dead*), asking his parents not a single question about themselves. He's only twenty-three, but the street-smart, mercurial idiolect feels practically fully formed (as does the rampaging egomania: 'I know you always get a kick out of me when I'm in the throes of creation').

It's not just in letters from the big personalities that we find echoes and glimmers of the work. In 1919, Franz Kafka – right at the other end of the Myers-Briggs spectrum – writes to his father. 'I have lived the high life ... and for this you have never demanded gratitude,' he says. 'But you expect some recognition, some sign of sympathy; instead of which I have always crawled away from you.' There are already many ways to read Kafka's 1915 novella, *Metamorphosis*, in which the 'monstrous insect' Gregor Samsa is pelted with apples by his father, but these lines surely provide another. Even in the letters of T.S. Eliot, who insisted that all art was 'impersonal', there are intimations of the poetry that was to come. Following a breakdown in his early thirties, Eliot is in Margate on doctor's orders, drafting the first fragments of what will become *The Waste Land*, when he writes to his friend Sydney Schiff: 'I have done this while sitting in a shelter on the front – as I am out all day except when taking rest. But I have written only some 50 lines, and have read nothing, literally.' In the poem, his hours on the seafront become 'On Margate Sands./I can connect/Nothing with nothing.' Other letters shed light on the practical side of a work's genesis. Edgar Allan Poe, hoping to capitalize on the surprise success of his poem 'The Raven', suggests some shrewd amendments for the next newspaper syndication. And D.H. Lawrence, provoked to fresh fury by United States customs' seizure of books by the sixteenth-century author François Rabelais, asks the Philadelphia bookseller Harold Mason if he can help to smuggle unexpurgated copies of *Lady Chatterley's Lover* into the US.

Many of the letters here give a strong sense of the social and artistic networks from which they emerged. Some of these have been characterized by high ideals, solidarity and intellectual exchange. 'Yes I am radical,' declares Victor Hugo, straight off the bat, in his letter to Alphonse de Lamartine. 'From all points of view, I understand, I want and I call for more.' Gustave Flaubert, writing to George Sand, offers her an axiom: 'Hatred of the Bourgeois is the Beginning of Virtue'. Even as the Nazis deprive him of his (already precarious) livelihood, Walter Benjamin, the visionary German-Jewish writer, wants to tell his friend Gershom Scholem all about his 'new theory of language'. That said, a mean-spirited, self-interested side to literary life can't be concealed: the sixteenth-century Chinese poet Tang Yin grumbles to a friend about 'upstart' young writers, and Jonathan Swift – that great iconoclast – can be seen ingratiating his way into the Hanoverian court, only to throw a tantrum when he doesn't get what he wants.

Generally, women come out of this better than men, who tend to want to cut anyone who looks remotely like a rival down to size (think of Byron and 'poor John Keats'). For instance, we have George Eliot and Harriet Beecher Stowe, two of the most famous women writers of the nineteenth century, offering each other moral support and constructive criticism. A theme that runs throughout this book is the importance of the letter as a platform for women – who, before the twentieth century, generally had few other outlets. Eliot, Austen, Brontë and Mary Shelley all had to publish their work anonymously or pseudonymously. In their letters, they are able to speak on their own terms (and under their own names). There's a striking contrast, in fact, between Shelley's letters, which are passionate and candid, and the ones she receives from her future husband – who, with a public image to uphold, can be touchy and self-justifying. (Elizabeth Barrett, likewise, proves to be the more nimble correspondent in her high-brow flirtation-by-letter with Robert Browning.) Even in 1955, the letter is still useful for Zora Neale Hurston. The controversial African-American novelist has fallen out with many of her old friends from the Harlem Renaissance, and her work is increasingly sidelined, but she's still stirring up debate – on the letters page of the *Orlando Sentinel*.

It's not all about writing, though. There's a lot of living going on in this book too. Several of the authors here, who would never have imagined spending their entire careers at a desk, had such outlandish experiences that you wonder why they ever felt the need to turn to fiction. Miguel de Cervantes was captured by pirates. Ben Jonson found himself tangled up with the Gunpowder plotters. By the time Daniel Defoe got round to writing the books for which he is remembered today, he'd built up a business, lost it, gone to prison, spied for England and more or less single-handedly invented opinion journalism (for better or worse). An argument could be made that, since about 1800, the literary life has become steadily more humdrum. But there are exceptions: Arthur Rimbaud, who finished his writing career early, then became a soldier, joined the circus and, finally, settled into arms dealing; or Gabriele D'Annunzio, the gaudy Italian poet, aviator and proto-fascist, who, between 1919 and 1920, ruled over the Adriatic city of Fiume, where the founding principle of the state was music.

Elsewhere, writers bear witness to epoch-defining events. Shortly after the end of the war in Europe in May 1945, the American soldier Kurt Vonnegut is in a Red Cross camp. He sends a long letter to his parents, who haven't heard from him for months and are almost certainly expecting the worst. In that time he has been taken prisoner by the Germans, bombed (accidentally) by the RAF, survived the firebombing of Dresden and been liberated by the Russians. Does he need to be a writer to tell this story? Obviously not – though the matter-of-fact style that he would deploy more than twenty years later in his novel *Slaughterhouse-Five* does help to ground these shattering historical moments, these almost unimaginable traumas, in human experience.

Samuel Johnson observed that 'no class of the human species requires more to be cautioned against … anticipation of happiness, than those that aspire to the name of authors.' Over the years, the literary business has had an unusually high rate of attrition.

There's a fair amount of pain spread across these pages (of the ninety-four writers here, seven took their own lives). But even in the darkest moments, the letter serves to provide reassurance. In 1919, Katherine Mansfield writes to her husband, John Middleton Murry. She is dying of tuberculosis and, though she doesn't know when the final day will come, she knows it will be sooner rather than later. It is a beautiful letter – heartbreaking but totally unsentimental: 'Don't let anybody mourn me. It can't be helped. I think you ought to marry again and have children. If you do give your little girl the pearl ring. Yours forever.'

In 2020, there was talk that letter-writing might make a comeback – aided, unpromisingly, by hashtags like #PandemicPenPals. This doesn't yet appear to have happened. We have no idea what collections of literary correspondence – collections of any correspondence – will look like in, say, a hundred years' time. But the flotsam and jetsam of day-to-day life deserve to live on; readers will still want to get behind the official stories. The final letter in this collection is by Patrick White, the tetchy Australian novelist (and Nobel Prize-winner). A librarian has asked him for some of his papers, and he's not playing ball. He destroys them, he says, and tells his friends to do the same with his letters. 'If there is anything of importance' in him, he adds, rather piously, it will be in his books. But it seems he didn't believe that, not really. He left plenty of papers behind.

Orlando Bird
London, March 2021

A note on the text

Each letter is presented in the form of a reproduction of one or more pages from the author's original manuscript or typescript. This is accompanied by a short commentary, followed by a transcript or translation of either the complete text of the letter (if it is reasonably short) or selected excerpts, with omissions marked by ellipses in square brackets. For longer letters, the transcripts and translations include content that can be matched with the reproduction on the facing page as well as text from other parts of the letter. With a few exceptions, such as letters from John Donne and Ben Jonson, who wrote before English orthography had become standardized, we have retained idiosyncratic spellings and unconventional or absent punctuation, with minimal editorial interpolations in square brackets. Published sources for existing translations and credits for new translations can be found on pages 222–3. We have grouped the letters into eight thematic chapters, within which (with one exception) they are arranged alphabetically by author surname. There is a chronological list of letters on pages 216–17.

Chapter 1

'Got my steam up'

Before They Were Famous

Bei Muthesius.
　　Berlin.
　　　Nikolassee.
　　　　Potsdamer Chaussee.
　　　　　49.

My dear Patience,
　　　I was very touched to get a card from you.
Its whiff of clean English Boyhood nearly gave me a stroke
and for nights I shant be able to sleep without three
orgasms.Berlin is the buggers daydream.There are 170 male
brothels under police control.I could say a lot about my
boy,a cross between a rugger hearty and Josephine Baker.
We should make D.H.Lawrence look rather blue.I am a mass
of bruises.Perhaps you can give me some news of Bill?
He is notlikely to write but I should like to know how
his health is.I am perfectly convinced tha disease is
psychological,and taking him to throat specialists a waste
of time and money .Perhaps a sanatorium life will be psych
ologically right but I doubt it.You are much more likely
to cure him than anyone else.
I am doing quite a lot of work.The German proletariat are
fine,but I dont like the others very much,so I spend most
of my time with Juvenile Delinquents.The conception of
England may be illustrated by the following story which
I read in a paper called 'The Third Sex'.The hero of the
story who writes in diary form says that his friend has
left him.He is Desolate.He will avenge himself by taking
another.A few days later he finds him.He is an Englishman,
athletic,rich,a lord.He is very good and doesnt ask for
anything but fills my room with flowers.A few days later.
He wants to possess me,but I wont as I love him too much.
Then the Englishman has to go to England,whence he sends
a ring on which is written. My only happiness is to know
your heart'At this point there is a footnote to the story
which saysV 'Der Englander hat immer Geschmack'ie Thax
TheEnglishman always has taste.
　　　After the 1st I am moving to live in a slum.My address is
　　　　bei Ginther
　　　　Berlin
　　　　　Hallescher Tor
　　　　　　Furbringer Strasse
　　　　　　　8.

Please write some time

　　　　　　love

W.H. Auden (1907–73) to Patience McElwee
31 December 1928

The twenty-one-year-old Wystan Auden has finished his English degree at Oxford, found his voice as a poet and, with an allowance from his doctor father, is spending a gap year in Berlin. Though he's long been aware of his sexuality, he has recently become engaged. Nothing has prepared him for the sexual freedom and self-realization he's finding in Berlin, during the city's brief, wild renaissance between the aftermath of the First World War and the Hitler era. It is, he writes to Patience McElwee, wife of his university friend William, 'the buggers daydream'.

A postcard from Patience, presumably bearing a teasingly conventional picture of 'clean English Boyhood', triggers a high-spirited riff on orgasms, brothels and Auden's Berlin 'boy', whom he compares to Josephine Baker, the American-born celebrity of Parisian cabaret, whose stage act was notoriously erotic. Describing some gay fiction he's been reading, Auden shifts from third person to first ('he finds him', 'he fills my room') – the kind of unconsciously revealing slip made famous by Freud (another recent, liberating discovery).

Auden's hints at the depravity of his Berlin life are – as Patience probably guesses – not the whole truth. In the end, he lets almost nothing interfere with his writing. He is doing 'quite a lot of work' on a poetic drama, *Paid on Both Sides: A Charade*, which he plans to submit to T.S. Eliot for publication in *The Criterion*. Eliot has praised Auden's student poetry; in 1930 he will publish *Paid on Both Sides* and, as editor at Faber & Faber, the debut collection, *Poems*, that will make Auden's name.

My dear Patience,

I was very touched to get a card from you. Its whiff of clean English Boyhood nearly gave me a stroke and for nights I shant be able to sleep without three orgasms. Berlin is the buggers daydream. There are 170 male brothels under police control. I could say a lot about my boy, a cross between a rugger hearty and Josephine Baker. We should make D.H. Lawrence look rather blue. I am a mass of bruises. Perhaps you can give me some news of Bill? […]

I am doing quite a lot of work. The German proletariat are fine, but I don't like the others very much, so I spend most of my time with Juvenile Delinquents. The German conception of England may be illustrated by the following story which I read in a paper called 'The Third Sex'. The hero of the story who writes in diary form says that his friend has left him. He is Desolate. He will avenge himself by taking another. A few days later he finds him. He is an Englishman, athletic, rich, a lord. He is very good and doesnt ask for anything but fills my room with flowers. A few days later. He wants to possess me, but I wont as I love him too much […]

After the 1st I am moving to live in a slum […]

love

Wystan.

c/o milward
RFD 1,
Chepachet, R.I.
26 June '63

Dear Allen & Isabella –

Bless you both for yr good letters.
Petrinelli are doing an anthology, so the
first appearance of that Song for you
may be in Italian; I haven't decided.
Yr ₱, then abt. the Songs delighted me,
it was so characteristic. Of course I am
wild to done & move on. I don't write
these damned things willingly, you know.
Each one takes me by the throat. I've
vowed 100 times: never again. So I
stall one, for hours, days, weeks;
then I've had it. I figure a few more
months or years will see the poem
through.
        Isabella I'm glad you don't
despise Rosy's boy and were kind to

John Berryman (1914–72) to Allen Tate and Isabella Gardner
26 June 1963

Fame came late to the American poet John Berryman. It wasn't that he hadn't wanted it. When Robert Frost died, he was desperate to know, 'Who's number one?' But for years he had been, at best, a competent apprentice – too obviously indebted to his two great heroes, William Shakespeare and W.B. Yeats (he used the payment for his 1942 *Poems*, a cheque for 50 cents, as a bookmark). Meanwhile, despite a decent academic career, his life was a mess – a grimy patchwork of alcoholism, depression and adultery. Then, shortly after turning forty, he started working on *The Dream Songs*, a series of semi-autobiographical poems combining delicate patterning, fragmentary syntax, pungent slang, scholarly allusion and raucous humour. Though uneven – sometimes impenetrable – they were unlike anything else in American literature.

Berryman is nearing the end of the first sequence, made up of seventy-seven poems, when he writes to his friends Allen Tate and Isabella Gardner – both poets, and leading lights of literary bohemia in Minneapolis – who had read a few samples. Tate, a loyal supporter, was unconvinced. But Berryman takes it in his stride, claiming that he isn't surprised. And anyway, he doesn't 'write these damned things willingly'. He also describes his new-found life of domesticity. After two failed marriages, he's settled with his third wife, Kate Donahue, with whom he has recently had a daughter, and is teaching at Brown University in Rhode Island.

77 Dream Songs appeared in 1964. It was a triumph, winning Berryman a Pulitzer Prize the following year. The second instalment, *His Toy, His Dream, His Rest* (1969), comprising the remaining 308 poems, cemented his reputation. But this wasn't enough to keep his demons at bay, the most destructive of which – the suicide of his father when he was a boy – haunts the *Songs* from start to finish.

. . . .

Dear Allen & Isabella –

Bless you both for yr good letters. Feltrinelli are doing an anthology, so the first appearance of that Song for you may be in Italian; I haven't decided. Yr [*scribble*], Allen, ab[ou]t the Songs delighted me, it was so characteristic. Of course I am wild to be done & move on. I don't write these damned things willingly, you know. Each one takes me by the throat. I've vowed 100 times: never again. So I stall one, for hours, days, weeks; then I've had it. I figure a few more months or years will see the poem through [...]

The baby is up on all fours, seeking what she may devour. It is so hot during the day we go under our falls three times, sometimes taking her. Do come try it. We also plan at least one Cape [Cod] trip – K's never been – & will pay our respects if we may on you & the lovely Wilsons [...]

I've been working here – on the poem, a review for the lousy Times, correspondence, a new book – and my papers (with no study) are in a tangle.

Love,

John

Monday, September 11, 1934.

My dear Louise:

I was so glad to hear from you, and I think you are a master of discreet and tactful criticism. Of course I don't agree with you entirely — but you have actually moved me to the point of making some changes — notably in my addition of small numbers. Margaret was very pleased to have the copy of your brother's article; I read it myself twice, exercising great concentration, but I'm sorry to say I still don't understand all of it. I got the theory, all right, but the equations, etc., puzzle me completely. Under Margaret's general supervision I've been reading various books on art — and I wonder if you've ever run across any of Wilenski? — particularly the Modern Movement in Art. He's a very cranky man and irritating — but I think he's awfully good and he makes one want to attempt classification even half so good and precise for poetry or writing in general. And if you'd enjoy seeing the Greeks completely exposed, as I do, read his book on sculpture —

When are you coming to New York? It must be pretty soon now, and I'm getting ready to receive you suitably. You must see me for more than a "lunch", — can't you? or are you going to be awfully busy? I should like to have you meet Margaret and I want to see you for a long time. You can come and stay with me any time you want to — I know that's an awful form of invitation, but I don't know your plans just now — but I have plenty of room and I'm all alone. Charles Street goes off Greenwich Avenue, between 11th and 10th Streets, and it's really very easy to find — just a couple of blocks off 5th Avenue. My telephone number is Chelsea 2-4717.

Jane Bryant is about to begin taking her pre-med courses — she is still being psycho-analyzed, and the other day she told me, to my great surprise and embarrassment, that I have a "positive" effect on her. I don't know what that means, but it sounds quite favorable I think. I am planning to take a course in either Physiology or Anatomy, — the latter, I guess, at Columbia. I think it will be very valuable in my business .... as undoubtedly psychology will be in yours. I don't really disapprove of it, Louise, — I distrust of pure psychology, it's the applied sort that I think is useless and somewhat indecent. I'm also busy on an enormous amount of sort of bit-or-miss reading, everything around — but I find it awfully hard to get books in New York. The Public Library scares the wits out of me, and the branch down here is just as nasty in a petty way, besides having so books to speak of. I hope to work my way very thoroughly through 19th century

Elizabeth Bishop (1911–79) to Louise Bradley
11 September 1934

Poetry, art history, short stories, Italian food ... twenty-three and living for the first time in New York, Elizabeth Bishop races through the experiences she's looking forward to sharing with Louise Bradley when her friend visits. She's also 'puttering around' with poems, 'little pearls of obscurity', that she offers to send Bradley in exchange for her stories. Bishop was encouraged in her writing by Marianne Moore, who taught her at Vassar College. She would publish her first collection, *North and South*, in 1946.

My dear Louise:

I was so glad to hear from you, and I think you are a master of discreet and tactful criticism. Of course I don't agree with you entirely – but you have actually moved me to the point of making some changes [...] I've been reading various books on art – and I wonder if you've ever run across any of *Wilenski*? – particularly *The Modern Movement in Art*. He's a very cranky man and irritating – but I think he's awfully good and he makes one want to attempt classifications even half so good and precise for poetry or writing in general [...]

When are you coming to New York? It must be pretty soon now, and I'm getting ready to receive you suitably [...]

I'm also doing an amazing amount of sort of hit-or-miss reading [...] I hope to work my way very *thoroughly* through 17th century poetry [...] I'm also puttering around as usual with a dozen or so poems none of which makes any sense, but on which I am sure my life depends [...]

Would you be so kind and courageous as to send me, or bring me, some more stories? I shall send you some poems if you will – *there* – and I'm sure you will feel quite rewarded by my little pearls of obscurity! –

It is such a nice day. I've just been down to the Italian market buying the romantic things: pomegranates and *scatoni* – at least that's the way I imagine it's spelt. Have you ever had it? An Italian squash – narrow, and small and green and white striped, very nice to look at and very delicious, a delicate flavor. I am getting awfully educated about out of the ordinary vegetables, or so I think, and by cultivating the family who run this little market I hope to learn a lot about Italian cooking. This morning the daughter ran up and popped an Italian potatoe cake, scorching hot, into my mouth – very crisp on the outside and soft on the inside, with garlic and parsley and other savoury things [...]

The man whose stories I liked so much is *William Saroyan*. His book is coming out soon – 'The Daring Young Man on the Flying Trapeze', and I really recommend it to you most highly [...]

I'm looking forward to seeing you –

With lots of love,

Elizabeth.

Brussels May 1st 1843

Dear B

I hear you have written a letter to me;
this letter however as usual I have never received
which I am exceedingly sorry for, as I have
wished very much to hear from you – are you
sure that you put the right address and that you
paid the English postage 1/6 without that, letters
are never ~~sent~~ forwarded. I heard from Papa a
day or two since – all appears to be going on rea
sonably well at home – I grieve only that ~~Emily~~ Papa is
so solitary but however you & Anne will soon be
returning for the holidays which will cheer the house
for a time – Are you in better health and spirits and
does Anne continue to be pretty well ? I under
stand Papa has been to see you – did he seem
cheerful and well ? Mind when you write to me
you answer these questions as I wish to know –
Also give me a detailed account as to how you
get on with your pupil and the rest of the family

Charlotte Brontë (1816–55) to Branwell Brontë
1 May 1843

In February 1842, the sisters Charlotte and Emily Brontë set off for Brussels, where they enrolled at the Pensionnat Héger school for girls, run by Zoë Héger. They hoped to learn the skills required to set up a school of their own in England. But then their aunt died, and by the end of the year they were back in Yorkshire.

The following year, Charlotte returned to the *pensionnat* by herself, this time to teach. She'd hated being a governess in England – but, as this vinegary letter to her brother Branwell shows, she didn't think much of Belgium either. Branwell was a wild child – an alcoholic and opium addict, he died aged thirty-one – but Charlotte felt she could be herself with him. Instinctively forthright, she was frustrated by the constraints imposed on women in 'polite' society, and has fun tearing into the taciturn Belgians. Yet she is holding something back too. While at the school she fell in love with Constantin Héger, the headmistress's clever, charismatic husband. Here she refers to the 'black Swan' with rather studied nonchalance, but, after leaving the school in 1844, she sent him a string of increasingly torrid letters – until Mme Héger intervened.

Literary acclaim followed, beginning with *Jane Eyre* (1847) and culminating in *Villette* (1853), the tale of a young Englishwoman who, while teaching at a Belgian school, falls in love with a male colleague, only for the devious headmistress to sabotage their relationship. Charlotte tried to stop the book being translated into French.

....

Dear B,

I hear you have written a letter to me; this letter however as usual I have never received which I am exceedingly sorry for, as I have wished very much to hear from you – are you sure that you put the right address and that you paid the English postage 1s/6 without that, letters are never forwarded [...]

I am very well and wag on as usual. I perceive however that I grow exceedingly misanthropic and sour – you will say this is no news [...] but the fact is the people here are no go whatsoever [...] I don't hate them – hatred would be too warm a feeling – They have no sensations themselves and they excite none – but one wearies from day to day of caring nothing, fearing nothing, liking nothing, hating nothing – being nothing, doing nothing [...] but don't think I ever scold or fly into a passion – if I spoke warmly, as warmly as I sometimes used to do at Roe-Head they would think me mad – nobody ever gets into a passion here – such a thing is not known – the phlegm that thickens their blood is too gluey to boil – they are very false in their relations with each other – but they rarely quarrel & friendship is a folly they are unacquainted with – The black Swan M. Héger is the sole veritable exception to this rule (for Madame, always cool & always reasoning is not quite an exception) but I rarely speak to M[onsieu]r now for not being a pupil I have little or nothing to do with him [...]

Madam,

Poets are such outré Beings, so much the children of way-ward Fancy and capricious whim, that I believe the world generally allows them a larger latitude in the rules of Propriety, than the sober sons of judgment and Prudence. — I mention this as an apology all at once for the liberties which a nameless Stranger has taken with you in the inclosed; and which he begs leave to present you with. — Whether it has poetical merit any way worthy of the Theme, I am not the fitchest judge: but it is the best my abilities can produce; and what to a good heart will perhaps be a superiour grace, it is equally sincere. —

The Scenery was nearly taken from real life; though I dare say, Madam, you don't recollect it for I believe you scarcely noticed the poetic Reveur, as he wandered by you. — I had roved out as Chance directed, on the favorite haunts of my Muse, the banks of Ayr; to view Nature in all the gayety of the vernal year. — The sun was flaming o'er the distant, western hills; not a breath stirred the crimson opening blossom, or the verdant spreading leaf. — 'Twas a golden moment for a poetic heart. — I listened the feathered Warblers pouring their harmony on every hand, with a congenial, kindred regard; and frequently turned out of my path lest I should disturb their little songs, or frighten them to another station. — "Surely," said I to myself,

Robert Burns (1759–96) to Wilhelmina Alexander
18 November 1786

What did Wilhelmina Alexander think when, four months after encountering a young neighbour on a woodland walk near the River Ayr, she received this letter? Burns enclosed a poem, in which, although he'd been trespassing on her brother's estate and the two hadn't even spoken, he rhapsodized about her 'charms':

> Her look was like the morning's eye,
> Her air like Nature's vernal smile ...

The poem goes on to imagine a simple rustic life, in which Burns will 'nightly to my bosom strain/The bonnie Lass o'Ballochmyle'. Anticipating Alexander's surprise and displeasure, he claims that poets can't be expected to follow the customary 'rules of Propriety'.

News may by now have reached Alexander that, following the publication of *Poems, Chiefly in the Scottish Dialect* in July, the 'outré' brother and former co-tenant of Gilbert Burns of Mossgiel Farm was being hailed as Scotland's brightest new poetic talent, as well as having fathered the twins recently born to a local girl, Jean Armour. She may have suspected that Burns's breathtakingly inappropriate letter and poem were insincere (in her early thirties – considered past marriageable age in eighteenth-century gentry circles – Alexander was not known for her looks). For whatever reason, she refused his request to include 'The Lass o'Ballochmyle' in the new edition of *Poems*. Burns was bitter and sarcastic; Alexander treasured this letter for the rest of her life.

Madam,

Poets are such outré Beings, so much the children of wayward Fancy and capricious Whim, that I believe the World generally allows them a larger latitude in the rules of Propriety, than the sober Sons of Judgment and Prudence. – I mention this as an apology all at once for the liberties which a nameless stranger has taken with you in the inclosed, and which he begs leave to present you with [...]

The Scenery was nearly taken from real life; though I dare say, Madam, you don't recollect it; for I believe you scarcely noticed the poetic Reveur, as he wandered by you. – I had roved out as Chance directed, on the favorite haunts of my Muse, the banks of Ayr; to view Nature in all the gayety of the vernal year. – The Sun was flaming o'er the distant western hills; not a breath stirred the crimson opening blossom, or the verdant spreading leaf. 'Twas a golden moment for a poetic heart. – I listened the feathered Warblers powring their harmony on every hand [...]

Such was the scene and such the hour, when in a corner of my Prospect I spyed one of the finest pieces of Nature's workmanship that ever crowned a poetic Landskip [...] What an hour of inspiration for a Poet! It would have raised plain, dull historic Prose to Metaphor and Measure!

The inclosed Song was the work of my return home: and perhaps but poorly answerd what might have been expected from such a scene. I am going to print a second Edition of my Poems, but cannot insert these verses without your permission [...]

A TASTE OF HONEY

A play by

Shelagh Delaney.

77 Duchy Rd.
Salford 6
Lancs.

Dear Miss Littlewood,   April 1958.

         along with this letter to you comes a play –
the first – I have written and I wondered if you would read it through
and send it back to me – because no matter what sort of theatrical
atrocity it might be it isn't valueless so far as I'm concerned.
         A fortnight ago I didn't know the
theatre existed but a young man, anxious to improve my mind,
took me along to the Opera House in Manchester & I came away
after the performance having suddenly realised that at last,
after nineteen years of life, I had discovered something that
means more to me than myself. I sat down on reaching home &
thought – the following day I bought a packet of paper & borrowed
an unbelievable typewriter which I still have great difficulty in
using – I set to and produced this little epic – don't ask me
why – I'm quite unqualified for anything like this. But at
least I finished the play and if, from among the markings
out, the typing errors and the spelling mistakes you can
gather a little sense from what I have written – or a little nonsense –
I should be extremely grateful for your criticism – though
I hate criticism of any kind.
         I want to write for the theatre –
but I know so very little about the theatre. I know nothing.
I have nothing – only a willingness to learn – and intelligence
         At the moment I seem to be caught
between a sort of dissatisfaction with myself & everything I'm
doing and an exasperated frustration at the thought of what I
am going to do – please can you help me? I don't really know
who you are or what you do – I just caught sight of your
name in the Deal Ham magistrates court proceedings – but please
help me – if you think I'm worth helping – I'm willing enough to
help myself.
         Yours sincerely
         Shelagh Delaney

Shelagh Delaney (1938–2011) to Joan Littlewood
April 1958

This letter launched Sheila Delaney as British theatre's new young star. It accompanied the script of her first play, *A Taste of Honey*. Dealing with poverty and aspiration, homosexuality and a mixed-race, teenage pregnancy, its taboo-busting realism instantly appealed to Joan Littlewood, director of the radical Theatre Workshop. A month after Delaney posted her package from Salford, *A Taste of Honey* opened on the London stage.

Though she writes from the heart ('enraptured frustration' captures something essential in teenage experience), Delaney's self-presentation as a wide-eyed ingénue – like her adoption in this letter of the Irish version of her name – is astutely pitched. In reality, she already loved the theatre and had been an usherette at Manchester Opera House, where she'd seen Samuel Beckett's *Waiting for Godot* in 1956. She did write *A Taste of Honey* in a fortnight, but recast much material from an unfinished novel. Delaney knew Littlewood was scouting for working-class talent and challenging official censorship (hence the magistrates' court summons for presenting a play that had not been licensed for performance). She also knew that – whatever Littlewood thought – she'd produced something original: *A Taste of Honey* was the first play to present British working-class life primarily through women's experience.

Dear Miss Littlewood,

along with this letter to you comes a play – the first I have written and I wondered if you would read it through and send it back to me – because no matter what sort of theatrical atrocity it might be it isn't valueless so far as I'm concerned.

A fortnight ago I didn't know the theatre existed but a young man, anxious to improve my mind, took me along to the Opera House in Manchester & I came away after the performance having suddenly realised that at last, after nineteen years of life, I had discovered something that means more to me than myself. I sat down on reaching home & thought – the following day I bought a packet of paper & borrowed an unbelievable typewriter which I still have great difficulty in using. I set to and produced this little epic – don't ask me why – I'm quite unqualified for anything like this. But at least I finished the play and if, from among the markings out, the typing errors and the spelling mistakes you can gather a little sense from what I have written – or a little nonsens – I should be extremely grateful for your criticism – though I hate criticism of any kind.

I want to write for the theatre but I know so very little about the theatre. I know nothing. I have nothing – only a willingness to learn – and intelligence

At the moment I seem to be caught between a sort of dissatisfaction with myself & everything I'm doing and an enraptured frustration at the thought of what I am going to do – please can you help me? I don't really know who you are or what you do – I just caught sight of your name in the West Ham magistrates court proceedings – but please help me – if you think I'm worth helping – I'm willing enough to help myself.

Yours sincerely
Shelagh Delaney

Furnivals Inn
　　Wednesday Evening

My dearest Kate

　　Macrone has urged me
most imperatively and
pressingly to "get on". I
have made considerable
progress in my "Newgate"
sketch, but the subject is
such a very difficult one
to do justice to, and I have
so much difficulty in
remembering the place, and
arranging my materials, that
I really have no alternative
but to remain at home
to-night, and "get on"
in good earnest. You know

Charles Dickens (1812–70) to Catherine Hogarth
25 November 1835

Throughout 1835 Charles Dickens kept up a punishing schedule as a political reporter and theatre reviewer. He also published entertaining topical sketches, which led to a job offer from George Hogarth, editor of the *Evening Chronicle*, whose nineteen-year-old daughter, Catherine, he was soon courting. November was a hectic month. Dickens was covering the Kettering by-election, where he described the intimidatory tactics of Conservative Party thugs to Catherine – 'a ruthless set of bloody-minded villains'. He was rushing back to London to file his copy, house-hunt for their future home and finish his first book, a collection of stories to be published by John Macrone as *Sketches by Boz*. On 5 November he spent a day in Newgate Prison, researching what he hoped would be a powerful new chapter for the book.

Almost three weeks later, with the Newgate piece still unfinished, Dickens writes to Catherine from his lodgings in Furnival's Inn, Holborn, to apologize that he won't be able to see her that evening. He'll have to work late, pressing on 'until I have got my steam up' – a brand new railway-era metaphor for creative energy, first recorded in 1832. Dickens entrusts his teenage brother and fellow lodger Fred with delivering the letter – a two-hour walk to Fulham – before, very possibly, getting up steam to write the harrowing passages in 'A Visit to Newgate', in which he imagines the night spent by a condemned man before his execution.

Dickens and Catherine married in April 1836. After twenty-two years of 'ill-sorted' life together and ten children, he would leave her for the young actress Ellen Ternan.

. . . .

My dearest Kate

Macrone has urged me most imperatively and pressingly to 'get on'. I have made considerable progress in my 'Newgate' sketch, but the subject is such a very difficult one to do justice to, and I have so much difficulty in remembering the place, and arranging my materials, that I really have no alternative but to remain at home to-night, and 'get on' in good earnest. You know I have frequently told you that my composition is peculiar; I never can write with effect – especially in the serious way – until I have got my steam up, or in other words until I have become so excited with my subject that I cannot leave off; and hoping to arrive at this state to-night, I have, after a great deal of combating with my wish to see you, arrived at the determination I have just announced – I hope to do a good deal

I will not do you the injustice to suppose that knowing my reason and my *motive* for exertion, *you* of all people will blame me one instant for my self-denial. You may be disappointed: – I would rather you would – at not seeing me; but you cannot feel vexed at my doing my best with the stake I have to play for – you and a home for both of us.

Write me by Fred and Believe me, my own love

Ever Yours most sincerely & aff[ectionatel]y

Charles Dickens

Ansd 6. Nov. 22 (T. S. Eliot)

THE ALBEMARLE HOTEL,
CLIFTONVILLE,
MARGATE.

TELEPHONE 117.

Friday night.

My dear Sydney

I am so sorry about the MSS – Vivien told me – but as you told me to keep it, and as I am always uneasy in the possession of other people's MSS, I had locked it up in my box at the Bank safes. I will get it out for you when I come up to town, and do hope you will not be grossly inconvenienced by the delay. It will not be very long now.

I hope that your being in

31.

T.S. Eliot (1888–1965) to Sydney Schiff
4 November 1921

Working as a clerk in a dungeon-like office at Lloyds Bank in London, his marriage under strain and his experimental verse unlikely to liberate him from the day job anytime soon, the young American poet T.S. Eliot suffered a nervous breakdown. In autumn 1921 he took three months' leave, decamping to the Albemarle Hotel in Margate on the Kent coast. Some of the time his wife, Vivien (or Vivienne), who was experiencing mental troubles of her own, stayed with him. Eliot walked the beaches, took up the mandolin and ensconced himself in a cavernous Victorian beach shelter to work on his new poem, a cinematic montage of voices and images.

He apologizes to his writer friend Sydney Schiff (pen-name Stephen Hudson) for not returning a manuscript of his (currently locked in a safe at the bank) and reports on progress with Part III of his poem. It evokes the disjunctive bleakness of modern London, intercut with flashbacks to a more poetic or meaningful past ('The pleasant whining of a mandoline') and containing a series of desultory sexual encounters, leading to a sense of disconnection and depression, until 'On Margate Sands./I can connect/ Nothing with nothing'. When *The Waste Land* was published in 1922, Schiff was among the first to congratulate Eliot. Vivien thanked him, explaining how the poem 'has become part of me (or I of it) this past year'.

My dear Sydney

I am so sorry about the MSS – Vivien told me – but as you told me to keep it, and as I am always uneasy in the possession of other people's MSS, I had locked it up in my box at the Bank safes. I will get it out for you when I come up to town, and do hope you will not be grossly inconvenienced by the delay. It will not be very long now [...]

I should have liked to hear from you, but of course did not expect to, knowing that you had much to do and bad health and worries. I have done a rough draft of part of part III, but do not know whether it will do, & must wait for Vivien's opinion as to whether it is printable. I have done this while sitting in a shelter on the front – as I am out all day except when taking rest. But I have written only some 50 lines, and have read nothing, literally – I sketch the people, after a fashion, and practise scales on the mandoline.

I rather dread being in town at all – one becomes dependent, too, on sea or mountains, which give some sense of security in which one relaxes – and hope to be only a day or two. I hope to have good news of you both from Vivienne – she tells me very little about her own health, inspite of my complaints. With best love to you and Violet

Yrs aff[ectionately],
Tom.

GREEN BANK HOTEL.
FALMOUTH.
10th May 1907.

My darling Mouse

This is a birth-day letter,
to wish you very many happy returns
of the day. I wish we could have
been all together, but we shall
meet again soon, & then we will
have treats. I have sent you two
picture-books, one about Brer
Rabbit, from Daddy, & one about
some other animals, from Mummy.
And we have sent you a boat,

painted red, with mast & sails, to
sail in the round pond by the
windmill — & Mummy has sent you
a boat-hook to catch it when it
comes to shore. Also Mummy has
sent you some sand-toys to play
in the sand with, and a card-game.

Have you heard about the
Toad? He was never taken prisoner
by brigands at all. It was all a
horrid low trick of his. He wrote
that letter himself — the letter saying
that a hundred pounds must be
put in the hollow tree. And he got
out of the window early one morning,
& went off to a town called Buggleton
& went to the Red Lion Hotel & there
he found a party that had just
motored down from London, &
while they were having breakfast he

Kenneth Grahame (1859–1932) to Alastair Grahame
10 May 1907

Kenneth Grahame was Secretary of the Bank of England when he began publishing children's stories of a new kind, in which – unlike Victorian classics such as Lewis Carroll's 'Alice' books – tales of adventure and fantasy unfold in everyday modern settings. *The Wind in the Willows* started life as bedtime stories for his son Alastair, or 'Mouse'.

Alastair was cast as the hero, in the guise of the impulsive Mr Toad. In this letter, Toad pretends to have been kidnapped, while scheming to collect the ransom he's persuaded his friends to deposit in a hollow tree. This heist didn't make it into the book, though the theft of a car that followed became a central episode. Still, who knows whether news of Toad's latest adventures consoled Alastair for the fact that his parents were neither with him nor with each other on his seventh birthday? Born prematurely with visual impairment, Alastair was idealized by his parents, who expected great things but packed him off to boarding school, where he was lonely and depressed. He died just before his twentieth birthday, after falling – or more likely jumping – under a train at Oxford station.

While Grahame's literary fame was growing, his distinguished financial career seemed to allow for plenty of time out. Before leaving for Cornwall in April 1907, he'd entertained the Prince of Wales's children at the Bank. In June, he received fan-mail from President Theodore Roosevelt, whose support would ensure that *The Wind in the Willows* found an American publisher. Toad's madcap escapades, in which he is repeatedly saved from disaster by loyal animal friends, became an enduring children's classic.

....

My darling Mouse

This is a birth-day letter, to wish you very many happy returns of the day. I wish we could have been all together, but we shall meet again soon, & then we will have *treats*. I have sent you two picture-books, one about Brer Rabbit, from Daddy, & one about some other animals, from Mummy. And we have sent you a boat, painted red, with mast & sails, to sail in the round pond by the windmill – & Mummy has sent you a boat-hook to catch it when it comes to shore. Also Mummy has sent you some sand-toys to play in the sand with, and a card-game.

Have you heard about the Toad? He was never taken prisoner by brigands at all. It was all a horrid low trick of his. He wrote that letter himself – the letter saying that a hundred pounds must be put in the hollow tree. And he got out of the window early one morning, & went off to a town called Buggleton & went to the Red Lion Hotel & there he found a party that had just motored down from London, & while they were having breakfast he went into the stable-yard & found their motor-car & went off in it without even saying Poop-poop! And now he has vanished & every one is looking for him, including the police. I fear he is a bad low animal.

Goodbye, from
    Your loving Daddy.

is on the boards, the stage ; reading it, much more acting it, is not its performance. The performance of a symphony is not the scoring it however elaborate ; it is in the concert room, with the orchestra, and then only. A picture is performed, or performs, when any one looks at it in the proper and intended light. A house performs when it is built and lived in. To come nearer : books, play, or perform, or are played and performed when they are read ; and ordinarily by one reader, alone, to himself, with the eyes only. Now we are getting to it, George. Poetry was originally meant for either singing or reciting ; a record was kept of it ; the record could be, was read, and that in time by one reader, alone, to himself, with the eyes only. This reacted on the art : what was to be performed under those conditions for these conditions ought to be and was composed and calculated. Sound-effects were intended, wonderful combinations even ; but they bear the marks of having been meant for the whispered, not even whispered, merely mental performance of the closet, the study, and so on. You follow Joseph ? You do : We are there. This is not the true nature of poetry, the darling child of speech, of lips and spoken utterance : it must be spoken ; till it is spoken it is not performed, it does not perform, it is not itself. Sprung rhythm gives back to poetry its true soul and self. As poetry is emphatically speech, speech purged of all dross like gold in the furnace, so it must have emphatically the essential elements of speech. Now emphasis itself, stress, is one of these : sprung rhythm makes verse stressy ; it purges it to an emphasis as much brighter, livelier, more lustrous than the regular but commonplace emphasis of common rhythm as poetry in general is brighter than common prose speech. But this it does by a return from the regular emphasis towards, not up to the more picturesque irregular emphasis of talk without however becoming itself lawlessly irregular ; then it could not be art ; but making up by regularity, equality, of a larger unit (the foot merely) for equality in the less, the syllable. Here it wd. be necessary to come down to mathematics and technicalities which time does not allow of, so I forbear. For I believe you now understand. Perform the Eurydice then see. I must however add that to perform it quite satisfactorily is not at all easy, I do not say I could do it ; but this is no kind nothing against the truth of the principle maintained. A composer need not be able to play his violin music or sing his songs. Indeed the higher wrought the art, clearly the wider severance between

Gerard Manley Hopkins (1844–89) to Everard Hopkins

5 November 1885

The most original voice in Victorian poetry, Gerard Manley Hopkins remained almost unpublished in his lifetime. As a Jesuit priest and teacher, he snatched time to write during an exhausting series of relocations to different pastoral and teaching posts, and bouts of depression. In this long letter to his artist brother Everard, Hopkins gives full play to his ideas about poetry and performance, momentarily slipping free from the self-doubt that tormented him particularly badly in 1885. In the context of his poem 'The Loss of the Eurydice', he explains his own innovatory poetics. Hopkins's 'sprung rhythm', which defines verse lines by a variable number of stressed syllables rather than regular metrical 'feet', gives his poetry a tensile, vocal quality, in which speech – in the beautiful image he coins on the page reproduced here – is 'purged of dross like gold in the furnace'.

Dear Everard, – I am taking a short rest after deadly work [...]

I am sweetly soothed by your saying that you could make any one understand my poem by reciting it well. That is what I always hoped, thought, and said [...]

Every art then and every work of art has its own play or performance. The play or performance of a stage play is the playing it on the boards [...] The performance of a symphony is not the scoring it however elaborately; it is in the concert room, by the orchestra, and then and there only. A picture is performed, or performs, when any one looks at it in the proper and intended light. A house performs when it is built and lived in. To come nearer: books play and perform, or are played and performed when they are read [...] Poetry was originally meant for either singing or reciting; a record was kept of it; the record could be, was, read, and that in time by one reader, alone, to himself, with the eyes only [...] This is not the true nature of poetry, the darling child of speech, of lips and spoken utterance: it must be spoken; *till it is spoken it is not performed*, it does not perform, it is not itself. Sprung rhythm gives back to poetry its true soul and self, as poetry is emphatically speech, speech purged of dross like gold in the furnace, so it must have emphatically the essential elements of speech. Now emphasis itself, stress, is one of these: sprung rhythm makes verse stressy; it purges it to an emphasis as much brighter, livelier, more lustrous than the regular commonplace emphasis of common rhythm as poetry in general is brighter than common speech [...] For I believe you now understand. Perform the *Eurydice*, then see. I must however add that to perform it quite satisfactorily is not at all easy, I do not say I could do it [...] A composer need not be able to play his violin music or sing his songs. Indeed the higher wrought the art, clearly the wider severance between the parts of the author and the performer [...]

Queridísimo Melchorito: Yo que me imagi-
-naba no sé porqué que tú estabas disgustado conmigo he tenido una
inmensa alegría cuando he visto tu carta de Zaragoza. Me explico que
la ciudad baturra no te haya gustado. Zaragoza está felipizada y
zarzuelizada como la jota, y para buscarla en su antiguo espíritu
hay que ir al Museo del Prado y admirar el exactísimo retrato
que le hizo Velázquez. Allí la torre de San Pablo y los tejados de la
Lonja, están ambientados sobre el cielo de perla y la original
silueta del caserío. Hoy la ciudad se ha mercadeado. Yo que he
pasado Aragón en el tren, creo que el viejo espíritu de Zaragoza debe
andar errabundo, amortecido Vale blancas Mérida, por los alrede-
-dores de Caspe, en las últimas grises rocas, donde el viento duro
tira al pastor y salvajiza la luz de las estrellas grandes.
En cambio Barcelona ya es otra cosa ¿verdad? Allí está el
Mediterráneo, el espíritu, la aventura, el alto sueño de amor
perfecto. Hay palmeras, gentes de todos países, anuncios comerciales
sorprendentes, torres góticas y un vivo pleamar urbano hecho
por las máquinas de escribir. ¡Qué a gusto me encuentro allí

Federico García Lorca (1898–1936)
to Melchor Fernández Almagro
February 1926

'How I enjoy being there,' Federico García Lorca – now back home in Granada – enthuses to his childhood friend Melchor Fernández Almagro about Barcelona. With its 'rich urban high tide' of literary life and erotic possibilities, the Catalan capital is so different from Zaragoza, from where Melchor has just written to him. Lorca contrasts Diego Velázquez's 1647 painting of Zaragoza with the present-day city, a touristic caricature of its former self.

Lorca is twenty-seven, has published two books of poetry, seen his first play staged, taken his law degree and is now working on a new play and a verse collection that will appear in 1928 as *Romancero gitano* (*Gypsy Ballads*). Family money means that there's no pressure to find paid employment: poet, playwright, even perhaps an artist (he decorates his letter with drawings of Pierrot figures) – he'll wait and see how his work develops. For his part, Fernández Almagro has become a literary critic and Lorca's most eloquent supporter.

Later in 1926, Lorca will – as he anticipates – pose for the eccentric young Catalan artist Salvador Dalí, with whom he'd made friends the previous year. The poet's sleeping head features in *Still Life (Invitation to Dream)*, painted after Dalí's first trip to Paris and meeting with Picasso in April.

. . . .

Dear Melchorito,

I, who imagined, I don't know why, that you were displeased with me, was overjoyed to see your letter from Zaragoza. I understand why the Aragonese city displeased you. Zaragoza is *falsified and turned into a comic operetta*, like the *jota* [Aragonese dance], and in order to find her ancient spirit you have to go to the Prado to admire the *exact portrait* done by Velázquez [...]

But Barcelona is very different, isn't it? There one finds the Mediterranean, the spirit, the adventure, the elevated dream of perfect love. There are palms, people from every country, surprising advertisements, gothic towers and a rich urban high tide created by typewriters. How I enjoy being there, with that air and *that passion*! [...]

I've kept up to date with that region through my friend and inseparable companion Salvador Dalí, with whom I carry on an abundant correspondence. He has invited me to spend another season at his house, which I'll certainly do, since I have *to pose* for him [...]

The *literary atmosphere* of Madrid seems to me too *stingy and mean*. Everything turns into gossip, cabals, calumnies and American banditry. I feel like refreshing my poetry and my heart in foreign waters, in order to produce greater riches and expand my horizons. I'm sure that a new period is beginning now for me.

I want to be a poet, from head to toe, living and dying by poetry. I'm beginning to *see clearly*. A high awareness of my future work is taking hold of me and an almost dramatic feeling of my responsibility constrains me ... I don't know ... it seems that *I'm giving birth* to new forms and an absolutely defined balance [...]

Dear Mother & Dad,

Sunday, March 10, 46

I just got an idea for the novel so I'll slip it to you while it's still hot, not bothering to explain who Red is. Red thinks of an eager kid who had wanted to see combat, and he's amused — there were so few of his kind. For a moment he felt a little pride. Where could you find an army like this one which fought with so little enthusiasm, so sure a knowledge that in the end they'd be fucked as they'd always been fucked before. Where almost everybody hated it, where everybody was afraid, when all they knew were the personal injustices wreaked against them, when they did not know the enemy and hated him without zeal as they hated the weather or the weight of a pack after a long march. You never could find such an army again, against a pack of crazy hopped-up bastards, and still beating them. Of course they had more of everything, food and men and arms, but inside they had nothing and still they won. It was only Americans who could do that, who had kept going not cause they were patriotic, or cause they understood anything, but because they wouldn't take any craps from anybody, and letting up meant taking craps from your buddies and the officers.

And then his thoughts turned sour. And wasn't that a hell uva reason — that was the same fuggin thing as standing on a street corner and whistling at women, or fighting with a gang against another gang when you didn't want to, but were more afraid to drop out. That's what they were really when you got down to it, a bunch of cowards who were afraid to drop away from the pack, yellow gutless cocksuckers who were so afraid of being found out that they ended by acting like men because they were afraid not to.

That wasn't all of it — they had to have that or they'd have nothing at all, but Red's moment of pride was gone, and his familiar mood imbued him again. He was sad and wistful and then bitter and dejected. Life was the shits. He felt as if he were breathing again the one thing you always came back to, the flat stench of cigar ashes in an old butt tray.

Sorry to take up the letter my dears, but I know you always get a peek out of me when I'm in the throes of creation. Save this, will you, hon — I think I'll be able to use it.

I'm feeling fine, sweating out the month or a little more, it still ahead of me before I pack my gear for the last trip.

All my love,
Norman

Norman Mailer (1923–2007) to Isaac and Fanny Mailer
10 March 1946

Having failed to persuade the US military authorities that he should be spared conscription in order to work on an 'important novel', Norman Mailer took part in the Philippines campaign of 1944–5. In 1946, serving the last of his time as a cook with the 112th Cavalry in Japan, he writes to his adoring parents, Isaac and Fanny, back in Crown Heights, Brooklyn. But he doesn't have time to talk about day-to-day things. He's had an idea.

Mailer goes on to describe – with the same spiky intelligence and self-mythologizing bombast that would characterize much of his work – the novel that would become *The Naked and the Dead*. Based on his own experiences, the book follows a brigade of soldiers in the South Pacific, viscerally evoking the waste and horror – also the boredom – of war. It was an immediate hit when it appeared in 1948, spending sixty-two weeks on the *New York Times's* bestseller list. Mailer was twenty-five. He had a long, if chequered, career ahead of him. But even he, with his unshakeable sense of being destined for great things, couldn't have imagined a better start.

Dear Mother & Dad,

I just got an idea for the novel so I'll slip it to you while it's still hot, not bothering to explain who Red is. Red thinks of an eager kid who had wanted to see combat, and he's amused there were so few of his kind. For a moment he felt a little pride. Where could you find an army like this one which fought with so little enthusiasm, so sure a knowledge that in the end they'd be fucked as they'd always been fucked before. Where almost everybody hated it, where everybody was afraid, where all they knew were the personal injustices wreaked against them, where they did not know the enemy and hated him without zeal as they hated the weather or the weight of a pack after a long march. You never could find such an army again, fighting against a pack of crazy hopped-up bastards, and still beating them. Of course they had more of everything, food and men and arms, but inside they had nothing and still they won. It was only Americans who could do that, who'd keep going not cause they were patriotic, or cause they understood anything, but because they wouldn't take any crap from anybody, and letting up meant taking crap, from your buddies and the officers [...]

Sorry to take up the letter my dears, but I know you always get a kick out of me when I'm in the throes of creation. Save this, will you, Mom. I think I'll be able to use it.

I'm feeling fine, sweating out the month or a little more, still ahead of me before I pack my gear for the last trip [...]

Dear Olwyn—

Ted and I are just back from climbing Mount Holyoke, one of our peaks of exercise, taking a good hour to get up, under a green network of leaves, but the view worth it from the porch of a hundred-year old hotel which housed Abraham Lincoln once, and Jenny Lind who named the view "The Paradise of America", although I suspect Jenny was over-ecstatic. She named our Smith frog-pool 'Paradise Pond.' From the top we can see north along the back of the broad winding Connecticut river, all the green patchwork of asparagus, strawberry & potato farms below. We're right in the middle of a great river-rich farming valley & so get vegetables & fruits fresh from the fields. I do like your sending those recipes of delectable things & will try this pepper & tomato & onion & sausage one soon. Try to get more such from the Hungarians! do any of them make a good borsch? Maybe Luke remembers the heavenly borsch the three of us had at the restaurant with the bitterly old waitress whose daughter (probably chained to the stove) was a wonderful cook. Tell Luke for me to send ahead his favorite menus & I'll cook them if he promises to visit us. We'd both love to see him this August & will be here till the end of the month.

Ted Thrives & so do I, with no jobs. Both of us are meant to be wealthy & have convinced our Boston landlord (dubious about our future rent-paying) that we are hourly having money pour in from magazines. As soon as I stopped work & started writing I sold my two longest poems to the New Yorker (my first acceptance from them) & we figure the check should total 3 months rent at least. This is very encouraging & especially so since I want to get a full first book of poems to the publishers this winter — I'm ditching old work at an amazing rate. Ted's second book is already magnificent — richness, depth, color & a mature force & volume. Slowly, slowly, we hope to sell the poems. I know he is the great poet of our generation & feel that the most important thing is to somehow clear these next five years for a tough & continuous apprenticeship to writing — his children's story has just come out — delightfully & sprightly illustrations with it. We will try for grants, too. Our work should begin to speak for itself. Then our Boston apartment is minute, but aesthetically fine with its light, air, quiet & superb view. The city is a delight to walk in. I'm extremely interested in the Scorpio book. Do send on the Scorpio book. I'm extremely interested in seeing it. Ted & I both love getting your letters, especially long ones like the last, so do write soon again. Tell us more about deGaulle. With love, Sylvia.

Sylvia Plath (1932–63) to Olwyn Hughes
30 June 1959

In the summer of 1959, Sylvia Plath writes to Olwyn Hughes, sister of her husband Ted, with an upbeat account of their travels around America. The couple had moved to the US shortly after their whirlwind romance and hasty marriage in London in 1956, settling in Plath's home state of Massachusetts, where she had secured a job at her alma mater, Smith College. After two years of teaching (and other things: Plath worked briefly as a receptionist at a psychiatric hospital), they have decided to give full-time writing a go. Hughes's work has already won acclaim, with the publication in 1957 of his debut collection, *The Hawk in the Rain*. And Plath, after several bouts of depression and writer's block, has had a breakthrough. Two of her poems, 'Mussel Hunter at Rock Harbor' and 'Nocturne' have been accepted by the illustrious (and well-paying) *New Yorker*, though she still has more confidence in Hughes's gifts than her own.

Given the chattiness of the letter, it's surprising that Plath and Olwyn Hughes did not, in fact, get on (Hughes, a blunt Yorkshirewoman, described her sister-in-law as 'pretty straight poison'). But in an odd twist, after Plath's suicide in 1963, Olwyn became her literary executor – as well as her brother's agent. When the long, bitter debate over their relationship began, with Plath's admirers blaming Hughes for her death, Olwyn found herself in the unusual position of defending both of their reputations – and was, by all accounts, formidably effective.

Dear Olwyn –

Ted and I are just back from climbing Mount Holyoke – one of our peaks of exercise, taking a good hour to get up, under a green network of leaves, but the view worth it from the porch of a hundred-year-old hotel which housed Abraham Lincoln once, and Jenny Lind who named the view 'The Paradise of America', although I suspect Jenny was over-ecstatic. She named our Smith frog-pool 'Paradise Pond'. From the top we can see north along the back of the broad winding Connecticut river, all the green patchwork of asparagus, strawberry & potato farms below [...]

Ted thrives & so do I, with no jobs. Both of us are meant to be wealthy & have convinced our Boston landlord (dubious about our future rent-paying) that we are hourly having money pour in from magazines. As soon as I stopped work & started writing I sold my two longest poems to *The New Yorker* [...] & we figure the dreck should total 3 months rent at least [...] Ted's second book is already magnificent – richness, depth, color & a mature force & volume. Slowly, slowly, we hope to sell the poems. I know he is the great poet of our generation & feel that the most important thing is to somehow clear these next five years for a tough & continuous apprenticeship to writing [...] We will try for grants, too. Our work should begin to speak for itself then [...]

Chapter 2

'My head is full of pebbles'

out scenery, dressing dolls,
a letter to you that was opene
ved, that I am a cocaine victir
ppreciate it. Please give my b
be boiled to a jelly in the hope
o lay the crown of Lilliput at y
a humane infirmary and they
and **Between Friends** I can sa
naster. I admired you before I
you can really perform the ex
rsake you, for if when I examir
hy couldn't you have taken m
xample, such a slack soft pla
since we like each other that
alls for my perticular thanks,
drivers exasperate the bourg
h candy like his aunty Gertrud
ould like to sit in the dust. I f

Henrietta St. Wednesday March 2

My dear Cassandra

You were wrong in thinking of us at Guildford last night, we were at Cobham. On reaching G. we found that John & the Horses were gone on. We therefore did no more there than we had done at Farnham, sit in the Carriage while fresh Horses were put in, & proceeded directly to Cobham, which we reached by 7, & about 8 were sitting down to a very nice roast fowl &c. — We had altogether a very good journey, & everything at Cobham was comfortable. — 'I could not pay Mr Herington.' That was the only alas! of the Business. I shall therefore return his Bill & my Mother's £2. — That you may try your Luck. We did not begin reading till Bentley Green. Henry's approbation hitherto is even equal to my wishes; he says it is very different from the other two, but does not appear to think it at all inferior. He has only married Mrs R. I am afraid he has gone through the most entertaining part. He took to Lady B. & Mrs N. most kindly, & gives great praise to the drawing of the Characters. He understands them all, likes Fanny & I think foresees how it will all be. I finished the Heroine last night & was very much amused by it. I wonder James did not like it better. It diverted me exceedingly. — We went to bed at 10: I was very tired, but slept to a miracle & am lovely today; — & at present Henry seems to have no complaint. We left Cobham at ½ past 8, stopt to bait & breakfast at Kingston & were in this House considerably before 2. — quite in the stile of Mr Knight.

Jane Austen (1775–1817) to Cassandra Austen

2 March 1814

'If Cassandra were to have her head cut off, Jane would insist on sharing her fate.' That's how Jane Austen's mother (also a Cassandra) is said to have described her relationship with her older sister. Jane wrote hundreds of letters to Cassandra, her closest confidante and a sounding board for her ideas. Yet when she died, Cassandra destroyed or censored much of their correspondence.

By 1814, Jane had published *Sense and Sensibility* and *Pride and Prejudice*. In this letter, describing a journey from the family home in Chawton, Hampshire, to London, she writes with the lightness of touch found in those novels. All the stuff of agreeable, upper-middle-class English life is here – tea, roast fowl, a trip to the theatre to see the famous tragic actor Edmund Kean – but every now and then an ironic edge cuts through ('Wyndham Knatchbull is to be asked for Sunday, & if he is cruel enough to consent, somebody must be contrived to meet him,' she complains towards the end of the letter).

She also alludes to her new novel, *Mansfield Park*, which would appear in July that year. The story of Fanny Price, a young girl sent to live as the poor relation with her forbidding uncle and aunt, Sir Thomas and Lady Bertram, it is, as Henry Austen observes, 'very different from the other two' – darker and more expansive in its themes. Cassandra had doubts about it. Perhaps it revealed a side of her sister that she didn't think the world should see.

My dear Cassandra

You were wrong in thinking of us at Guildford last night, we were at Cobham. On reaching G. we found that John & the Horses were gone on. We therefore did no more there than we had done at Farnham, sit in the Carriage while fresh Horses were put in, & proceeded directly to Cobham, which we reached by 7, & about 8 were sitting down to a very nice roast fowl &c. – We had altogether a very good Journey, & everything at Cobham was comfortable. – I could not pay Mr Herrington! – That was the only alas! of the Business. I shall therefore return his Bill & my Mother's £2. – that you may try your Luck. –

We did not begin reading till Bentley Green. Henry's approbation hitherto is even equal to my wishes; he says it is very different from the other two, but does not appear to think it at all inferior [...]

And now, how do you all do? You in particular after the worry of yesterday & the day before. I hope Martha had a pleasant visit again, & that you & my Mother could eat your Beefpudding. Depend upon my thinking of the Chimney Sweeper as soon as I wake tomorrow. – Places are secured at Drury Lane for Saturday, but so great is the rage for seeing Keen that only a 3[r]*d* & 4*th* row could be got. As it is in a front box however, I hope we shall do pretty well [...]

HOTEL DE PARIS
MONTE-CARLO
ADRESSE TÉLÉGRAPHIQUE: PARISOTEL
TÉLÉPHONE: 018-11

Chère Julia, vous
ne m'en voudrez pas de
vous avouer ma fatigue ?
Maurice m'a amenée
ici pour la rendre
avouable, et nous
sommes invités ici pour
un mois par Tchamy
Hussein Pacha. Je
ne suis bonne qu'à
me reposer, et je
n'en ai pas de honte
devant vous. Que de
fleurs, déjà, dans cet

Sidonie-Gabrielle Colette (1873–1954) to Julia Ruc
21 June 1951

Midsummer in Monte Carlo, 1951. Sidonie-Gabrielle Colette and her husband, Maurice, are staying in the luxurious seafront Hôtel de Paris as guests of an expat Turkish grandee, Ilhamy Hussein Pasha. Now in her seventies, disabled by osteoarthritis, Colette is in a wheelchair. She confides to her friend Julia Ruc that she feels 'good for nothing but taking a rest'. Except that she and Maurice have a project – to adapt her most famous novella, *Gigi*, for the stage.

Colette's semi-autobiographical 'Claudine' stories (1900–4), charting the coming-of-age of a girl from rural Burgundy in turn-of-the-century Paris, had struck a popular chord. When she separated from her first husband, Henry Gauthier-Villars, however, he retained the copyright (the 'Claudine' series had initially been published under his pen-name, Willy). But Colette was a born survivor. After performing in music hall and embarking on a series of lesbian relationships, she remarried in 1912 and returned to full-time writing. Her novels of the 1920s, including *Chéri* and *Sido*, explore themes of female sexuality and the pressures of social convention on women. By her early fifties, when Colette met her third husband, Maurice Goudeket, she was the most celebrated female author in France.

The couple survived in Paris during the Nazi occupation of 1940–4. Maurice, who was Jewish, was under constant threat of arrest; the ever-resourceful Colette, meanwhile, wrote for the anti-Semitic right-wing press. In 1944, she published *Gigi*. Dealing with the relationship between a teenage courtesan, Gigi Alvar, and her rich lover, it caught the widespread yearning for youthful freedom and glamour after years of war.

Also in Monte Carlo in summer 1951 was a young British actress, Audrey Hepburn, who was starring in a modest Anglo-French comedy film, *Monte Carlo Baby*. Not long after this letter was written, Colette was introduced to Hepburn, who immediately struck her as perfect for the part of Gigi. The play duly opened on Broadway in November, in an adaptation by the screenwriter Anita Loos, with Hepburn in the title role. Her success in *Gigi* was soon followed by Hollywood stardom.

Dear Julia, you won't mind me admitting how tired I am? Maurice has brought me here so that it can become admissible, and we've been invited to stay here for a month by Ilhamy Hussein Pasha. I'm good for nothing but taking a rest, and I can say this to you without shame. What flowers there are already in this strange country! If I receive just a few words from you here, I'll be happy. We're going to try, Maurice and I, to adapt *Gigi* for the stage. But for the time being, I'm not up to anything except wondering at what is eternally wonderful, the colours, the gentleness of the air. Dear friend, three lines from you would give such happiness to your friend, who embraces you with all her heart.

Colette

Sunday night.

Dear Mr Bowles.

I am much
ashamed. I misbehaved
tonight. I would like
to sit in the dust.
I fear I am your little
friend no more, but
Mr Jim Crow.

I am sorry I smiled
at women.

Indeed I were hot
ours, like Mrs A.F.
and Miss Nightingale.

I will never be giddy
again. Pray forgive
me now. Respect little
Bob o'Lincoln again!

My friends are a very
few. I can count—

Emily Dickinson (1830–86) to Samuel Bowles
c.1860

Of the 1,800 poems Emily Dickinson wrote, only ten were published during her lifetime – anonymously, and without her consent. Of these, seven appeared in the *Springfield Daily Republican*, a progressive and influential New England newspaper edited by the charismatic Samuel Bowles.

No one knows exactly how these 'surreptitiously communicated' poems ended up on his desk, but Bowles was a friend of Emily's brother, Austin, and his wife, Susan. He'd met them on a trip to look at agricultural machinery in Amherst, Massachusetts, where the Dickinsons had been a prominent family for generations. From the late 1850s he was a regular guest at their house, next door to where Emily lived with her parents and younger sister, Lavinia. Emily kept her social circle small, but she made an exception for Bowles. In many ways it was an unlikely match: Bowles, worldly and sociable, was often puzzled by Emily's reticence (he addressed her as 'Queen Recluse'). But she opened up to him, and sent him many of her poems during the 1860s (none of them published), when she was going through a personal crisis. In this letter, she apologizes for her behaviour during one of his visits. It seems she had been dismissive of Elizabeth Fry and Florence Nightingale, social reformers whose work Bowles would have admired. She fears that this abolitionist now sees her as 'Mrs Jim Crow', but hopes that she can return to being 'Bob o' Lincoln' – another name for the bobolink, an American songbird that appears in her poetry.

There has been much speculation about Dickinson's relationship with Bowles. He has been suggested as the 'Master' to whom she addressed a series of tormented, cryptic – and unsent – letters. After several years, their correspondence ended abruptly. It picked up again, but in a rather businesslike manner, after the death of Dickinson's father in 1874.

Dear Mr Bowles

I am much ashamed. I misbehaved tonight. I would like to sit in the dust. I fear I am your little friend no more, but Mrs Jim Crow.

I am sorry I smiled at women.

Indeed, I revere holy ones, like Mrs Fry and Miss Nightingale. I will never be giddy again. Pray forgive me now: Respect little Bob o'Lincoln again!

My friends are very few. I can count them on my fingers – and besides, have fingers to spare.

I am gay to see you – because you come so scarcely, else I had been graver.

Good night, God will forgive me – Will you please to *try*?

Emily.

Twentieth Century-Fox Film Corporation

STUDIOS
BEVERLY HILLS, CALIFORNIA

September
14
1940

Dear Gerald:

I suppose anybody our age suspects what is emphasized--so
let it go. But I was flat in bed from April to July last year
with day and night nurses. Anyhow as you see from the letterhead
I am now in official health.

I find, after a long time out here, that one develops new
attitudes. It is, for example, such a slack soft place--even its
pleasure lacking the fierceness or excitement of Provence--that
withdrawal is practically a condition of safety. The sin is to
upset anyone else, and much of what is known as "progress" is attained
by more or less delicately poking and prodding other people. This
is an unhealthy condition of affairs. Except for the stage-struck
young girls people come here for negative reasons--all gold rushes
are essentially negative--and the young girls soon join the vicious
circle. There is no group, however small, interesting as such. Everywhere there is, after a moment, either corruption or indifference.
The heroes are the great corruptionists or the supremely indifferent--
by whom I mean the spoiled writers, Hecht, Nunnally Johnson, Dotty,
Dash Hammet etc. That Dotty has embraced the church and reads her
office faithfully every day does not affect her indifference. She
is one type of commy Malraux didn't list among his categories in
Man's Hope--but nothing would disappoint her so vehemently as success.

I have a novel pretty well on the road. I think it will baffle
and in some ways irritate what readers I have left. But it is as
detached from me as Gatsby was, in intent anyhow. The new Armageddon,
far from making everything unimportant, gives me a certain lust for
life again. This is undoubtedly an immature throw-back, but it's
the truth. The gloom of all causes does not affect it--I feel a
certain rebirth of kinetic impulses - however misdirected.

Zelda dozes--her letters are clear enough--she doesn't want
to leave Montgomery for a year, so she says. Scottie continues at
Vassar--she is nicer now than she has been since she was a little girl.
I haven't seen her for a year but she writes long letters and I feel
closer to her than I have since she was little.

I would like to have some days with you and Sara. I hear
distant thunder about Ernest and Archie and their doings but about
you I know not a tenth of what I want to know.

With affection,

Scott

1403 N. Laurel Avenue
Hollywood, California

F. Scott Fitzgerald (1896–1940) to Gerald Murphy
14 September 1940

With the publication of his debut novel, *This Side of Paradise*, in 1920, F. Scott Fitzgerald found himself famous. He was just twenty-four. The ensuing decade was one long party, split between the United States and the French Riviera. Then came the hangover. With the arrival of the Great Depression, Fitzgerald's work fell out of fashion, accused of the very vices it satirized: decadence, flippancy, solipsism. By 1936, his income was a third of what it had been. His marriage to Zelda was long over, and she was in and out of mental institutions. And there was the drinking. Even after cutting down on gin, Fitzgerald was putting away almost forty beers a day and stuck in a dismal cycle of dry-outs, relapses, arrests and hospitalizations.

In 1937, he was offered work in Hollywood, at that time teeming with gifted novelists trying their hand (not always successfully or soberly) at screenwriting. Fitzgerald, who'd had an unhappy stint there in the early 1930s, cleaned up his act, using Coca-Cola as a stand-in for booze and earning more than he had for a decade (though his only credit was for a screen adaptation of Erich Maria Remarque's novel *Three Comrades*). But in 1939, he toppled off the wagon and spent several months under medical supervision.

The following year, in remission once more, he writes to Gerald Murphy, a friend from the Riviera days (Gerald and his wife, Sara, are thought to be the inspiration for Dick and Nicole Diver in *Tender Is the Night*). He's over the worst, he says, but that's no thanks to Los Angeles. The sickness he diagnoses in the city – a kind of moneyed inertia – will be familiar to readers of *The Great Gatsby*. Despite his valiant efforts to look on the bright side – relations with his much-neglected daughter Scottie have improved, he's got a novel on the go, and the 'new Armageddon' of world war has strangely revived his 'lust for life' – there's a sense that Fitzgerald the writer has admitted defeat, settling for 'what readers I have left'. He didn't have the physical robustness of his friend Hemingway (to whose latest rampages he alludes) to keep him going. Three months later, he died of a heart attack.

Dear Gerald:

[...] I was flat in bed from April to July last year with day and night nurses. Anyhow as you see from the letterhead I am now in official health.

I find, after a long time out here, that one develops new attitudes. It is, for example, such a slack soft place – even its pleasure lacking the fierceness or excitement of Provence – that withdrawal is practically a condition of safety [...] Except for the stage-struck young girls people come here for negative reasons – all gold rushes are essentially negative – and the young girls soon join the vicious circle [...] Everywhere there is, after a moment, either corruption or indifference. The heroes are the great corruptionists or the supremely indifferent – by whom I mean the spoiled writers [...]

I have a novel well on the road. I think it will baffle and in some ways irritate what readers I have left. But it is as detached from me as Gatsby was, in intent anyhow. The new Armageddon, far from making everything unimportant, gives me a certain lust for life again [...]

L'Exposition seule "occupe tous les esprits"
et les Cochers défiance exaspèrent tous
les bourgeois. ils ont été bien beaux, (les
bourgeois) pendant la grève des tailleurs.
on aurait dit que la Société allait
crouler.

Axiome: la Haine du Bourgeois est le
commencement de la Vertu. Mais je
comprends dans ce mot de bourgeois, les
bourgeois en blouse comme les bourgeois
en redingotte. C'est nous, nous seuls, c'est
à dire les Lettrés qui sommes le Peuple—
ou pour parler mieux: la tradition
de l'Humanité.

Oui je suis susceptible de colères désintéressées
et je vous aime encore plus depuis m'aimons
v= cela. La Bêtise & l'injustice me font
rugir. — & Je gueule, dans mon
coin contre un
tas de choses

Gustave Flaubert (1821–80) to George Sand
17 May 1867

When Gustave Flaubert met George Sand (pen-name of Amantine-Lucile-Aurore Dudevant; see page 59) in April 1857, he had just published his first novel, *Madame Bovary*. With more than thirty novels behind her, Sand was one of the most successful writers of her day. She was also notorious for dressing as a man (for which a woman technically required an official permit) and for her love affairs with, among others, the writers Alfred de Musset and Prosper Mérimée and composer Frédéric Chopin. By now, however, Sand was in her fifties, and things had quietened down. Despite the fact that her brand of romantic fiction offered very much the sort of reading that fatally warps the impressionable mind of Flaubert's heroine Emma Bovary, the two novelists struck up a friendship. They met at literary dinners in Paris and corresponded regularly in between times. The much younger Flaubert addressed Sand affectionately as 'master'.

The Exposition Universelle of 1867 was the second vast world's fair staged in Paris, featuring new inventions and some 50,000 exhibitors. In his previous letter, Flaubert reported to Sand, 'I went twice to the Exposition. It is amazing. There are splendid and extraordinary things there.' A couple of weeks later, the incessant middle-class chatter about the spectacle is making him sick. 'Hatred of the Bourgeois is the beginning of Virtue,' he growls, nursing the 'selfless rages' that powered much of his fiction.

I am going back to my mother next Monday, dear master. I'm not very hopeful that I will see you before then!

When you are in Paris, however, what is there to stop you continuing on to Croisset, where everyone, including me, adores you? [...] There's no more talk about the war, or about anything at all. The Exposition is the sole 'talk of the town', and the cab drivers exasperate the bourgeoisie. They were quite a sight (the bourgeoisie) during the tailors' strike. You would have said that *Society itself* was falling apart.

Axiom: Hatred of the Bourgeois is the beginning of Virtue. But what I mean by this word bourgeois is the bourgeois in smocks as well as in dress suits [i.e. lower and upper middle classes]. It is we, and we alone – that's to say literary folk – who are the People, or rather: the tradition of Humanity.

Yes, I'm prone to selfless rages and I love you all the more for loving me because of that. Stupidity and injustice make me roar & I *howl*, in my corner, about a load of things 'that have nothing to do with me'.

It's so sad not to be living together, dear master. I admired you before I knew you. From the day I first saw your kind, lovely face, I have loved you. There you are – and I embrace you warmly.

Your old
Gustave Flaubert

To *Mr Barker* at Mrs Clapp's
Bishop Stortford Hertfordshire

Dear Francis

    I am at last sat down to write to you, and
should very much blame myself for having neglected
you so long, if I did not impute that and many
other of my failings to want of health. I hope
not to be so long silent again. I am very well
satisfied with your progress, if you can really
perform the exercises which you are set, and I hope
Mr Ellis does not suffer you to impose on him
or on yourself.

    Make my compliments to Mr Ellis and to
Mrs Clapp, and Mr Smith.

    Let me know what English books you want
for your entertainment. You can never be wise

Samuel Johnson (1709–84) to Francis Barber
25 September 1770

Francis Barber was born a slave on a plantation in Jamaica. When he was seven, the plantation failed, and its owner, Colonel Richard Bathurst, brought him to England. He was given his freedom after Bathurst's death in 1754. It was through the colonel's son, Dr Richard Bathurst, that he found himself working in the rackety London home of Samuel Johnson, a giant of the eighteenth-century literary world. Johnson, a widower since the death of his wife Tetty two years earlier, was toiling over his *Dictionary*, the first in English (eventually published in 1755).

Dr Bathurst and Dr Johnson were staunch opponents of slavery, decades before the first stirrings of the abolitionist movement, and Johnson treated Barber as a companion – even a surrogate son – rather than an employee. His less free-thinking friends were bemused by his refusal to make Barber perform menial tasks ('Diogenes himself never wanted a servant less,' one remarked). He insisted, for example, on trudging to the fish market himself to buy oysters for his cat, Hodge, arguing that Barber did not deserve to be 'employed for the convenience of a quadruped'.

In 1767, when Barber was in his twenties, Johnson sent him to Bishop's Stortford grammar school, run by the Reverend William Ellis. It would have been a strange experience for Barber, who was many years older than his classmates and certainly the only black pupil in the school. But Johnson's affection – and ambitions – for him are clear in this letter: 'You can never be wise unless you love reading. Do not imagine that I shall forget or forsake you.'

Barber returned to London and, in 1773, married Elizabeth Hall. They had five children, and for a while the whole family lived in Johnson's house (other residents included a quack doctor and a retired prostitute). When Johnson died in 1784, Barber was his principal heir.

. . . .

Dear Francis

I am at last sat down to write to you, and should very much blame myself for having neglected you so long, if I did not impute that and many other of my failures to want of health. I hope not to be so long silent again. I am very well satisfied with your progress, if you can really perform the exercises you are set, and I hope Mr Ellis does not suffer you to impose on him or on yourself [...]

Let me know what English books you read for your entertainment. You can never be wise unless you love reading.

Do not imagine that I shall forget or forsake you, for if when I examine you, I find that you have not lost your time, you shall want no encouragement, from, yours affectionately,

SAM. JOHNSON

71, RUE DU CARDINAL LEMOINE. VI

Paris V

Dear Miss Weaver : apparently we were both
alarmed and then relieved for different
reasons. I can only repeat that I am glad
it is not any trouble of yours own and
as for myself having been asked what I
have to say why sentence of death
should not be passed upon me I should
like to rectify a few mistake.
                        A nice collection could
be made of legends about me. Here is
one. They fancy in Dublin believe
that I enriched myself in Switzerland
during the war by espionage work for
one or both combatants.. Trieste, seeing
me emerge from my relative's house
occupied by my furniture for about
twenty minutes every day and walk
to the same point the G.P.O and back
(I was writing Nausikaa and the Oxen
of the Sun in a dreadful atmosphere)
circulated the rumour, now firmly
believed, that I am a cocaine victim.
The general rumour in Dublin was
(All the proprietors of Ulysses stopped
it) that I could write no more,
had broken down and was dying
in New York. A man from Liverpool
told me he had heard that I
was the owner of several cinema
theatres all over Switzerland. In
America there appear to be a have
been two versions: one that I was

James Joyce (1882–1941) to Harriet Shaw Weaver
24 June 1921

Harriet Shaw Weaver was understandably disturbed to hear from the artist and novelist Wyndham Lewis and the writer Robert McAlmon that James Joyce had been on an all-night bender with them – and had insisted on picking up the tab. Weaver had been supporting Joyce while he worked on his first great experimental novel, *Ulysses*. In June 1921, he received a reproachful letter from his longstanding and generous patron.

It's possible that Lewis – said to have envied Joyce – was stirring things up, though nobody who knew Joyce (at this point living in a plush apartment in Paris) would have described him as a paragon of moderation. Either way, Joyce refuses to deny the charge outright. Instead, he reels off a series of outlandish 'legends' supposedly circulating about him, before acknowledging, bafflingly, that Lewis and Weaver are 'both probably right'. It's a virtuoso performance: at once self-justifying and self-lacerating, infuriating yet disarmingly funny. Joyce also claims in his defence that he has been left 'unbalanced' by *Ulysses* – a book that, with its multiple perspectives, calls the nature of truth into question. Which, on a smaller scale, is exactly what his letter does. 'An impossible person!', as Buck Mulligan says of Stephen Dedalus, the alter-ego hero of *Ulysses*.

Dear Miss Weaver: apparently we were both alarmed and then relieved for different reasons [...]

A nice collection could be made of legends about me. Here are some. My family in Dublin believe that I enriched myself in Switzerland during the war by espionage work [...] Triestines, seeing me emerge from my relative's house occupied by my furniture for about twenty minutes every day and walk to the same point the G.P.O. and back [...] circulated the rumour, now firmly believed, that I am a cocaine victim. The general rumour in Dublin was (till the prospectus of *Ulysses* stopped it) that I could write no more, had broken down and was dying in New York [...] I suppose I now have the reputation of being an incurable dipsomaniac [...]

What Mr Lewis and Mr McAlmon told you is, I am sure, right but at the same time you may have misunderstood what they said. I do not attach the same importance to the 'excess' mentioned as you do and as Mr Lewis does, apparently. And yet you are both probably right [...]

I hate pose of any kind and so I could not [write] a highflown epistle about nerve tension and relaxation, or asceticism the cause and the effect of excess etc etc. You have already one proof of my intense stupidity. Here now is an example of my emptiness. I have not read a work of literature for several years. My head is full of pebbles and rubbish and broken matches and bits of glass picked up 'most everywhere. The task I set myself technically in writing a book from eighteen different points of view and in as many styles, all apparently unknown or undiscovered by my fellow tradesmen, that and the nature of the legend chosen would be enough to upset anyone's mental balance [...]

Manuel,

      vamos a conversar.Es la hora en que yo miro caer la tarde;pe-
ro te miraré a ti,como se mira un cielo profundo i dulcísimo.
      Son las seis;acaba de irse tu primo,don Custodio.Estuvo desde
las dos,con su hija.Conversamos mucho.Alguien le mostró unas manchas,i él
habló de ti.Aproveché para preguntarle si te hallaba enfermo i de eso pa-
só él a otro cosa,i a otras,i a otras,hasta caer en tu estado de ánimo i
tu situación espiritual i sus causas.Te justificó plenamente,i su hija tam
bien.Habló ella de la vida triste que te había visto hacer en setiembre.Te
vi,a través de su palabra,que dejaba caer descuidadamente,dar de comer a
las palomas.En cada detalle te reconocía la dulzura,la del hombre bueno,ma-
yor que tu misma inmensa dulzura de poeta.Tu primo dijo por ahi:-Si,pues,
un alma necesita sentir la palpitación de otra alma(aleteo,fué su palabra)
aunque sea a través de un muro,i yo sentí que hai algo de eso en nosotros
El muro es espeso i terco;es el mundo,son las costumbres,es lo fatal que tú
sabes.Dijo ella por ahi,al hablar de que eran imprudentes contigo,lo de una
carta para ti que habian abierto .Pensé en la mia perdida.Es mui necesario
que tú te prevengas,que lo hagas por ti i por mí.Talvez eres descuidado
por exceso de seguridad.Comprendo i justifico:yo haria lo mismo;talvez haria mucho más.Te repito que es preciso que veles mucho por esto.

      Hai un derramamiento de brasas hacia el poniente;es una tarde dema-
siado ardiente.Yo estoi cansada.Conversar me cansa más que trabajar fisi-
camente,porque hasta en la conversación sencilla pongo demasiada vehemencia
i porque una emoción me quiebra como el levantar una montaña.Además,ha hecho calor.Como a ti me daña el calor.Tengo algo al corazón i me ahogan es-
tas siestas espesas de aire,densas como un humo,emboZan un poco.Uno de mis
temores de Buenos Aires es el clima.

      He pasado con el ánimo distinto hace tres dias;reaccioné con una vi-
sita a la Cárcel,un matadero humano,una cosa no para contada sino para
vista.Una enfermeria en la que los presos se pudren entre un hedor de cua-
dra;cinco meses sin remedios i sin médico los presos;unos rostros de pesa-
dilla,Manuel.La colonia española ha reunido fondos para darles una enfermeria humana.Me pidieron que los acompañara.I ese horror me hizo bien.Sentí
en la cara arderme la verguenza de toda la ciudad que tiene semejante putre
facción en su seno.He salido a la calle estos dias,porque me dieron lo de
la adquisicion de la ropa (están desnudos en el lecho),lo delas camas etc.
Cura Manuel,mirar el dolor verdadero i horrible de otras vidas;mira una a
la propia,compara i da gracias a Dios,i despúes ve el cielo más hermoso i,
sobre todo,sale de sí misma i se pone a vivir en la vida de los otros.La
noche antes habia estado en la Casa del Pueblo,para hablar los obre-
ros.Les hablé contra el odio,i horas despúes,en la Cárcel,lo justificaba.Voi
a hacer algo antes de irme de aqui,en el Dispensario,en el presidio i en la
Casa del Pueblo.Si en la última me dejan,porque me hallaron reaccionaria...
Te cuanto,como ves,mis dias.

      Ahora el cielo está amoratado i rojo:es el color de la violencia,del
odio trenzado con la amargura;parece que estuviera aquella parte estendido
el dolor de todo el pueblo infeliz.
      De los presos enfermos que nos repartimos,tomé uno,un tal Parra,un
tisico.El médico dice que no se salva.A ver.Va a tener aire pleno,por prime
ra vez;se van a abrir grandes ventanas con barrotes en lo alto.Va a ver el

cielo.
     Ro

Gabriela Mistral (1889–1957) to Manuel Magallenes Moure
8 February 1921

In 1914, Lucila Godoy Alcayaga, a Chilean teacher writing under the pseudonym of Gabriela Mistral, was awarded first prize in the Floral Games literary contest with *The Sonnets of Death*. The poems were a response to the suicide of her first love, and they made her name – or, rather, her pen name. As Gabriela Mistral (a tribute to the Italian poet Gabriele D'Annunzio and the French poet Frédéric Mistral), she went on to publish prolifically: poetry, essays, journalism.

One of the Floral Games judges was Manuel Magallenes Moure, a poet, playwright and artist. He and Mistral became friends, corresponding often. In 1921, she writes to him from Temuco, where she is teaching at a girls' school. Touching on the themes that animate her work – nature, spirituality, social justice – she describes a visit from Moure's cousin, and her visit to a prison. The nature of her relationship with the married Moure is unclear. While they kept their letters secret, it isn't known if they were romantically involved (though Mistral's later correspondence suggests she was more attracted to women).

After Mistral published her first collection, *Desolation*, in 1922, she embarked on a new, itinerant life as a diplomat, university tutor and human rights campaigner. Her work, balanced against a Franciscan lifestyle, took her from Cuba to Nice, Mexico to New York. She never returned to Chile for long. Yet despite her ambivalence towards the country, as her literary reputation grew, she turned into something of a national hero: 'la divina Gabriela'. In 1945, she became the first Latin-American writer to win the Nobel Prize.

Manuel,

[...] It is the time of day when I watch the night fall, but I will look for you as one looks for a deep and sweet sky [...]

Your cousin has just left [...] I asked him whether you were ill and that led to one thing and another and another, until he spoke of your state of melancholy and your spiritual life [...] Your cousin let it slip – Yes a soul needs to feel the beating of another soul [...] I felt that there is something of that essence in ourselves [...] When hearing that others were impudent towards you, the matter of a letter to you that was opened, I thought of my loss. It is very important that you are careful [...]

I have had a different mindset these past three days after I visited the jail, which was a human slaughterhouse [...] There was an infirmary where the prisoners rotted in a terrible stench. They had been there for five months without any medicine or doctor [...] The Spanish colony has gathered funds to provide them with a humane infirmary and they asked me to join them [...] It is healing, Manuel, to look upon the true and horrifying pain of other lives. One compares them to one's own and gives thanks to God, and then one looks upon a beautiful sky and most of all comes out of oneself and puts oneself in another's place [...]

Il paraît que tu étudies le
pignouf. moi je le suis, je le
connais trop. j'aime le paysan
bourichon qui ne lit pas, qui
ne lit jamais, même quand
il ne vaut pas grand chose;
le mot pignouf a sa profondeur
il a été créé pour le bourgeois
gandinocrate, n'est ce pas?
Dans cent bourgeoises de
province, quatre-vingt dix sont
pignouflardes renforcées, même
avec de jolies petites mines;
qui annonçaient des instincts
délicats - on est tout surpris
de trouver un fonds de
suffisance grossière dans ces

fausses dames. où est le
bonne maintenant? qu'est devenu
une spontanéité Dans le monde.

Bonsoir mon troubadour
Je t'aime et je t'embrasse
bien fort, Maurice aussi.
G Sand

Nohant 17 Janvier 69.

George Sand (1804–76) to Gustave Flaubert
17 January 1869

The first thing Baroness Dudevant (better known by her pen-name George Sand) did on New Year's Day 1869 was to dash off a note to 'my great friend and my dear, big child' Gustave Flaubert (see page 51). It was one in the morning, she was 'tired from having spent the night making a complete costume for a large doll' for her granddaughter, but, she wrote, 'I don't want to turn in without embracing you.'

Sand was at Nohant, the picture-book country estate in the Indre region she had inherited in her teens. Here she lived for eight years with her lover Frédéric Chopin, penned a series of popular novels and entertained many of the radical creatives of her day, including Franz Liszt, Eugène Delacroix, Honoré de Balzac (see page 155) and Flaubert. Now, though, Nohant was primarily a family home. In this letter, writing again to Flaubert two weeks later, Sand – once notorious for her cross-dressing and love affairs – describes her new life as a super-gran, sewing dresses, making scenery and just enjoying time with her namesake, 'little Aurore'.

With her 'old troubadour' Flaubert, however, Sand slips back into her masculine persona, musing about that other life, when 'he' had 'the folly to be young'. She frankly admits that, as novelists, she and Flaubert are 'the two most different workers that exist'. Which is, paradoxically yet naturally, the basis for their deep friendship – the kind of relationship in which 'we complete ourselves'.

....

[...] The individual named George Sand is well: he is enjoying the marvellous winter which *reigns* in Berry, gathering flowers, noting interesting botanical anomalies, making dresses and mantles for his daughter-in-law, costumes for the marionettes, cutting out scenery, dressing dolls, reading music, but above all spending hours with the little Aurore who is a marvellous child. There is not a more tranquil or a happier in his domestic life than this old troubadour retired from business, who sings from time to time his little song to the moon, without caring much whether he sings well or ill [...] It has not always been as nice as this. He had the folly to be young; but as he did no evil nor knew *evil passions*, nor lived for vanity, he is happy enough to be peaceful and to amuse himself with everything.

This pale character has the great pleasure of loving you with all his heart, and of not passing a day without thinking of the other old troubadour, confined to his solitude of a frenzied artist, disdainful of all the pleasures of this world [...] We are, I think, the two most different workers that exist; but since we like each other that way, it is all right. The reason each of us thinks of the other at the same hour, is because each of us has a need of his opposite; we complete ourselves, in identifying ourselves at times with what is not ourselves [...]

Good night, my troubadour: I love you, and I embrace you warmly [...]

G. Sand

27 Rue de Fleurus
1908

My dear Jinné(?),

Many thanks for the three Dilios and the papa and the mama. Seems to me Dilio looks a good deal like his papa Julie. What does he say about it, he looks like a tolerably happy little Dilio not as contented with life as his papa and his mama. Please say merry christmas to him and did he eat too much already, like his aunty Gertrude and

his uncle Leo, and has he got a little pain in his head in consequence like his aunty Gertrude and a little pain in his tummy in consequence like his uncle Leo, and does he have to take Hunyadi's to get rid of the same as has been afflicting some of his revered relations. Oh Dilio, you are young but we are never too young to learn.

Gertrude Stein (1874–1946) to Hortense and Dicky Moses
27 December 1908

Gertrude Stein followed her brother, Leo, to Paris, where they shared an apartment in Montparnasse. Liberated from strait-laced provincial Baltimore, Gertrude felt free to explore both her lesbian sexuality and literary ambitions. Leo was eagerly collecting modern art and befriending artists, including a young Spanish painter, Pablo Picasso, whose career Gertrude was soon promoting through the weekly salon she hosted. In 1905, Picasso began painting what would become the definitive portrait of Stein. Brown-robed, her face a grimly androgynous mask, she leans forwards on one elbow, part avant-garde influencer, part primitive seer. In real life, as this letter to friends back in Baltimore reveals, Stein could be much warmer and sillier than the artist's famous image suggests.

Hortense Guggenheim had married Judge Jacob (Jakie) Moses in 1903 and now had a young son, Dicky. At Christmas 1908, she updated Stein with some recent family photos, including three of Dicky. Stein's thank-you letter echoes the stream-of-consciousness mode of writing with which she was experimenting around this time: 'Dicky Dicky listen to the words as they tumble off your wise auntie's pen … don't ever mix up such sweet cake and sweet candy with salt pickles.' She must have imagined Hortense reading this vigorously scrawled advice aloud to her infant son, smiling at Aunty Gertrude's virtuoso exercise in one of the great themes of the avant-garde – the grown-up artist's ability to recover the unschooled immediacy of childhood. The Hunyadi János mineral water mentioned in the letter was marketed for constipation and other 'evil consequences of indiscretion in diet'.

My dear people

Many thanks for the three Dickies and the papa and the mama. Seems to me Dickie looks a good deal like his papa Jakie. What does he say about it, he looks like a tolerably happy little Dickey most as contented with life as his papa and his mama. Please say merry christmas to him for me and did he eat too much candy like his aunty Gertrude and his uncle Leo, and has he got a little pain in his head in consequence and a little pain in his tummy like his uncle Leo [...] Oh Dicky, you are young but we are never too young to learn. Dicky Dicky listen to the words as they tumble off your wise auntie's pen, never, no never when the Merry Christmas time comes round don't you ever eat too much sweet cake and sweet candy and above all Dicky, and let these words sink well into you, don't ever mix up such sweet cake and sweet candy with salt pickles. Dicky a lady what never tells lies tells you that that's a bad way to do. She did it, her big brother did it, and they both know Dicky, and you can believe a great deal of sweet cake, a great deal of candy and a great many salt pickles makes a combination that makes Hunyadie very necessary [...] Dicky, a lady what never tells lies tells you that that's a bad way to do [...]

Newark in Nottinghamshire.
No: 28. 1726

Madam.

My correspondents have informed
me that Your Lady.p has done me the honour to
answer severall objections that ignorance, malice
and party have made to my Travells, and bin
so charitable as to justifie the fidelity and veracity
of the Author. This Zeal you have shown for
Truth calls for my perticular thankes, and at
the same time encourages me to beg you would
continue your goodness to me by reconcileing
me to the Maids of Honour whom they say
I have most greviously offended. I am so stupid

Jonathan Swift (1667–1745) to Henrietta Howard
28 November 1726

Countess of Suffolk, mistress of the Prince of Wales (later George II) and a skilful operator in the Hanoverian court, Henrietta Howard was also a patron of the arts and a potentially useful friend to writers she admired. She and Jonathan Swift had been carrying on a gossipy correspondence for several years when *Gulliver's Travels* – Swift's great satire of human nature – was published in October 1726. At first, he tried to preserve authorial anonymity. The book is presented as Captain Lemuel Gulliver's true account of his voyages to Lilliput, Brobdingnag and beyond. But readers had their suspicions: Swift was widely known as a brilliant, often brutal satirist, with a track record of using alter-egos in works like *A Tale of a Tub* (1704). Howard was one fan of *Gulliver's Travels* who saw through his tricks.

The month after it was published, Howard sent Swift a letter replete with teasing references to Yahoos and Houyhnhnms, the savage humanoids and ultra-rational horses Gulliver encounters in Part IV of his travels. In his reply, on 27 November, Swift feigned ignorance, claiming that he'd had to buy a copy of the book in order to understand her 'unaccountable' references. But the following day, she received this letter, signed Lemuel Gulliver, apparently posted from the character's hometown of Newark, Nottinghamshire, and written in Gulliver's obsequious, point-missing style. In a typically Swiftian joke, he thanks Howard 'for being so charitable as to justifie the fidelity and veracity of the Author', as well as enclosing a toy crown from the kingdom of Lilliput, where the people are only about one-twelfth the size of normal humans.

When George II came to the throne, it became clear that Swift might have been looking for more than entertaining letters from Howard. Frustrated in Dublin, where he was Dean of St Patrick's Cathedral, he'd hoped that she could secure a position for him elsewhere. When she failed to do so, he turned nasty. Their correspondence fizzled out, with Swift opining that Howard only had 'as much of that Virtue as could be expected in a Lady, a Courtier and a Favourite'.

Madam

My correspondents have informed me that Your Lady[ship] has done me the honour to answer severall objections that ignorance, malice and party have made to my Traveills, and bin so charitable as to justifie the fidelity and veracity of the Author. This zeal you have shown for Truth calls for my perticular thanks, and at the same time encourages me to beg you would continue your goodness to me by reconciling me to the Maids of Honour, whom they say I have most greviously offended. I am so stupid as not to find out how I have disobliged them [...] But I submit myself and my cause to your better judgment, and beg leave to lay the crown of Lilliput at your feet, as a small acknowledgement of your favour to my book and person [...]

Monks House
Rodmell   29th Dec.
Lewes.   1929

My dear Frances,

I liked your letter so much that Nell I
really couldn't answer it in the Chaos of London
but must wait for a little peace down here.
That little book was rather a jump in the dark
full of queens & dashes & everything had to be
boiled to a jelly in the hope that the young
women would swallow it.   I'm very happy
that a wise & distinguished woman, with
growing daughters, should find some sense in it.
Yours is so much more important a contribution
to life than mine.

No, no, far from being compact &
united & only giving the right parents to
the right person, I am, or was till
Christmas Eve, a 'harassed' middle class
middle aged (47 to your 43) woman,
drifting into Hawleys toyshop & buying

Virginia Woolf (1882–1941) to Frances Cornford
29 December 1929

Virginia Woolf published her polemical essay *A Room of One's Own* in September 1929. Serving as a riposte to the idea – expressed by the priggish Charles Tansley in her 1927 novel *To the Lighthouse* – that 'women can't write, women can't paint', it explored the prejudices and prohibitions that had excluded women from British cultural life, concluding that 'a woman must have money and a room of her own if she is to write fiction'.

A *Room of One's Own* is one of the great feminist texts of the twentieth century. It came as a fitting end to a productive decade for Woolf. As well as *To the Lighthouse*, she'd produced *Mrs Dalloway* (1925) and *Orlando* (1928). Yet she is dismissive of these achievements in her response to an admiring letter from the poet Frances Cornford, one of the writers published by Hogarth Press, which Woolf ran with her husband, Leonard. Relieved to be back in Sussex after the 'chaos' of Christmas in London, Woolf describes her travails as a 'middle class middle aged' woman traipsing around toyshops in search of gifts for her nieces and nephews. It's often said that, in *A Room of One's Own* and indeed much of her work, Woolf failed to acknowledge her social privilege. But there's a note of genuine self-deprecation in her insistence that Cornford's 'contribution to life' as a mother is more important than Woolf's writing.

My dear Frances,

I liked your letter so much that I felt I really couldn't answer it in the chaos of London but must wait for a little peace down here. That little book was rather a jump in the dark full of guesses & dashes & everything had to be boiled to a jelly in the hope that the young women would swallow it. I'm very happy that a wise & distinguished woman, with growing daughters, should find some sense in it. Yours is so much more important a contribution to life than mine.

No, no, far from being compact & united & only giving the right presents to the right person, I am, or was till Christmas Eve, a harassed middle class middle aged (47 to your 43) woman, drifting into Hamleys toyshop & buying spotted horses for my nephews & nieces, whose wheels come off, & I then have to go to Hamleys & ask for wheels to be sent to Putney. I only point this out to correct your poetic impressions [...]

Perhaps you will write some more poems [...] & then we can hold a disembodied communion. I like your poems – I wish you did write more of them, or, if your children prevent, why not prose?

But, as you see, I am ending every sentence with a question mark. Why this & why not that – anyhow I was all of a heap when I read your letter with pleasure that you should have liked my book.

Yours Ever
Virginia Woolf

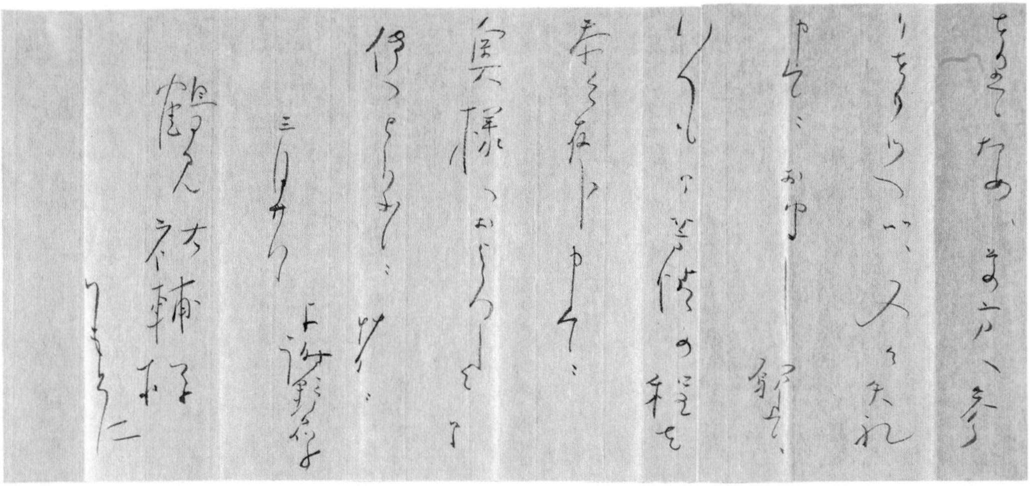

Akiko Yosano (1878–1942) to Yusuke Tsurumi
28 March 1927

Unless you can read *kuzushiji* script (not taught in Japanese schools since 1900), you might imagine that the elegant calligraphy in this letter represents one of the love lyrics for which Akiko Yosano made her name. In fact, it's a routine note relating to a visit to her adult son Hikaru, who was living in another part of Tokyo. It's not clear how she can have offended Yusuke Tsurumi, a former railway official, now Japanese delegate to the Pacific Conference. Maybe 'rudeness' was too strong to a word for whatever happened.

Yosano wasn't known for an apologetic take on life. Born Shō Hō into a strict patriarchal household, she began writing poetry in her teens and was twenty-two when her first book, *Midaregami* (*Tangled Hair*), came out. In a long series of *tanka* (a classic thirty-one-syllable form), she explored her sexual awakening and love affair with the poet and editor Hiroshi Yosano (known as Tekkan), whom she married the same year, as well as giving birth to their first child, Hikaru. She took the pen-name Akiko, meaning 'crystal child'.

Her frank celebration of female desire caused uproar. In traditional Japanese culture, references to the female body tended to be associated with ideals of meekness and motherhood. Yosano wrote of 'the flowers/of my breasts cupped,/offered with both my hands', portraying herself as an active partner in a sexual relationship:

> I whisper, 'Good night,'
> slipping silently from his room
> in the spring evening,
> and pause at his kimono,
> and try it on for size.

She went on to publish twenty more poetry collections and eleven prose works. She also spent three years translating *The Tale of Genji*, by the eleventh-century noblewoman Murasaki Shikibu, into modern Japanese. During this time, she gave birth to the seventh, eighth and ninth of her thirteen children. On a trip to Paris in 1913, she presented her translation to the sculptor Auguste Rodin. Yosano was politically controversial too. Her opposition to the Russo-Japanese War of 1904–5 led her to become the first Japanese poet to criticize the emperor in public. Outraged patriots stoned her house. In later life, her politics lurched to the right; she wrote poetry in praise of military valour. But she remains a founding figure of modern Japanese literature and feminism.

To Mr Yusuke Tsurumi,

I would like to express deepest apologies for my rudeness. I went to the suburbs to see my eldest son on that day because he had become sick. Please forgive me. Thank you very much for always being so kind. I very much appreciate it. Please give my best regards to your wife.

Sincerely yours,

Akiko Yosano

Chapter 3

'Yes I am radical'

hey have found a Little Roun
d our unmarked train. They ki
al contact means nothing unl
not overflowing with riches,
re, most noble Prince, that yo
teel ship, the railroad, the per
, who not only apprehended
ties

This Is History

& then into
in from hysteria and neurasth
an a book based on fraternity
e Front – a fact which I some
urge me to counter-acting tho
out send me dotty. I get the h
s, a religion which accepts he
good job of it, & the bullet m
climb down into the ferrybo
oks rather as if he'd like to ret
driatic to be a thorn in our si

1ST London General Hospital.
Camberwell, S.E.

Monday Nov. 8th 1915.

Most estimable, practical, unexceptional Adjutant,

I suppose I ought to congratulate you on the attainment of the position, even temporally But I don't know that I do. I suppose also I ought to thank you for your letter, since apparently one has to be grateful now-a-days for being allowed to know you are alive. But all the same, my first impulse was to tear that letter into small shreds, since it appeared to me very much like an Epistolary expression of the Quiet Voice, only with indications of an even greater sense of personal infallibility than the Quiet Voice used to contain. My second impulse was to write an answer with a sting in it which would have

Vera Brittain (1893–1970) to Roland Leighton
8 November 1915

Vera Brittain has cut short her studies at Oxford to volunteer as a nurse. Her fiancé, Roland Leighton, is in the trenches in France. A few days ago, after a long silence, she received a letter from him, full of excuses and dull army news, including his appointment as acting adjutant. He could be killed any moment – she should be sympathetic. But his restraint and lack of romantic fire make her want to 'tear that letter into small shreds'. Extreme situations, she seems to suggest, demand naked honesty, not reticence. Her outpouring of hurt and anger comes as close as she and Leighton can to having a long-distance row.

Yet she sees the big picture too: 'the War kills other things beside physical life.' She could cry, but would never have tears enough 'to wash away the pitiableness of it all'. On 27 December, news will come that Leighton has been killed by a sniper. Brittain will relive the impossible circumstances of their love in her 1933 autobiography, *Testament of Youth*.

....

Most estimable, practical, unexceptional Adjutant,

I suppose I ought to congratulate you on the attainment of the position, even temporally. But I don't know that I do. I suppose also I ought to thank you for your letter, since apparently one has to be grateful now-a-days for being allowed to know you are alive. But all the same, my first impulse was to tear that letter into small shreds [...] My second impulse was to write an answer with a sting in it [...] But I can't do that. One cannot be angry with people at the Front – a fact which I sometimes think they take advantage of – and so when I read 'We go back into the trenches to-morrow,' I literally dare not write you the kind of letter you perhaps deserve, for thinking that the world might end for you on that discordant note [...]

[A]lthough in this life I render material services and get definite and usually immediate results which presumably ought there to be satisfying, I cannot yet feel as near to Light and Truth as I did when I was 'wasting my time' on Plato and Homer. Perhaps one day when it is over I shall see that there was Light and Truth behind all, but just now, although I suppose I should be said to be 'seeing the world,' I can't help feeling that the despised classics taught me the finest parts of it better [...]

[T]he War kills other things besides physical life, and I sometimes feel that little by little the Individuality of You is being as surely buried as the bodies are of those who lie beneath the trenches of Flanders and France. But I won't write more on the subject. In any case it is no use, and I shall probably cry if I do, which must ever be done, for there is so much both personal and impersonal to cry for here that one might weep for ever and yet not shed enough tears to wash away the pitiableness of it all [...]

Eccellenza,

m'è ottima questa occasione
di guerra per esprimerLe
la gioia fidente che tutti i
sinceri amatori della nostra
Marina provarono quando
ne furono rimesse le sorti
nella Sua mano ferma e
sapiente.

Gabriele D'Annunzio (1863–1938) to Camillo Maria Corsi
10 November 1915

The poet, novelist, playwright, compulsive showman and First World War fighter pilot Gabriele D'Annunzio writes to Admiral Camillo Maria Corsi to request permission for a reconnaissance flight over the port of Zadar (Zara) in Croatia, at that time under Austrian (i.e. enemy) control. Corsi may be Commander in Chief of the Italian navy, but D'Annunzio makes it clear that – should he hesitate to endorse his plan – Corsi's peers and superiors have allegedly given it their blessing. In this apparently practical letter, he manages to sound both sycophantic and bullying, and to display symptoms of two obsessions for which he became notorious: flying and ultra-nationalism.

D'Annunzio's writing career began early, with a volume of poems published at nineteen, and peaked in the years around 1900 with novels such as *L'Innocente* (*The Intruder*) and plays including *Francesca da Rimini*, written for his celebrity lover, the actress Eleanora Duse. A parallel political career took off in 1897 with D'Annunzio's election to the Italian parliament as a deputy. In 1910, however, his debts forced him into exile in France, where he collaborated with the composers Claude Debussy and Pietro Mascagni. As a writer, D'Annunzio's purple Romanticism locates him firmly in the *fin de siècle*. In other ways, he embraced the spirit of modernity in the forms of powered flight (he took lessons from pioneer aviator Wilbur Wright) and polarized politics.

Returning to Italy at the outbreak of war in 1914, D'Annunzio volunteered as a naval pilot, joining a new breed of national hero – the flying ace. The sortie over Dalmatia, which he's proposing in this letter, was followed by other exploits, most famously his flight over Vienna in August 1918, dropping 50,000 propaganda leaflets that announced (in Italian) 'Destiny … turns towards us with an iron certitude'. Outraged at the failure of the Treaty of Versailles to assign the Adriatic port of Fiume to Italy, D'Annunzio invaded with a force of black-shirted *Arditi* shock troops. Here, during a sixteen-month dictatorship, he established a proto-fascist mini-state. His poseur's charisma (his catchphrase was '*Me ne frego*' – 'I don't care'), right-wing populism and instinct for seizing every 'opportunity provided by the war' would soon inspire Benito Mussolini to try something similar.

Excellency,

this opportunity provided by the war is the best possible chance for me to express to you the faithful joy that every true lover of our Navy experienced when fate was placed in your strong, wise hands.

Admiral Thaon di Revel did me the honour of communicating to you my plan to fly over Zara and at the same time explore part of the Dalmatian Archipelago, which should be ours if we don't want the Adriatic to be a thorn in our side forever. This plan, considered and studied for a long time, has the approval of His Majesty the King, of the Chief of Staff General Cadorna, and of His Highness the Duke of Aosta who commands that Third Army, in which I have the honour of serving [...]

tou jours parler de moi à   ostende ce lundi 27
nos ... — comme vous,
à vendre, je pense ce que vous dite

tonte la grosse artillerie et arrivée on
voir que dans la derniere affaire ce tont le
françois qui ont eu l'avantage mais pour
celle de camp de famars elle est claire
presque les françois sont déposte, aucun
habitant d'ostende ne peut aller se
promener aux por de la ville sans un
ordre du commandant c'est un
Donc maintenant la signature du
bailli de la ville et du commandant
anglois apposé à mon passeport que
j'attends pour partir — retenes tout ce
que je vous dis et prenes garde autre à
une echelle j'ai laquelle on descend à
bords dans le paquebot à la tête tourne
en descendant on tombe dans la mer
mon Dieu aures vous soin de vous mon
ange je vous en prie je ne veux pas mourir
je vais envoye une lettre de h'o rest ce
je me chage de bolman directement cela se peut faire
me d'range le moins du monde — ah que
ne je tout à coure un meilleur au plus
grand des hommes que je t'aime
Dim cent les
boyd à l'adresse
lendre le 5 56

cela fait bien mal de vous quitter phisiquement
et moralement je n'ai jamais tant souffert
de ma vie je suis arrivée ici avec la pine
hier à midi, et je me leve seulement
à présent pour vous dire adieu et partir
partir par la route d'allemagne car moi
je ne puis désobéir à ce que j'aime et
j'ai besoin de croire que ma vie luis est
nécessaire ah la tienne est tout mon
bien tout, me le jurer je te conjure
aux disens qu'en une tiens aux personnes
dont j'entends parle et toute la nature en
un éloge pour toi — la garde officielle
de bruxelles dit que les autrichiens ont
pris le camp de famars après avoir tué mille
hommes aux françois à camp et pris en
une position excellente — d'un autre
côte on assure qu'à contray les françois
ont fait 800 hollandais

Germaine de Staël (1766–1817) to Louis de Narbonne
27 May 1793

The daughter of Louis XVI's finance minister Jacques Necker, Germaine Necker was introduced to enlightened thinkers and politicians at her parents' home in Paris. By her early twenties, she was publishing plays and *belles lettres*. After marrying the Swedish diplomat Baron de Staël-Holstein, she hosted an influential political salon during the early phase of the French Revolution. With the September Massacres of 1792, Germaine fled to Switzerland, then to England to rejoin her lover, the exiled former war minister Louis de Narbonne. On 26 May 1793, she sailed for Ostend, from where she wrote immediately to de Narbonne. She tells him about the latest developments in the Coalition Wars, her husband's ultra-radical secretary, Pierre Signeul, and a treacherous quayside ladder at Dover, enclosing £50 (about £4,000 today). Interspersed with war news, the emotional high notes of this letter ('all nature sings your praises') reveal de Staël's deep debt to the Romanticism of Jean-Jacques Rousseau.

It was awful leaving you, I have never suffered so much physically and mentally. I arrived here at midday yesterday with a fever, and I have got up now only to say goodbye to you and to set off, set off on the way to Germany because I am unable to disobey the one I love and I need to believe that my life is essential to him. Ah your life is all that is dear to me [...] all nature sings your praises [...]

[T]he Austrians have taken the camp at Famars after killing a thousand men[,] for the French I've heard that this camp is an excellent position. On the other hand I'm assured that at Courtrai the French have taken 600 Dutch prisoners [...]

M. de S. doesn't seem to be thinking of returning to London. It looks rather as if he'd like to return to Sweden to undertake great democratic schemes at least the ones that Signeul has in mind. You can imagine that, if this is their plan, I'll be far from seconding it. I've had my fill of France, not to mention the feeling that irresistibly draws me both towards where you are and to your wishes [...]

The English control Ostend and it's said that in general the soldiers of every nation wish for peace. All the same, the coalition army between here and Luxembourg is 120,000 strong and all the heavy artillery has arrived. I've heard that in the most recent business the French have had the upper hand but in the case of the camp at Famars the situation's clear, since the French have been expelled [...]

Remember everything I tell you, and watch out for a ladder you have to climb down into the ferryboat at Dover, if you lose your balance you fall into the sea. Dear God please look after yourself my angel I don't want to die [...]

Ah why do I not have more to give the most generous of men – how I love you adieu [...]

Comfort I got from him since — &
now I am again oblige to leave on more
than before if possible — as I have a Wife.

    may God ever keep you &
me from a tachement to this evil
World, & the things of it — I think I
shall be happy when time is no
more with me, as I am resolved
ever to look to Jesus Christ & submit
to his preordainations —

    Dr Sir I am with Christian
    Love to you & Wife — &c.
      Gustavus Vassa
        The African

J. Gurnell

Edinbury may 28th 1792

Dr Sir &c &c

    With respect I take this oppor-
tunity to acquaint you (by Mr. Ford an
acquaintance of mine who is to go to
Day for London) that I am in health — hope that you & Wife
is well — I have sold books at Glasgow
& Paisley, & came here on the 10th ult.
I hope next month to go to Dunde, Perth,
& Aberdeen — Sir I am sorry to tell you
that some Rascals have asserted in the
news papers viz oracle of the 25th of april,
& the Star 27th — that I am a native of a
Danish Island, Santa Cruz, in the West Indies
the assertion has hurted the sale of my
Books — I have now the afore said oracle
& will be much obliged to you, to get me
the Star, & take care of it till you see or

Olaudah Equiano (c.1745–97) to a friend
20 May 1792

In 1789, a former slave, now a free man, published his autobiography. *The Interesting Narrative of the Life of Olaudah Equiano* contained one of the earliest first-hand accounts of the Atlantic slave trade seen through a captured African's eyes. It provided powerful ammunition for the British anti-slavery campaign. Equiano was born in West Africa, kidnapped as a child and shipped to Virginia, where an English naval officer bought him, renaming him Gustavus Vassa. He served in the Seven Years' War between Britain and France, learned to read, reached London, was sold into Caribbean slavery again, then finally bought his freedom. After voyages to the Mediterranean and Arctic, he returned to London and became a leading abolitionist. In 1788, he petitioned Queen Charlotte (wife of George III) on behalf of all enslaved Africans.

The Interesting Narrative sold well, bringing Equiano income and fame. Here he describes a Scottish book tour, dealing with the press (he is furious at attempts to question his African identity) and losing a precious brooch in his lodgings. He'd recently married a young Cambridgeshire woman, Susannah Cullen. The loss of a substantial bad debt, together with his new responsibilities as a breadwinner, make him reflect that, although he is now a fêted author, he is 'obliged to slave on more than before'.

D[ea]r Sir, etc. etc.

With respect I take this oppertunity to acquaint you [...] that I am in health – hope that you & Wife is well – I have sold books at Glasgow & Paisley, & came here on the 18th ult [i.e. last month]. I hope next month to go to Dunde[e], Perth, & Aberdeen – Sir, I am sorry to tell you that some Rascal or Rascals have asserted in the news parpers [...] that I am a native of a Danish Island, Santa Cruz, in the W[es]t Indias. the assertion has hurted the sale of my Books [...] Pray ask Mr & Mrs Peters who Lodged in the next Room to me, if they have found a Little Round Gold Breast Buckel, or broach, sett in or with fine stones – if they have, I will pay them well for it. – & if they have found it pray write to me on that account Directly [...] I was in the General assembley of the Church of Scotland, now Convened & they agreed unanimously on a petition, or an address to the House of Lords to abolish the Slave Trade – & on which account I gave them an address of thanks in two news papers [...] Mr Lewis wrote me a Letter within 12 Days after I Left you & acquaint[e]d me of that villain who owed me above £200 – Dying on the 17th of april – & that is all the comfort I got from him since – & now I am again obliged to slave on more than before if possible – as I have a Wife [...]

D[ea]r Sir, – I am with Christian Love to you & Wife - etc.
Gustavus Vassa

The Priory,
21 North Bank.
Regents Park.

Sep. 15. 1870

My dear Mrs Pattison

I have abstained
a long while from troubling you
with any report of ourselves or
any inquiries about you, from
an impression that you prefer
being left uninterrupted by
such small claims on your
attention. But the painful,
too engrossing thoughts raised
by the War urge me to counter-
acting thoughts of all friendly
bands. It seems to me more
than ever that in all our

George Eliot (1819–80) to Emilia Francis Pattison
15 September 1870

Marian Evans and Emilia Francis Pattison (known as Francis) were contemporaries on the London literary scene. Francis was a critic; Marian, after starting out as a journalist, had published several novels under the pen-name George Eliot. The success of *Adam Bede*, *Romola* and *The Mill on the Floss* made her one of the highest-paid writers in Victorian England. In 1863 she and her partner, the writer George Henry Lewes, moved into a mansion near Regent's Park, where they entertained in style. The scandal that had dogged their first ten years together – they lived openly as a couple despite a legal bar on Lewes divorcing his wife – simmered down. Eliot refers to recent travels 'in search of health for my husband' (Lewes suffered from chronic headaches and nausea).

She was working on two stories that she would combine in her next novel, set in a fictional town in the Midlands in the 1830s. Writing to Francis, however, she's preoccupied by news of the Franco-Prussian War. Following the catastrophic French defeat at Sedan, Prussian forces had encircled Paris. On 14 September 1870, *The Times* – one of the papers Eliot and Lewes have been compulsively reading – carried a harrowing report. 'Incidents of the War' described wounded French soldiers laid out in railway yards: 'The clattering of the colossal munitions trains which go by, stirs in their wounds. They lie on the ground helpless.' Eliot's 'counter-acting' reflection, 'that in all our affectionate relations we have some of the moral treasure of the world under our charge', prefigures the theme of redemptive ordinary integrity and kindness that she would explore in the new novel, her masterpiece, *Middlemarch*.

My dear Mrs Pattison

I have abstained a long while from troubling you with any report of ourselves or any inquiries about you, from an impression that you prefer being left uninterrupted by such small claims on your attention. But the painful, too engrossing thoughts raised by the War urge me to counter-acting thoughts of all friendly bonds. It seems to me more than ever that in all our affectionate relations we have some of the moral treasure of the world under our charge. And thus the impulse to write to you & ask for a little news of you has become at last stronger than any diffidence [...]

Probably, like us, you spend a good deal of the day in reading the papers & discussing events contained in the telegrams & correspondence. I read through two daily papers, the Times & the Daily News – an excess in journal-reading that I was never drawn into before.

Very shortly after we parted from you we began wandering again, first into northern counties & then into southern, in search of health for my husband. At last we have won some of that good, & we are settled here with the hope of being able to enjoy our home corners for a long while. Perhaps I should be consulting only my own pleasure if I wished that you should not be equally stationary, but should find occasion to come to London [...] I am always affectionately yours

M E Lewes

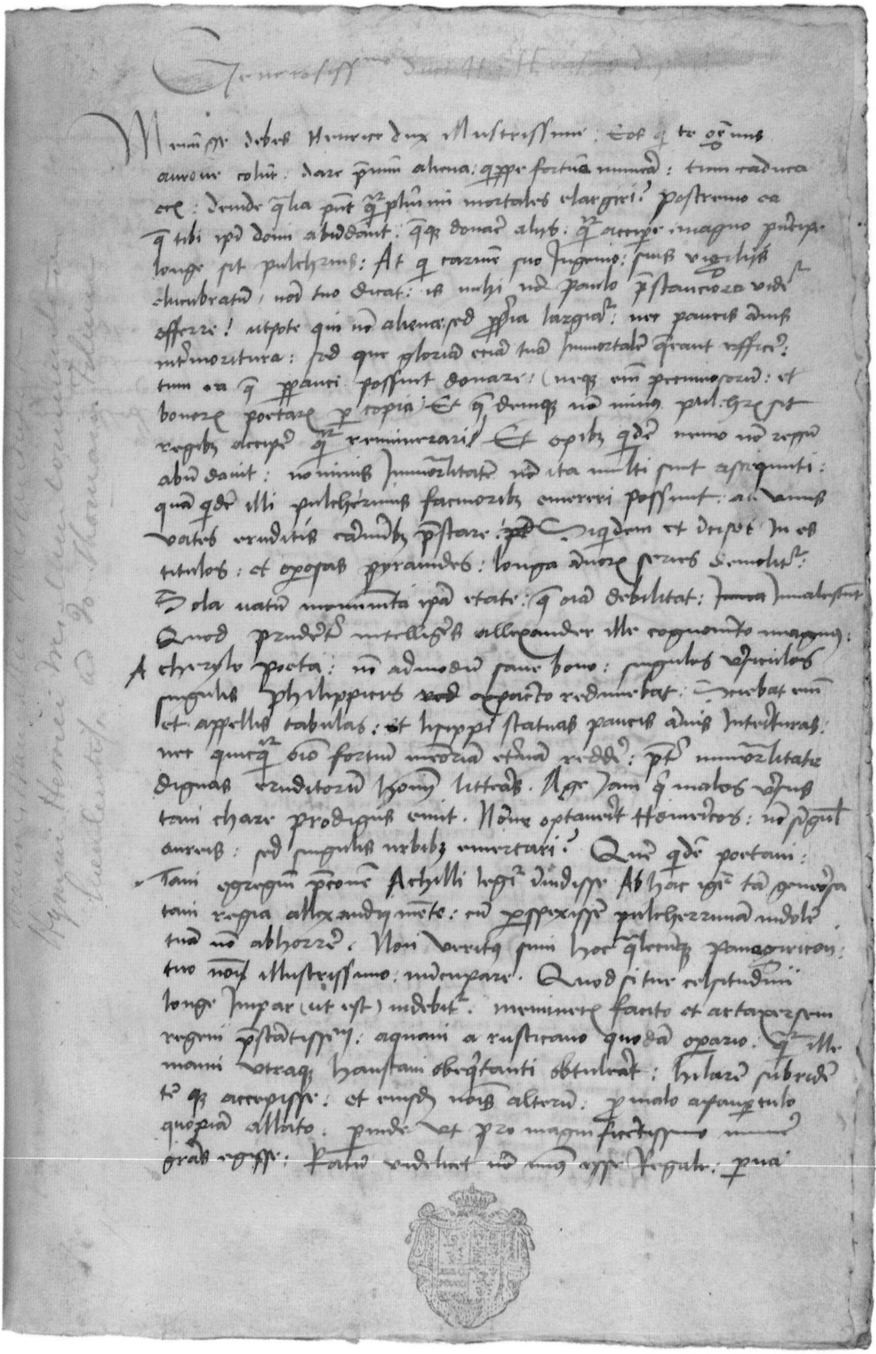

Desiderius Erasmus (1466–1536) to Prince Henry
Autumn 1499

Invited to England in 1499, the Dutch humanist philosopher and writer Desiderius Erasmus was introduced by Sir Thomas More to the eight-year-old Prince Henry (the future Henry VIII). More presented the prince with a poem, but hadn't forewarned Erasmus, who found himself embarrassingly empty-handed. In just three days, he composed a poem of 150 lines, which he duly presented to Henry with this letter. He seems to be addressing the future king rather than the child prince, making a case that still has to be made for the value of literature in a material world, where 'the supply of good poets by no means matches that of wealthy men'.

....

To the most noble boy, Prince Henry, from Erasmus the theologian, greetings

Illustrious Prince: you ought to remember that those persons who honour you with presents of jewels or of gold are giving you, firstly, what is not their own, for such gifts belong to Fortune, and are, moreover, perishable; further these gifts are such as the greater part of mankind can amply bestow, and lastly they are but what you yourself possess in abundance, and better beseem a great prince to give away than to receive. Whereas he who dedicated to you a poem which is the fruit of his own talent and toil seems to me to offer a present that is more distinguished by far; inasmuch as he lavishes upon you what belongs to himself, not to another, and will not fade away in a few years but may even bring you everlasting renown, and can be given to you by few indeed (for the supply of good poets by no means matches that of wealthy men) [...] And while there never was a king who was not overflowing with riches, not so many have achieved immortal fame. Kings may indeed earn such fame by their glorious deeds, but poets alone can confer it [...] for whereas waxen effigies, and portraits and geneaologies, and golden statues, and inscriptions on bronze, and pyramids laboriously reared, decay one and all with the passing of long years, only the poets' memorials grow stronger with the lapse of time, which weakens all things else [...]

    At the same time I am not unaware that most princes in modern times enjoy literature the less, the more they fail to comprehend it. They think it equally foolish, equally shameful, for a nobleman either to be schooled or to receive scholars' praise [...] The reason why they think it unseemly to accept a poet's praise is simply that they have ceased to do praiseworthy deeds, not that this prevents them from accepting the flattery of their parasites [...] It is because I am aware, most noble Prince, that your generous nature recoiled from such folly [...] that I have ventured to dedicate this laudatory poem, such as it is, to you [...]

    May you illuminate good literature by your high distinction, protect it with your royal authority, and encourage it by your generosity [...]

Hauteville house — 24 juin 1862

Mon illustre ami,

si le radical, c'est l'idéal pur,
je suis radical. Oui, à tous les points
de vue, je comprends, je veux ce
que j'appelle le mieux ; le mieux, n'est
pas l'ennemi du bien

et surtout n'est pas du mal.
Oui, une société qui admet la misère,
oui, une religion qui admet l'enfer,
oui, une humanité qui admet la guerre,
me semblent une société, une religion
et une humanité inférieures, et c'est
vers la société d'en haut, vers
l'humanité d'en haut, et vers la religion
d'en haut que je tends ; société sans
roi, humanité sans frontières, religion
sans livre. Oui, je combats le prêtre
qui vend le mensonge et le juge qui
rend l'injustice ;

c'est à
dire arriver à ce but : tout homme pro-
priétaire et aucun homme maître, voilà
pour moi la véritable économie sociale
et politique. J'abrège et je me résume.
Oui, autant qu'il est permis à l'homme
de vouloir, je veux la fatalité
humaine ; je condamne l'esclavage, je
chasse la misère, j'enseigne l'ignorance,

Victor Hugo (1802–85) to Alphonse de Lamartine
24 June 1862

Victor Hugo writes to the poet Alphonse de Lamartine from St Peter Port, Guernsey, where he lived between 1855 and 1870 as a political exile from the France of Napoleon III. Elected to the National Assembly as a conservative member in 1848, Hugo became progressively more left-wing, campaigning for educational reform, universal suffrage, the abolition of capital punishment and an end to poverty.

Published in 1862, his novel *Les Misérables* charts the extremes of wretchedness and prosperity experienced by the former convict and everyman figure Jean Valjean in the turbulent political landscape of early ninteenth-century France. It culminates in the June Rebellion of 1832, when government troops brutally suppressed an uprising in Paris. Smarting from the hostile reaction *Les Misérables* has received from the press, Hugo explains to Lamartine – a 'dazzling' role model of his youth – how the novel reflects his deeply held belief in 'fraternity' and social progress. He hopes the older writer will understand, though he may 'wish for a gentler slope' of reform than the radical Hugo.

....

My illustrious friend,

If being radical is the ideal, yes I am radical. Yes, from all points of view, I understand, I want and I call for more; more, although denounced by the proverb, is not less. Yes, a society which accepts poverty, yes, a religion which accepts hell, yes a humanity which accepts war, seems to me to be a society, a religion and a humanity which is inferior, and what I am seeking is a higher society, a higher humanity and a higher religion; a society without a king, a humanity without borders, a religion without a book. Yes I fight the priest who sells lies and the judge who delivers injustice[.] Universalizing property, which is the opposite of abolishing it, by eliminating parasitism, namely, for this purpose putting an end to: all owners and masters, that for me is the true social and political economy. I'll come to the point and summarize. Yes, as long as man is permitted to wish, I wish to eradicate human adversity; I condemn slavery, I seek to drive out poverty, I inform ignorance, I treat illness, I light up the night, I hate hatred. You most likely didn't bring the book back with you when you returned to us, and lived magnificently, untiringly leading the struggle, so I thought I'd like to replace the 'imprisoned copy'.

That is what I am, and that is why I wrote Les Misérables.

In my way of thinking, Les Misérables is nothing more than a book based on fraternity, with progress as its pinnacle [...]

Now judge me. Literary competition between men of letters is ridiculous, but political and social debate between poets, that's to say between philosophers, is serious and fruitful. You obviously want what I want, for the most part at least; you just perhaps wish for a gentler slope [...]

Dear Lamartine, a long time ago, in 1820, my first stuttering adolescent poetry was a cry of enthusiasm in the light of your dazzling dawn rising on the world [...] Make what you will of my book and me. Nothing can come out of your hands but light.

Your Old friend Victor Hugo

Route 1, Box 86-E
Eau Gallie, Florida, U.S.A.
Dec. 3, 1955.

Dear Madam Sabloniere:

Please excuse my writing you by hand, but no sooner did I get the envelope addressed to you, than my typewriter go out of order. I am conscious that my handwriting is not very good.

A million thanks for your kind and understanding letter. I have been astonished that my letter to The Orlando Sentinel has caused such a sensation over the whole United States. But when I realized the intense and bitter contention among some Negroes for physical contact with the Whites, I can see why the astonishment that one (myself) should hold that physical contact means nothing unless the spirit is also there, and therefore see small value in it. I actually do feel insulted when a certain type of white person hastens to effuse to me how noble they are to grant me their presence. But unfortunately, many who call themselves "leaders" of Negroes in America actually are unaware of the insulting patronage and rejoice in it. It is not that I have any race prejudice, for it is well known that I have numerous white friends, but they are <u>friends</u>, not merely some who seek

Zora Neale Hurston (1891–1960) to Margrit de Sablonière
3 December 1955

Zora Neale Hurston was a leading figure in the Harlem Renaissance, a flowering of African-American literature, music and art that took place in the Manhattan neighbourhood during the 1920s and 1930s. The first African-American to graduate from Barnard College, she was a true Renaissance woman: novelist, anthropologist, filmmaker. She was also a gifted provocateur, with detractors on both sides of America's racial divide. Her 1937 novel, *Their Eyes Were Watching God*, which explores African-American life in a lively vernacular, earned her many enemies among black readers, with the critic Ralph Ellison condemning its 'blight of caricature and burlesque'.

By 1955, after several flops and fall-outs, Hurston's career as a novelist was over. She'd returned to her home state of Florida, where she was living in a cabin. But she was back in the public eye. The previous year, the US Supreme Court had ruled that segregation in schools was unlawful – and Hurston had written a letter to the *Orlando Sentinel* attacking the verdict. She argued that such gestures could only go so far, and that it was more important to focus on the quality of education available to black children, whether segregated or not. 'How much satisfaction can I get from a court order,' she asked, 'for somebody to associate with me who does not wish me near them?'

She revisits the theme in this letter to the Dutch translator Margrit de Sablonière, but turns her satirical fire on well-meaning white people, who 'grant [her] their presence' in order to feel good about themselves (she referred to them elsewhere as 'Negrotarians'; today she might call them 'virtue-signallers'). She also alludes to a new, typically irreverent, project – a revisionist history of Herod, the ancient Judean king. Intriguing though it sounds, it failed to reverse her fortunes.

Dear Madame Sablonière:

Please excuse my writing you by hand, but no sooner did I get the envelope addressed to you than my typewriter go out of order. I am conscious that my handwriting is not very good.

A million thanks for your kind and understanding letter. I have been astonished that my letter to The Orlando Sentinel has caused such a sensation [...] But when I realized the intense and bitter contention among some Negroes for physical contact with the Whites, I can see the astonishment that one (myself) should hold that physical contact means nothing unless the spirit is also there, and therefore see small value in it. I do actually feel insulted when a certain type of White person hastens to effuse to me how noble they are to grant me their presence. But unfortunately, many who call themselves 'leaders' of Negroes in America actually are unaware of this insulting patronage and rejoice in it. It is not that I have any race prejudice, for it is well known that I have numerous White friends, but they are *friends*, not merely some who seek to earn a spurious 'merit' by patronizing Negroes [...]

My most honorable Lord.

May it please yo[r] Lo: to vnderstand, I haue done no want in mee, eyther of Labor or sincerity in the discharge of this busines. to the satisfaction of yo[r] Lo: and the State. And wheras, yesterday, vpon the first mention of it, I tooke the most ready course (to my present thought) by the Venetian Ambassadors Chaplin, who not only apprehended it well, but was of mind with mee, that no Man of Conscience, or any indifferent Loue to his Country would deny to doe it; and What engaged himselfe to find out one, absolute in all Numbers, for the purpose; with he will'd me (before a Gent. of good Credit, who is my Testimony) to signifie to yo[r] Lo: in his Name: It fals out since, that that Party will not be found, (for so he returnes answere.) vpon w[ch] I haue made attempt in other Places, but can speake with no one in Person (all being eyther remoou'd, or so conceal'd, vpon this present Mischeise) but by some Meanes, I haue receaud answere of doubts, and Difficulties, that they will make it a Question to the Archpriest, with other such like Suspicions: So that to tell yo[r] Lo: playnely my heart, I thinke they are all so enwoaud in it, as it will make 500 Gent: lesse of the Religion within this weeke, if they carry theyr vnderstanding about them. For my selfe, if I had bene a Priest, I would haue put on wings to such an Occasion, and haue thought it no aduenture, wheare I might haue done (besides his Maiesty, and my Country) all Christianity so good seruice. And so much I haue sent to some of them.

If it shall please yo[r] Lordsh: I shall yet make farder triall, and What you comaund in the meane time to pro-vided: I doubt not but I will toudgnesse offer my seruice, but will performe it with as much integrity, as yo[r] particular Fauor, or his Maiesties Right in any subiect he hath, can exact.

yo[r] Ho: most perfect
seruant in Law
Ben: Jonson.

Ben Jonson (1572–1637) to Robert Cecil
8 November 1605

On 5 November 1605, a plot to blow up the House of Lords during the State Opening of Parliament, with King James I present, was narrowly intercepted. In the manhunt that followed, while Guy Fawkes was being tortured to reveal the names of his co-conspirators, the playwright Ben Jonson was enlisted to track down a certain Catholic priest. In this letter to the statesman, spymaster and royal confidante Lord Robert Cecil, who was leading the investigation, Jonson explains in rather studied, courtly prose that he hasn't yet managed to collar the elusive cleric but is doing everything he can.

The previous month – as Cecil must have known – Jonson had had dinner with a group of the plotters. Like them, he was a Catholic – a large persecuted minority in early seventeenth-century England. Though it's possible he was present as a government spy rather than a secret sympathizer, he clearly needed to convince Cecil of his loyalty and wholehearted commitment to the task in hand. The spectacular masques he wrote for James I's court would make Jonson a royal favourite. But these were dangerous times, and a false step might easily have led to Jonson sharing the Gunpowder Plot conspirators' barbaric death by hanging, drawing and quartering.

My most honourable Lord.

May it please your Lordship to understand, there hath bene no want in mee, either of labor or sincerity in the discharge of this busines, to the satisfaction of your Lordship and the state. And wheras, yesterday, upon the first Mention of it, I took the most ready Course (to my present thought) by the Venetian Ambassadors Chaplin, who not only apprehended it well, but was of mind with me, that no Man of Conscience, or any indifferent Love to his Countrey would deny to doe it [...] It falls out since, that that Party will not be found [...] upon which I have made attempt in other Places, but can speake with no one in Person (all being either remov'd or so conceal'd; upon this present Mischeife) [...] So that to tell your Lordship playnly my heart, I thinke they are All so enwean'd [deeply involved] in it, as it will make 500 Gentlemen less of the Religion within this weeke, if they carry their understanding about them. For my selfe, if I had been a Preist, I would have put on wings to such an Occasion, and have thought it no adventure, where I might have done (besides his Maiesty, and my Countrey) all Christianity so good service [...] If it shall please your Lordship I shall yet make farther trial, and that you cannot in the meane time be provided: I do not only with all readynesse offer my service, but will performe it with as much integrity, as your particular Favor, or his Maiesty's Right in any subject he hath, can exalt.

Your Honour['s] most perfect servant and Lover

Ben Jonson

Spelling partly modernized

Sambrook Ward.
4th London Hosp.
Denmark Hill.

Tuesday .24th. (1917)

My dear Uncle.

(when I see the corpses again; last
week was beyond anything I had been
up against before. I should love
to have the Hardy letter. The
book of poems will really be out
next week they say. Binders work slow.
love from Sigi.

I was very nearly your (late) nephew, as the
sniper only just ~~failed to~~ makes a good job of it, &
the bullet missed my jugular by a fraction of an inch,
& the spinal column by not too much. But, as
I wrote in the Head Sister's album, (by request).

"Good luck to the him
Who got out his gun
And dealt me a wound so auspicious;
May a flesh-hole like mine
Send him home from the Line
And his Nurses be just as delicious"—

(An effort which aroused delighted simpers of female
gratification).
"The Line" was the Hindenburg (not the "Siegfried"!)
& we were trying to take Fontaine-les-Croisilles,
(which is still holding out, curse it) (7m. dstk. of Arras).

This is Lotus-Land, with Dones & Mrs Gosse
& other sweet people drifting in of an afternoon laden
with gifts — & the only bad thing a bad Gramophone.
which grinds out excruciations of Little Grey homes in
the West. etc. Mother is busy being massaged, & is
not allowed to come up. I expect to be here another
week or more. It has healed up all right in front;
but not behind. I think another dose of the war
will just about send me dotty. I get the horrors at night

Siegfried Sassoon (1886–1967) to William Hamo Thornycroft
24 April 1917

Siegfried Sassoon enlisted in the British army on the day war was declared in August 1914. Before that, he'd been a literary country gentleman, writing romantic verse and hunting. As an officer in the Royal Welch Fusiliers, 'Mad Jack' Sassoon gained a reputation for suicidal courage on the Western Front. In July 1916, he was awarded the Military Cross for recovering dead and wounded soldiers under fire. Advice from poet and brother officer Robert Graves led Sassoon to abandon his earlier lyricism and write plainly about the brutal facts of war. *The Old Huntsman*, published in 1917 with a dedication to Thomas Hardy (see page 161), was the first of his books to feature the war poems on which his reputation now stands.

The Old Huntsman was at the printers when Sassoon was shot in the neck, narrowly escaping paralysis or death – as he writes to his maternal uncle from hospital in London. William Thornycroft was an eminent sculptor of public monuments and friend of Hardy. Sassoon tries to sound nonchalant, copying a jingle he's penned for the nurses and complaining about a loud gramophone, but also confesses to suffering traumatic flashbacks. Within weeks, he would write an open letter to the press, denouncing official hypocrisy about the war, which was read aloud in the House of Commons. Sassoon expected to be court-martialled but was instead transferred to Craiglockhart military hospital, where a pioneering approach to the effects of 'shell shock' (now called post-traumatic stress disorder) was being developed. Another Craiglockhart inmate was Wilfred Owen, whose poetry Sassoon did much to publicize after the war.

My dear Uncle,

I was very nearly your (late) nephew, as the sniper only just failed to make a good job of it, & the bullet missed my jugular by a fraction of an inch, & the spinal column by not too much. But, as I wrote in the Head Sister's album, (by request),

> 'Good luck to the hun
> Who got out his gun
> And dealt me a wound so auspicious;
> May a flesh-hole like mine
> Send him home from the Line,
> And his Nurses be just as delicious' –

(An effort which aroused delighted simpers of female gratification).

'The Line' was the Hindenburg (not the 'Siegfried'!) & we were trying to take Fontaine-lez-Croisilles, (7m south of Arras) [...]

This is Lotus-Land [...] & the only bad thing a bad Gramophone, which grinds out excruciations of Little Grey homes in the West, etc [...] It has healed up all right in front, but not behind. I think another dose of the war will just about send me dotty. I get the horrors at night [top of page] (when I see the corpses again; last week was beyond anything I had been up against before. I should love to have the Hardy letter. The book of poems will *really* be out next week they say. Binders were slow.

Love from Sig.

La Favière, par Bormes
(Var)
Villa Wrangel
6го iюля 1935г., суббота

Милый Тихоновъ,

Мне страшно жаль, что не удалось съ Вами проститься. У меня отъ нашей короткой встречи осталось горькое чувство. Я уже писала Борису: Вы мне предстали идущимъ навстречу - какъ мостъ, и - какъ мостъ, заставляющимъ идти въ своемъ направленiи. (Ибо другого - нетъ. На то и мостъ.)

Что Вамъ этотъ край - по сердцу и по силамъ - я верю и вижу. Вы самъ - этотъ край. Фактъ своего края, а не свидетельство о немъ. Вы самъ - тотъ мостъ, - изъ техъ, что сейчасъ идетъ много спорятъ. Видите - какъ съ иносказательного моста, похожа Достоевскихъ, и рада, какъ всему, что - само.

Съ Вами - свидимся.

Ибо В. - у меня смутное чувство. Онъ для меня порученъ темъ, что всё, что для меня - право, для него - его, Борисомъ, порокъ, болезнь.

Какъ мне - тогда (Васъ, видимо, не дело, - тогда

Marina Tsvetaeva (1892–1941) to Nikolai Tikhonov
6 July 1935

In June 1935, the International Congress for the Defence of Culture took place in Paris. Against a backdrop of fascist ascendancy in Germany and Italy, and fears of another European war, left-wing writers gathered to show solidarity. The Russian poet Marina Tsvetaeva, living in exile in France, was overjoyed at the prospect of seeing Boris Pasternak, one of the great lyric poets of her generation. They had met only briefly in 1918, but after 1922, when Tsvetaeva left Russia, they'd maintained a passionate creative correspondence. Pasternak, however, seemed withdrawn and depressed, trapped in the political quicksands of Stalin's Russia. After their 'non-meeting', she wrote advising him to 'think less of yourself'.

The following month, Tsvetaeva writes from the south of France to Nikolai Tikhonov, a conference delegate now back in Russia. Homesick and saddened by her encounter with Pasternak, she thanks Tikhonov for acting as a 'bridge' between them. Unlike either Pasternak or Tsvetaeva, Tikhonov – a former Red Army soldier – has found favour with the Soviet state. She teases him with a reference to *kolkhoz* (collective farms) – let's be upbeat and patriotic, she seems to say, instead of giving in to emotion.

Three years later, as Europe descended into war, Tsvetaeva returned to Russia. Soon afterwards, her husband, Sergei Efron, and their daughter, Alya, were arrested as spies. On 31 August 1941, isolated and possibly being pressured to turn informer for the NKVD (secret police), Tsvetaeva hanged herself.

Dear Tikhonov,

I'm terribly sorry that I couldn't say goodbye to you. Our short meeting left me with a wonderful feeling. I have already written to Boris: it seemed to me that you were coming towards me – like a bridge, and – just like a bridge – making me walk in that direction. (Any other direction – no. That's what a bridge does.)

What this land is for you – for your heart and your strength – I believe and see. You yourself are this land [...] You yourself are that bridge, not those bridges that are being built everywhere these days. You see – starting with a metaphorical bridge, I ended up – with a real one, and I'm glad, as I am about everything that is really itself.

You and me – we will see each other [...]

How about me – then (you, apart from anything else, were not there – then there would be no tears) – weeping. 'Why are you crying?' 'I'm not crying, it's the eyes that are crying' – If I'm not crying now, it's because I decided absolutely to refrain from hysteria and neurasthenia. (I was so surprised that I immediately stopped crying) – You will love the collective farms!

– In response to my tears – 'Collective farms!' [...]

And I cried because Boris, the best lyric poet of our time, betrayed the Lyric before my eyes, calling himself and everything in himself diseased. Let's call it 'loftiness', but that's not what he said. He also didn't say that this disease is dearer to him than health itself [...]

I'd love to hear from you, but if you don't want to write or cannot, I will understand that too.

M.T.

Hartford, May 24/89.

To Walt Whitman:

You have lived just the seventy years which are greatest in the world's history & richest in benefit & advancement to its peoples. These seventy years have done much more to widen the interval between man & the other animals than was accomplished by any five centuries which preceded them.

What great births you have witnessed! The steam press, the steamship, the steel ship, the railroad, the perfected cotton-gin, the telegraph, the telephone, the phonograph, the photograph, photo-gravure, the electrotype, the gaslight, the electric light, the sewing machine, & the amazing, infinitely varied & innumerable products of coal tar,

Mark Twain (1835–1910) to Walt Whitman
24 May 1889

Towards the end of his life, Walt Whitman was being fêted as America's greatest living poet. It hadn't happened overnight. His 1855 collection, *Leaves of Grass*, had been dismissed as 'a mass of stupid filth', due to its experimental technique and homoerotic overtones. But by 1889, although Whitman still had his detractors, his poetry was increasingly seen as a paragon of American art: rugged, questing, nobly individualistic.

Whitman was in poor shape. Since narrowly surviving a stroke in 1873, he'd been living quietly in Camden, New Jersey, writing little. Just before his seventieth birthday, however, he was deluged with letters from admirers, including a fifty-three-year-old Mark Twain. By this point, Twain was also a grand old man of letters: his *Adventures of Huckleberry Finn* (1884) had been extolled as 'the Great American Novel'. But where Whitman was rough-edged, transcendental and wary of the 'learn'd astronomer', Twain was urbane, satirical and a cheerleader for science (he had assisted in some of his friend Nikola Tesla's experiments with electricity). Here, though, his tone takes on an almost religious fervour as he recounts the innovations that have occurred during Whitman's lifetime – and predicts (a little naively) that in thirty years' time technology will have enabled humanity to reach its 'full stature'.

Twain also enthuses about the sweeping changes that have taken place in America over the past century. This former assortment of colonies was now well on the way to becoming the world's most powerful nation. And, between them, Twain and Whitman had helped lay the foundations for America to become a dominant literary force in the twentieth century too.

....

To Walt Whitman:

You have lived just the seventy years which are the greatest in the world's history & richest in benefit and advancement to its peoples. These seventy years have done much more to widen the interval between man & the other animals than was accomplished by any five centuries which preceded them.

What great births you have witnessed! The steam press, the steamship, the steel ship, the railroad, the perfected cotton gin, the telegraph, the telephone, the phonograph, the photograph, photo-gravure, the electrotype, the gaslight, the electric light, the sewing machine [...] And you have seen even greater births than these; for you have seen the application of anaesthesia to surgery-practice, whereby the ancient dominion of pain, which began with the first created life, came to an end in this earth forever; you have seen the slave set free, you have seen monarchy banished from France, and reduced in England to a machine which makes an imposing show of diligence & attention to business, but isn't connected with the works. Yes, you have indeed seen much – but tarry here a while, for the greatest is yet to come. Wait thirty years, & then look out over the earth! You shall see marvels upon marvels added to these whose nativity you have witnessed & conspicuous above them you shall see their formidable Result — Man at almost his full stature at last! [...]

To: KURT VONNEGUT
WILLIAMS CREEK
INDIANAPOLIS, IND.

From:
PFC. K. VONNEGUT, JR.
12102964 U.S. ARMY
PAGE ONE

(CENSOR'S STAMP)   See Instruction No. 2   (Sender's complete address above)

DEAR PEOPLE!

I'M TOLD THAT YOU WERE PROBABLY NEVER INFORMED ①
THAT I WAS ANYTHING OTHER THAN "MISSING IN ACTION."
CHANCES ARE THAT YOU ALSO FAILED TO RECEIVE ANY
OF THE LETTERS I WROTE FROM GERMANY. THAT
LEAVES ME A LOT OF EXPLAINING TO DO — IN PRÉCIS:

I'VE BEEN A PRISONER OF WAR SINCE DECEMBER
19TH, 1944 WHEN OUR DIVISION WAS CUT TO RIBBONS
BY HITLER'S LAST DESPERATE THRUST THROUGH LUXEMBURG
AND BELGIUM. SEVEN FANATICAL PANZER DIVISIONS HIT US
AND CUT US OFF FROM THE REST OF HODGES' FIRST
ARMY. THE OTHER AMERICAN DIVISIONS ON OUR FLANKS
MANAGED TO PULL OUT: WE WERE OBLIGED TO STAY
AND FIGHT. BAYONETS AREN'T MUCH GOOD AGAINST
TANKS: OUR AMMUNITION, FOOD AND MEDICAL SUPPLIES
GAVE OUT AND OUR CASUALTIES OUTNUMBERED THOSE
WHO COULD STILL FIGHT — SO WE GAVE UP. THE
106TH GOT A PRESIDENTIAL CITATION AND SOME BRITISH
DECORATION FROM MONTGOMERY FOR IT, I'M TOLD, BUT
I'LL BE DAMNED IF IT WAS WORTH IT. I WAS
ONE OF THE FEW WHO WEREN'T WOUNDED. FOR THAT
MUCH THANK GOD.

HAVE YOU FILLED IN COMPLETE ADDRESS AT TOP?

REPLY BY
V---MAIL

HAVE YOU FILLED IN COMPLETE ADDRESS AT TOP?

Kurt Vonnegut (1922–2007) to family
29 May 1945

Three weeks after the end of the war in Europe, Kurt Vonnegut is in a Red Cross camp in north-west France. He writes to his family in the States, who haven't heard from him for months.

Vonnegut was taken prisoner in the Battle of the Bulge, the Germans' last major offensive, in December 1944. He gives a matter-of-fact account of what happened next, quietly emphasizing the extraordinary fact that he's still alive. His experience in Dresden, where he and other soldiers survived the Allied firebombing of the city by sheltering in an underground meat-locker, would form the basis of his 1969 novel *Slaughterhouse-Five*, one of the greatest anti-war books of the century.

Dear People:

I'm told that you were probably never informed that I was anything other than 'missing in action' [...] That leaves me a lot of explaining to do [...]

I've been a prisoner of war since December 19th, 1944, when our division was cut to ribbons by Hitler's last desperate thrust through Luxemburg and Belgium [...] Bayonets aren't much good against tanks [...]

The supermen marched us, without food, water or sleep to Limberg [...] where we were loaded and locked up, sixty men to each small, unventilated, unheated box car [...] On Christmas eve the Royal Air Force bombed and strafed our unmarked train. They killed about one-hundred-and-fifty of us. We got a little water Christmas Day and moved slowly across Germany to a large P.O.W. Camp in Muhlburg, south of Berlin. We were released from the box cars on New Year's Day. The Germans herded us through scalding delousing showers. Many men died from shock [...] But I didn't.

Under the Geneva Convention, Officers and Non-commissioned Officers are not obliged to work when taken prisoner. I am, as you know, a Private. One-hundred-and-fifty such minor beings were shipped to a Dresden work camp [...] I was their leader by virtue of the little German I spoke [...] After desperately trying to improve our situation for two months and having been met with bland smiles I told the guards just what I was going to do to them when the Russians came. They beat me up a little [...]

On about February 14th the Americans came over, followed by the R.A.F. their combined labors killed 250,000 people in twenty-four hours and destroyed all of Dresden – possibly the world's most beautiful city. But not me [...]

When General Patton took Leipzig we were evacuated on foot to [...] the Saxony-Czechoslovakian border. There we remained until the war ended [...] On that happy day the Russians were intent on mopping up isolated outlaw resistance in our sector. Their planes (P-39's) strafed and bombed us, killing fourteen, but not me.

Eight of us stole a team and wagon. We traveled and looted our way through Sudetenland and Saxony [...] The Russians picked us up in Dresden. We rode from there to the American lines at Halle in Lend-Lease Ford trucks. We've since been flown to Le Havre [...]

Chapter 4

'I turn to look on you'

All for Love

ne, but I am hoping that you a
take any step that would pe
ny sicknes as that I cannot sti
eart oh my love you have no fr
t the sickness in my heart has
to make each other happy o
camarade', without reference t
our vassal; but bu
larling love, this will be one a
at is so close to my heart, be
ny lodging but only one tram
into a terribly strung-out stat
few well-chosen, heartfelt wor
eet poison from your lips to s
vas the mysterious twilight hou
less longings, instinctive des
d have whiskers, or not? My w
passion; but I know no passi

Guillaume Apollinaire (1880–1918)
to Louise de Coligny-Châtillon
2 June 1915

Shortly before joining the French army in December 1914, the poet and art critic Guillaume Apollinaire had a passionate fling with Louise de Coligny-Châtillon, a glamorous pioneer aviator. De Coligny refused to leave her long-term lover Gustave Toutant (Toutou), and they split up in March 1915, when Apollinaire was posted to the Western Front. From the trenches, he wrote obsessively to de Coligny, vividly reimagining their short-lived sex life. In this letter, he plays on the French word *rose* (a rose, the colour pink); *feuilles de rose* (rose leaves) refers to both an actual gift from de Coligny and a sexual practice ('you do that incredibly well my Lou'). As his fantasies unfold, Apollinaire's letter gradually becomes less graphic, more tender. He ends with a new poem: 'Lou, you're my rose/Isn't your wonderful backside the loveliest of roses/ Aren't your breasts roses your darling breasts/And roses, aren't they pretty little Lous/ Whipped in the same way the breeze/Castigates the undersides of roses/In the abandoned garden.'

In March 1916, Apollinaire received a shrapnel wound in the head. Returning to Paris, he was assigned non-combatant duties and reimmersed himself in the art world. Weakened by his injury, he died in the Spanish Flu epidemic that swept Europe in the winter of 1918.

....

Amazing, my Lou

The idea of sending me rose leaves and finding that unsuitable! [...] It made me laugh for an hour at least and at the same time stirred me up forcefully [...] because you do that incredibly well my Lou [...] We'll come back, Toutou and I, and you'll see what good care we'll take of you and we'll make you very very happy while leaving you to your own devices as far as gardening is concerned. My li'l sweetest Lou, the long sexy kiss you sent me put me into a terribly strung-out state [...] I saw myself again as Lou's master, I dominated her completely; Lou was turned on to the point of sickness [...] and she madly loved her dominator Gui. Lou was just a little boy I whipped for pleasure [...] while little Lou shook with desire and love, Lou was just a naughty little boy [...] I pulled down his little sailor trousers the better to see your big rosy arse [...] one of my arms slipped under your waist and pressed hard against your little hard, smooth belly [...] while with the other hand I whipped hard very very hard, forcing you to lift your big rosy arse, right up in the air [...]

However, all things considered, I'm afraid that the war still won't be over, on this subject, little darling, I'd like to know what you think [...] When I have these feelings for you, I dream of only one thing: taking you in my arms and rocking you gently, very gently while I hug you, I want to see you sleeping my dearest dear, me right beside you, watching your lovely swelling tits, pink as eglantines [...]

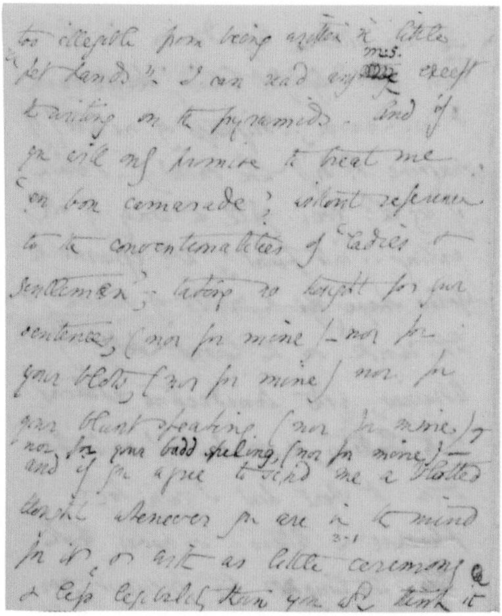
too illegible from being written in little
'fat hands'. I can read any MS. except
the writing on the pyramids. And if
you will only promise to treat me
'en bon camarade', without reference
to the conventionalities of 'ladies &
gentlemen', taking no thought for your
sentences, (nor for mine) — nor for
your blots, (nor for mine) nor for
your blunt speaking (nor for mine) nor for your badd speling, (nor for mine) —
and if you agree to send me a blotted
thought whenever you are in the mind
for it, & with as little ceremony
& less legibility than you would think it

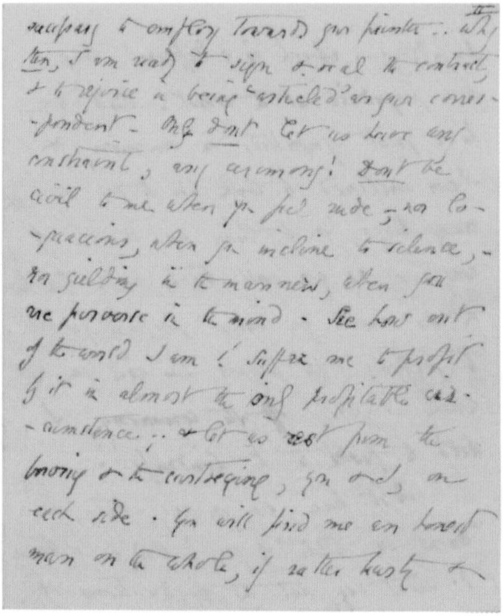
necessary to employ towards your printer. — Why,
then, I am ready to sign & seal the contract,
& to rejoice in being 'articled' as your corres-
-pondent. Only don't let us have any
constraint, any ceremony! Don't be
civil to me when you feel rude, — nor com-
-placent, when you incline to silence, —
nor yielding in the manners, when you
are perverse in the mind. See how out
of the world I am! Suffer me to profit
by it in almost the only profitable cir-
-cumstance, & let us rest from the
bowing & the curtsying, you and I, on
each side. You will find me an honest
man on the whole, if rather hasty &

Elizabeth Barrett (1806–61) to Robert Browning
3 February 1845

Elizabeth Barrett and Robert Browning (see page 103) had long admired each other in print, but in early 1845 something else was happening. The two poets – also known for their support for progressive social causes – were exchanging letters. In his first, Browning held nothing back: 'I love your verse … and I love you too.' Barrett's response was more cautious, but soon enough they were in touch almost every day. On 3 February, writing about a month into their correspondence, Barrett mostly sticks to literary matters, asking Browning whether he thinks poetry can be separated from the personality of the poet, and whether reviews should be taken seriously (she alludes to the lingering rumour that Keats had been killed by a bad one; see page 201). But her tone is often playful; and, for all the little jokes, the long list of conditions she makes in this extract for their future correspondence – 'promise to treat me "en bon camarade" … taking no thought for your sentences (nor for mine) … nor for your badd speling (nor for mine)' – suggests that she knows this is going to be an important relationship.

Browning dropped heavy hints that he wanted to meet in person. Barrett was resistant. Six years older than him, and increasingly frail, she insisted that her poetry was the most attractive thing about her. But on 20 May, Browning visited her at her home in Westminster – and declared his love. They married the following year.

. . . .

[…] I write this to you to show how I can have pleasure in letters, & never think them too long, nor too frequent, nor too illegible […] I can read any m.s. except the writing on the pyramids. And if you will only promise to treat me 'en bon camarade', without reference to the conventionalities of 'ladies & gentlemen' […] taking no thought for your sentences, (nor for mine) – nor for your blots, (nor for mine) nor for your blunt speaking (nor for mine), nor for your badd speling, (nor for mine) – and if you agree to send me a blotted thought whenever you are in the mind for it, & with as little ceremony & less legibility than you wd think it necessary to employ towards your printer – why then, I am ready to sign & seal the contract, & to rejoice in being 'articled' as your correspondent. Only dont let us have any constraint, any ceremony! Dont be civil to me when you feel rude, – nor loquacious, when you incline to silence, – nor yielding in the manners, when you are perverse in the mind […] You will find me an honest man on the whole, if rather hasty & prejudging […] which is a different thing from prejudice at the worst. And we have great sympathies in common, & I am inclined to look up to you in many things, & to learn as much of everything as you will teach me. On the other hand you must prepare yourself to forbear & to forgive – will you? […]

Saty night. March 1.

Dear Miss Barrett — I seem to find of a middle—
—worthy I knew before — anyhow, I do find now,
that with the octaves on octaves of quite new
golden strings you enlarged the compass of
my life's harp with, there is added too, such
a tragic chord — that which you touch'd, so
gently, in the beginning of your last sad gift
this morning = just escaping &c. But if my
truest heart's wishes avail, as they have
hitherto done, you shall laugh at East
winds yet, as I do — Put now: this
sad feeling is so strange to me, that
I must write it out, must — and you
might give me great, the greatest pleasure
for years and yet find me as passive
as a stone used to wine-libations, and

Robert Browning (1812–89) to Elizabeth Barrett
1 March 1845

Robert Browning and Elizabeth Barrett (see page 101) were two of the nineteenth century's great nonconformists. When they began exchanging love letters, they did it their way. Their correspondence, which began in January 1845, five months before they met in person, contains as much Greek poetry as grand passion.

Both were wary of the honeyed phrase, the beguiling but empty gesture. In this letter, Browning goes to frenzied lengths to say exactly what he means and ends up tying himself in knots. He's disturbed by Barrett's claim in her last letter that she had 'just escaped with her life' from the cold weather and feels he must explain the sorrow this caused him. (Barrett later assured him that it was a throwaway remark; her letters tended to be more lighthearted than his.) He's on surer ground discussing Barrett's youthful translation of Aeschylus's *Prometheus Bound*, to which she had also referred ('If I ever get well I shall show my joy by making a bonfire out of [it]'). Yet the story had unhappy resonances for them both. Barrett's father, though supportive of her creative endeavours, forbade any of his twelve children to marry. The housebound Barrett often compared herself to the mythological figure of Prometheus, chained to his rock.

Dear Miss Barrett – I seem to find of a sudden – surely I knew before – anyhow, I *do* find now, that with the octaves on octaves of quite new golden strings you enlarged the compass of my life's harp with, there is added, too, such a tragic chord, that which you touched, so gently, in the beginning of your letter I got this morning: 'just escaping' &c [...] See now: this sad feeling is so strange to me, that I must write it out, *must* [...] I have been 'spoiled' in this world – to such an extent, indeed, that I often *reason* out – make clear to myself – that I might very properly, so far as myself am concerned, take any step that would peril the whole of my future happiness – because the past is gained, secure, and on record; and, tho' not another of the old days should dawn on me, I shall not have lost my life, no! [...] How strangely this connects itself in my mind with another subject in your note! I looked at that translation for a minute, not longer, years ago, knowing nothing about it or you [...] but the original makes Prometheus (telling over his bestowments towards human happiness,) say [...] that he stopped mortals μη προδερκεσθαι μορον [from foreseeing their doom] —το ποιον εὑρων, asks the Chorus, τησδε φαρμακον νοσου [what cure did you discover for this affliction]? Whereto he replies 'τυφλας εν αυτοις ελπιδας κατἔωκισα [I planted blind hopefulness firmly in their hearts] (what you hear men dis[s]ertate upon by the hour, as proving the immortality of the soul apart from revelation, undying yearnings, restless longings, instinctive desires which, unless to be eventually indulged, it were cruel to plant in us, &c. &c.) [...]

Yours *ever*,
R.B.

Sr

I a very respectiue feare of yor displeasure, and a
doubt, that my L: whom I knew owt of yor worthines to loue yo^u much,
would be so compassionate wth yo^u, as to add his anger to yo^{rs} did not
so much increase my sicknes, as that I cannot stir I had taken the
boldnes to haue donne the office of this letter by wayting vpon yor self
my self. To haue giuen yo^u truthe, and clearnes of this matter
between yor daughter and me; and to show to yo^u plainly the limits
of o^r fault, by wch I know yor wisdome wyll proportion the punishm^t.
So long since as at her being at yorkhouse this had foundation: and so
much then of promise and contract built vpon yt as wthowt violence
to Conscience might not be shaken. At her lyeng in town this last
parliam^t, I found meanes to see her twice or thrice: we both knew
the obligations that lay vpon vs, and wee aduentured equally, and about
three weeks before Christmas we married. And as at the doinge, there
were not vsd aboue fyue persons, of wch I protest to yo^u by my saluation
there was not one that had any dependence or relation to yo^u, so in all the
passage of it did I forbear to vse any such person, who by furtheringe
of yt might violate any trust or duty towards yo^u. The reasons why
I did not forracquaint yo^u wth it, (to deale wth the same plainnes that I
haue vsd) were these. I knew my present estate lesse then fitt for her; I
knew (yet I knew not why) that I stood not right in yor opinion; I
knew that to haue giuen any intimacion of yt had been to impossibilitate
the whole matt^r. And then hauing these purposes in o^r harts, and those
fetters in o^r Consciences, me thinke we should be pardoned, if o^r fault be but
this, that wee did not by fore-reuealinge of yt, consent to o^r hindrance
and torment. S^r I acknowledge my fault to be so great, as I dare scarce
offer any other prayer to yo^u in myne own behalf, then this, to beleeue this
truthe, that I neyth^r had dishonest end nor meanes. But for her
whom I tender much more then my fortunes or lyfe (els I would I might
neyth^r ioy in this lyfe, nor enioy the next) I humbly beg of yo^u, that she
may not, to her danger, feele the torror of yor sodaine anger. I know
this letter shall find yo^u full of passion: but I know no passion can
alter yor reason and wisdome; to wch I aduenture to comend these
perticulers; That yt ys irremediably donne. That if yo^u incense
my L, yo^u destroy her and me; That yt is, vie may cause to giue vs happines; And
that my endeuors and industrie, if it please yo^u to prosper them, may
soone make me somewhat worthyer of her. If any take the

John Donne (1572–1631) to George More
2 February 1602

After Oxford University, followed by legal training and volunteering in naval expeditions against Spain, John Donne's career was at last taking off. In 1597, he was appointed secretary to Sir Thomas Egerton, a leading political figure of the late Elizabethan era. Though Donne was already writing poems on which his modern fame would rest – including some of the greatest English erotic verse – these were known during his lifetime only from handwritten copies shared among a small literary circle.

At Egerton's London mansion, York House, Donne met and fell in love with Ann, the teenage daughter of Sir George More, a Surrey landowner and politician known for his killjoy views (including an attempt to shut down ale-houses). Justifiably anxious that More would 'impossibilitate' their relationship, they married secretly in December 1601. When Ann temporarily returned home, Donne finally explained the situation to More. His eloquent attempt to calm his father-in-law's 'passion', flattering his 'wisdome and reason' and appealing to his better paternal feelings, had no effect. More used his influence to have Donne imprisoned. 'John Donne, Ann Donne, Undone' was how, with characteristically wry wordplay, Donne summed up the troubled but resolute start to their married life.

Sir,

If a very respective feare of your displeasure [...] did not so much increase my sicknes as that I cannot stir I had taken the boldness to have done the office of this letter by waiting upon you myself: To have given you truthe and clearness of this matter between your daughter and me [...] At her lying in town this last Parliament, I found meanes to see her twice or thrice [...] and about three weeks before Christmas we married [...] The reasons why I did not foreacquaint you with it [...] were these. I knew my present estate lesse than fitt for her; I knew (yet I knew not why) that I stood not right in your opinion; I knew that to have given any intimacion of it had been to impossibilitate the whole matter. And then having these honest purposes in our hearts and those fetters in our consciences, me thinks we should be pardoned, if our fault be but this, that wee did not, by fore-revealinge of it, consent to our hindrance and torment. Sir, I acknowledge my fault to be so great, as dare scarse offer any other prayer to you in mine own behalf, than this [...] that I neither had dishonest end nor meanes. But for her whom I tender much more, than my fortunes, or lyfe [...] I humbly beg of you, that she may not, to her danger, feele the terror of your sudaine anger. I know this letter shall find you full of passion: but I know no passion can alter your reason and wisdom [...] I have truly told you this matter, and I humbly beseeche you so to deale in it, as the persuasions of nature, reason, wisdome and Christianity shall informe you [...]

Spelling partly modernized

Red Cross
St. Martin's Buildings
Alexandria
25.4.17

Dear Lytton,

You have written at last, if in the New Statesman. What, besides you, has come over that paper? Coming back from the dead soldiers, I picked up a special Christian number, all about Easter. Has it been bought by Button Broth? I lay reading it up the office stairs, whose ridges in my spine raised other reminiscences. Steps were heard ascending. Had after all the Corporal — — It was Miss V. Grant Duff, though.

I shall be more typical however in describing a typical day. This morning, after breakfast, I took tram to the office where, 850 wounded having arrived in the hospitals as the result of our second Gaza victory, there was work. At 1.0 I gave an English lesson to a Venezelo-International-Socialist, our lent books being Le Jardin d'Épicure and The Silver Box. We lunched. He saw no reason why Europe should not be federated like Switzerland. Then I went to No 15 G.H., whose O.C. is brother to Monty James. The Missing lists from the two victories, which are rumoured tremendous, have not yet come out, but I learnt something about the country, disposition of Regts. etc. and got materials for a map. All the time a man whose hands had been shot to bits was whimpering and whistling "I'm in a fix, I'm in a fix." Another man, a stranger to him and quite a boy, bent over and

E.M. Forster (1879–1970) to Lytton Strachey
25 April 1917

E.M. Forster spent the First World War working for the Red Cross in Egypt. His job was to track down details of British soldiers listed as missing in battle. Apart from his annoying boss, Victoria Grant Duff, he found wartime life in Alexandria congenial, not least because he was able to express his sexuality in ways that would have been impossible in England. In March 1917, he fell in love with an Egyptian tram conductor, Mohammed el Adl. Not knowing from day to day which service el Adl would be working on, Forster hung around the terminus until his tram appeared.

Even when writing to Lytton Strachey, a flamboyant habitué of the sexually liberated Bloomsbury Group, Forster's confessional gossip is very veiled ('other reminiscences', 'a certain tram'), no doubt because he expected his letters to be read by a censor. 'Your situation sounds all that could be wished,' Strachey airily observed. He was an unenthusiastic correspondent, privately considering Forster (who had so far published four novels, including *A Room with a View* and *Howards End*) to be a 'second rate' writer.

In April 1917, the British garrison at Gaza decisively defeated an attacking Ottoman army. When the casualties reached Alexandria, 'there was work' for Forster, although – in the 'typical day' he describes to Strachey – there was still time to give an English lesson, based on light contemporary fiction, and to ride the tram with el Adl.

Dear Lytton,

You have written at last, if in the New Statesman. What, besides you, has come over that paper? Coming back from the dear soldiers, I picked up a special Christian number, all about Easter [...] I lay reading it up the office stairs, whose ridges in my spine raised other reminiscences. Steps were heard ascending. Had after all the Corporal – It was Miss V. Grant Duff, though.

I shall be more typical however in describing a typical day. This morning, after breakfast, I took tram to the office where, 850 wounded having arrived in the hospitals as a result of our second Gaza victory, there was work. At 10 I gave an English lesson to a Venz[u]elo-International-Socialist, our text books being Le Jardin d'Epicure and The Silver Box [...] The Missing lists from the two victories, which are rumoured tremendous, have not yet come out, but I learnt something about the country, disposition of Regts &ct and got material for a map. All the time a man whose hands had been shot to bits was whimpering and whistling 'I'm in a fix, I'm in a fix'. Another man, a stranger to him and quite a boy, bent over and kneeling gazed into his eyes [...] Went to the tram terminus to wait for a certain tram. All trams go to my lodging but only one tram does, and it has no fixed hour. The voyage this evening was marred by other passengers [...] Looking over this day it seems quite unlike any other. But you'll see what I'm like, which is my grim aim.

Yours ever
EM Forster

9.

For what a minute did I see
you yesterday – is this the
way my beloved that we
are to live Till the sixth
in the morning I look for you
and when I awake I turn to
look on & you – dearest Phee
ly you are solitary and un
comfortable why cannot I
be with you to cheer you
and to press you to my heart
oh my love you have no
friends why then should
you be torn from the
only one who has affection
for you – But I shall
see you to night and that
is the hope that I shall

Mary Godwin (1797–1851) to Percy Bysshe Shelley
25 October 1814

Mary Wollstonecraft Godwin met Percy Bysshe Shelley in 1812. She was the fifteen-year-old daughter of the radical philosopher William Godwin and the writer and proponent of women's rights Mary Wollstonecraft (see page 213). He was one of Godwin's disciples, recently sent down from Oxford for publishing a pamphlet on 'The Necessity of Atheism'. By 1814, they were in love. But Shelley was married and, despite some success as a firebrand poet and polemicist, he was heavily in debt – including to Godwin, who had serious doubts about the match.

In July, the couple eloped to Europe, accompanied by Mary's step-sister, Claire Clairmont. They travelled to France, which was still reeling from the Napoleonic Wars, then on to Switzerland and the Netherlands. But tensions emerged as Shelley became a little too close to Clairmont, and by September they had run out of money. Back in London, even like-minded friends turned their backs on them, and they entered into an exhausting, unsettled existence, moving from house to house. Mary was pregnant, but Shelley was mostly absent, on the run from irate creditors and bailiffs. In this letter, she looks forward to meeting him outside a coffee house and finding some privacy in St Paul's Cathedral nearby. It's clear that the constant upheavals are getting to her – though she doesn't blame the 'solitary and uncomfortable' Shelley, with whom she is still deeply in love. Worse was to come, however: their baby didn't survive.

....

[...] For what a minute did I see you yesterday – is this the way my beloved that we are to live till the sixth in the morning I look for you and when I awake I turn to look on you – dearest Shelley you are solitary and uncomfortable why cannot I be with you to cheer you and to press you to my heart oh my love you have no friends why then should you be torn from the only one who has affection for you – But I shall see you tonight and that is the hope that I shall live on through the day – be happy dear Shelley and think of me – why do I say this dearest & only one I know how tenderly you love me and how you repine at this absence from me – when shall we be free from fear of treachery? [...]

I was so dreadfully tired yesterday that I was obliged to take a coach home forgive this extravagance but I am so very weak at present & I had been so agitated through the day that I was not able to stand a morning rest however will set me quite right again and I shall be quite well when I meet you this evening – will you be at the door of the coffee house at five oclock as it is désagreable to go into those places and I shall be there exactly at the time & we will go into St Pauls where we can sit down [...]

Ah ma chere quel contretemps! Le Duc a changé
de plan et nous ne partirons qu'en 8 jours:
J'en serois assez content, car il y a encore
toutes sortes de choses a voir ici et nous connoitrons
mieux notre monde en partant, si ce n'étoit
pas ces terribles six heures qu'il faut passer
tous les jours a table.

Aujourd'hui nous avons fait un tour forcé
pour voir la galerie de Saltsdalen il y a de
tres belles choses que ji souhaitterois de
contempler avec toi, surtout un Everdingen
de la plus grande perfection, et quelques
autres dont ji te ferai un jour la description.

Je finis par un vers allemand qui sera placé
dans le Poeme que ji cheris tant, parceque j'y pourrai
parler de toi; de mon amour pour toi sous mille
formes sans que personne t'entende que toi seule.

Gewiss ich waere schon so ferne ferne
Soweit die Welt nur offen liegt gegangen
Bezwaengen mich nicht uebermaechtge Sterne
Die mein Geschiz an deines angehangen
Dass ich in dir nun erst mich kennen lerne
Mein Dichten, Trachten, Hoffen und Verlangen
Allein nach dir und deinem Wesen draengt
Mein Leben nur an deinem Leben haengt.

Ce 24 d'Aout 1784.

G.

Johann Wolfgang von Goethe (1749–1832) to Charlotte von Stein
24 August 1784

Travelling on a diplomatic mission, Goethe writes from the court of Brunswick to Charlotte von Stein at the court of Weimar. She is a lady-in-waiting; he is Weimar's intellectual prodigy – poet, scientist, senior councillor and trusted adviser to Duke Karl August. Charlotte's loveless high-society marriage in 1764 was followed by ten children in ten years, only three of whom survived. In 1783, her son Fritz went to live with Goethe, who undertook his education. Goethe is in love with Charlotte. If she feels the same for him, she still treats him more like a soulmate.

During the summer of 1784, Karl August is touring German princely courts, negotiating an alliance to counter the hegemonic ambitions of the Habsburg emperor Joseph II, with Goethe in tow. Goethe complains that his employer has extended their stay in Brunswick by eight days, involving many more tedious hours at the dinner table. They have visited the palace of Salzdahlum, with its celebrated art collection – 'which I was hoping to see with you,' he confides – including a landscape painting attributed to the seventeenth-century Dutch artist Allart van Everdingen.

Goethe writes in French, the language of diplomacy and cosmopolitan high culture, but he adds a love poem in German, one of several he addressed to Charlotte. It's intensely private ('no one but you yourself will understand'), but also part of Goethe's lifelong project to transform German into a great European literary language.

....

Ah, my dear, how unfortunate! The duke has changed his plans and we won't be leaving for 8 days. I would be quite happy with that, since there are still all kinds of things to see here and we will know our world better when we leave, if it were not for the six awful hours we have to spend at the table every day.

Today we were obliged to take a detour to see the gallery of Sahlsdalen [Salzdahlum] there are some beautiful things which I was hoping to see with you, above all an Everdingen of the very highest quality and other things that I will describe to you one day.

I'll finish with some verses in German that will be inserted into the Poem that is so close to my heart, because in it I can speak of you, of my love for you, in many ways that no one but you yourself will understand.

> I'd be so far away, for sure – so far,
> Travelling the open world's wide distances,
> Not letting myself be conquered by those stars
> That joined together our two destinies.
> Through you I first discovered my own nature,
> My poetry, my striving – hopes, desires –
> Towards you alone, and all you are, they tend.
> My life on yours in every part depends.

Sunday Night.

My sweet Girl,

I hope you did not blame me much for not obeying your request of a Letter on Saturday: we have had four in our small room playing at cards night and morning leaving me no undisturbed oportunity to write. Now Rice and Martin are gone I am at liberty. Brown to my sorrow confirms the account you gave of your ill health. You cannot conceive how I ache to be with you: how I would die for one hour — for what is in the world? I say you cannot conceive; it is impossible you should look with such eyes upon me as I have upon you: it cannot be. Forgive me if I wander a little this evening, for I have been all day employd in a very abstract Poem and I am in deep love with you — two things which must excuse me. I have believe me, not been an age in letting you take possession of me, the very first week I knew you I wrote myself your vassal, but burnt the Letter as the very next time I saw you I thought you manifested some dislike to me.

John Keats (1795–1821) to Fanny Brawne
25 July 1819

John Keats had already attracted attention – not all of it favourable – as a leading figure among the second wave of Romantic poets. But in 1819, after many experiments with style and subject matter, he found his mature voice. During a spell of febrile productivity, he wrote his great odes 'To a Nightingale', 'On a Grecian Urn' and 'To Autumn'.

In his personal life, there was less cause for optimism. Though he wouldn't be diagnosed until the following year, he was showing symptoms of tuberculosis, which had killed his mother, brother and uncle. His debts were piling up. And he was in an intense relationship with the girl next door, Fanny Brawne – but many of his friends disliked her, and her parents disapproved of him.

These disturbances found their way into poems like 'La Belle Dame Sans Merci', with its undercurrent of decay and death. They also run through this mercurial letter, veering between ardent devotion (echoing his sonnet 'Bright Star', addressed to Brawne) and gnawing insecurity. Keats sent it to Brawne while visiting his friends James Rice and Charles Brown on the Isle of Wight, hoping to write but often tempted to stay up all night playing cards.

Keats and Brawne are thought to have reached an 'understanding' on Christmas Day 1818 and become quietly engaged in October 1819. But Keats's health was worsening: in February 1820 he coughed up arterial blood. As a former surgeon's apprentice, he knew the signs: 'I cannot be deceived in that colour – that drop of blood is my death warrant.'

....

My sweet Girl,

I hope you did not blame me much for not obeying your request of a Letter on Saturday: we have had four in our small room playing at cards night and morning leaving me no undisturbed opportunity to write [...] I have, believe me, not been an age in letting you take possession of me; the very first week I knew you I wrote myself your vassal; but burnt the Letter as the very next time I saw you I thought you manifested some dislike to me. If you should ever feel for Man at the first sight what I did for you, I am lost. Yet I should not quarrel with you, but hate myself [...] You say speaking of Mr Severn 'but you must be satisfied in knowing that I admired you much more than your friend'. My dear love, I cannot believe there ever was or ever could be any thing to admire in me especially as far as sight goes [...]

I have two luxuries to brood over in my walks, your Loveliness and the hour of my death. O that I could have possession of them both in the same minute. I hate the world: it batters too much the wings of my self-will, and would I could take a sweet poison from your lips to send me out of it [...] I will imagine you Venus tonight and pray, pray, pray to your star like a Heathen [...]

Queen's Chambers
Belfast,

7 June 1951.

Dear graminivore,

  I'm not sure what you are
doing in this picture except preparing supper.
However, I'm sure you are comfortably of.
Do you think you should have whiskers,
or not? My whiskers are an integral part
of me:

  However. I am feeling
very June-like tonight, that is, a pulp
of my ordinary self. Hay fever has opened

Philip Larkin (1922–85) to Monica Jones
7 June 1951

Installed in a dingy flat in Belfast and working as a librarian at the university, Philip Larkin writes to his girlfriend Monica Jones, an English lecturer in Leicester. It was early in their relationship. They'd known each other since the mid-1940s – sharing a love of gin, animals and literary character assassination – but things had only recently turned romantic after Larkin broke off his engagement with another woman, Ruth Bowman.

For all the gloominess of Larkin's public persona, he had a tender, whimsical side. He soon came up with pet names for himself and Jones – she was a 'rabbit', he was a 'seal' – and many of his letters to her feature Beatrix Potter-esque drawings like the ones here (accompanying the hypochondriacal ruminations and gripes about colleagues).

This was the most important relationship of Larkin's life. Despite his fear of commitment and periodic betrayals, Jones stayed loyal to him as a lover, confidante and critic. It was in Belfast that Larkin, with her help, hit his stride as a poet – that distinctive mixture of wistful regret and tentative hope – and his reflections on the joy of solitude and the oppressiveness of work seem to contain the first glimmers of his famous poem 'Toads'. In 1955, Larkin included it in his first major collection, *The Less Deceived* – dedicated to Jones.

....

Dear graminivore,

I'm not sure what you are *doing* in this picture except preparing supper. However, I'm sure you are comfortably off. Do you think you should have whiskers, or not? My whiskers are an integral part of me.

However. I am feeling very *June-like* tonight, that is, a pulp of my ordinary self. Hay fever has opened an offensive without throwing all its troops into battle but quite nastily enough to keep me busy [...]

Yesterday however I had the morning off, & after completing a few commissions in town & being unluckily *collared by Bradley* for coffee, I got my bike and rode up the Lagan towpath. The weather was hot and splendid, & the riverside deserted except for a horse-drawn barge. It's almost entirely unspoilt, no houses anywhere, only lock gates & occasional refreshment-stalls (shut). I saw something I imagined to be a magpie, *heard* waterrats clopping in & out of the shallows, & hardly sneezed [...]

I proceeded to Lisburn, a small town, & failing to find anywhere to eat bought bread, cheese, onions & an apple, & sat in the gardens, reading *I leap over the wall*. The tar was oozing on the roads, & altogether it was a happy few hours. It is surprising how one's whole attitude changes on being released from work. My step was firm, my eye buoyant, my voice unfaltering; I wasn't thinking about the grave, or how miserable my lot was; no, I got up early, embracing the day eagerly like a groom his bride, and sang like Toad to the noise of my wheels – & all because I had *a few hours to myself* [...]

I know you are very busy
but may I nevertheless
point out that I haven't
had a letter from you since
(I think) July. I know too
that I didn't write for a
long time, but I am hoping
that you are not cross with
me. Vous ne m'en voulez pas?

Iris Murdoch (1919–99) to Raymond Queneau
29 October 1949

Iris Murdoch playfully upbraids Raymond Queneau for failing to reply to her last letter. She sketches herself trying to attract his attention, while he sits impervious at his editorial desk at the publishers Gallimard, churning out the pages of his next book, *Petite cosmogonie portative* (*A Pocket Cosmogony*).

Murdoch and Queneau first met in Innsbruck, Austria, in 1946, while she was working for the United Nations Relief and Rehabilitation Administration, which provided aid for millions of people displaced by war. Murdoch was yet to publish a novel of her own (an early manuscript was turned down by T.S. Eliot at Faber), but Queneau had been producing experimental fiction and poetry since the 1930s. After years of wartime insularity, she was excited by what continental literature and philosophy had to offer. She and Queneau struck up a close friendship – more than a friendship on Murdoch's part.

In October 1949, barred from taking up a scholarship at Vassar College, New York, because of her former membership of the Communist Party, Murdoch is back in Oxford, where she'd had a brilliant undergraduate career. She is teaching philosophy, but tiring of the narrowness of the curriculum and the dry, analytical tradition that holds sway in Britain. Preferring the 'kick' of French existentialism, she quizzes Queneau on Jean-Paul Sartre, about whom she would publish her first book in 1953.

The art of letter-writing, Murdoch observed, requires a balance between 'being earnest and sounding damned silly'. In this case, she manages both. On the one hand, her question '*Vous ne m'en voulez pas?*' ('Have you had enough of me?') is jokily melodramatic. But there's a lingering sense of anxiety too, hinting at Murdoch's unrequited feelings for the married Queneau. Subsequent letters suggest that, on the rare occasions when they met, she tried unsuccessfully to take things further (in 1952, she wrote, 'I would do anything for you, be anything you wished me … you don't need me in the way in which I need you'). It appears that she destroyed his letters to her.

· ·

I know you are very busy but may I nevertheless point out that I haven't had a letter from you since (I think) July. I know too that I didn't write for a long time, but I am hoping that you are not cross with me. *Vous ne m'en voulez pas?*

I am doing quite a lot of work too – apart from teaching, I mean, which doesn't count. I hope to get this thesis organised soon. Something on *meaning*, based chez Hegel, bringing in Sartre, refuting [Gilbert] Ryle. (Ryle is the reigning professor here. His book on Mind, just published, summarises the post-Wittgensteinian empiricism which *is* British philosophy at present. I'll send you a copy.) [...]

What's doing in Paris about peace? I suppose the P[artie] C[ommuniste] is organising conferences and so on. But does it extend beyond Communist circles? (Does Sartre lend himself to any such organisation?) Here, regrettably, peace is regarded as a Communist racket. Everyone seems to be becoming madder and madder [...]

our lives are dominated by Choice - with
a capital C. In everything we are implicated
in a matter of choice - even in love, we have
to make up our minds on which side of the barricades we
are to be.

 You used to make the mistake - I
believe - of identifying deep, passionate need
with weakness, and despising it. Certainly I
wanted strength - your strength. That is not
to say that I had none of my own. Weakness
is not the only quality that seeks out the
strength of another. Surely, there is a kind of
burning ovidity of mind that seeks
something as powerful as itself, strength seeing
out strength. The strongest creatures of this
world are the loneliest. The sycophants, the
timid, the pusillanimous at least have
the comforts of the poor and the hard, whatever
else they may have to fear. The voice that
cries out does not have to be a weakling's.
It may be that of the artist, the visionary.

 Perhaps this is claiming a lot for
myself. I am only trying to clear away an

John Osborne (1929–94) to Pamela Lane
1954

John Osborne returns to London after visiting his estranged wife, Pamela Lane, in Derby, where she's acting in a play and dating a local dentist. He hopes they can make their marriage work again. In his analysis of their relationship in this letter, he sounds very like Jimmy Porter, the main character in his play *Look Back in Anger*. Intelligent, working-class and scathingly impatient at the social status-quo, Jimmy goads his upper-middle-class wife, Alison, to the point where she returns to her family, reappearing in the final scene for a tender yet uneasy reconciliation.

Several passages in Osborne's long letter – the contempt for 'pusillanimous' people, the loneliness of the strong – are echoed in the script he was about to write. When *Look Back in Anger* premièred at the Royal Court Theatre in London in 1956, audiences loved its up-to-the-minute realism and atmosphere of youthful rebellion. The phrase 'Angry Young Man' came to stand for a generation empowered by postwar educational reforms but profoundly frustrated by the British class system.

My darling –

I do hope you got back all right. You must have been worn out, poor dear. I wonder if your back is any better. I got home last night, dazed and utterly exhausted [...]

Today everything is different. It is an utterly different day to the ones that have made up these past weeks. Perhaps neither of us seem to be really much better off. What is going to happen I don't know. I can't tell whether we shall be able to make each other happy or not. At least, one can be certain that failure can never be quite so bitter the second time. All I know is that when I was with you again yesterday, not even the strength of all my old fears could prevent me wanting you all over again, and today I am feeling more peace than I have known for many, many months [...]

Learning to love is not easy [...]

You used to make the mistake – I believe – of identifying deep passionate need with weakness, and despising it. Certainly I wanted strength – your strength. That is not to say that I had none of my own. Weakness is not the only quality that seeks out the strength of another. Surely, there is a kind of burning virility of mind that seeks something as powerful as itself, strength seeking out strength. The strongest creatures of this world are the loneliest. The sycophants, the timid, the pusillanimous at least have the comforts of the pack and the herd, whatever else they may have to fear. The voice that cries out does not have to be a weakling's. It may be that of the artist, the visionary [...]

All I know at the moment is that the sickness in my heart has gone. Yesterday, I was on my own. Today, it seems, I have a wife. I can't wait to be with you again [...]

Oh, darling, I hope you are all right [...] I'll write later. I do love you.

Johnny

München, Blütenstr. 8/I.
13. Mai 1897

Gnädigste Frau,

Es war nicht die erste Dämmerstunde gestern, die ich mit Ihnen verbringen durfte. Da gibt in meiner Erinnerung eine, die mich arg verlangen machte, Ihnen ins Auge zu sehen. So war im Winter und mein ganzer Sinnen und Streben, das der Frühlingswind in tausend Weiten weht, war in die enge Stube und die stille Arbeit gezwängt. Da kam mir, von Dr. Conrad gesandt, das Aprilheft 96 der „Neuen Deutschen Rundschau". Ein Brief Conrads verwies mich auf einen darin befindlichen Essay „Jesus der Jude". Warum? Dr. Conrad hatte damals ein paar Theile meiner „Christus-Visionen" (fünf sollen demnächst in der „Gesellschaft" erscheinen) gelesen und meinte, daß mich jene geistvolle Abhandlung interessiren dürfte. Er hat sich getäuscht. Nicht Interesse war es, was mich tiefer und tiefer in diese Offenbarung zieht, ein gläubiges Vertrauen ging mir auf dem ersten Wege voran, und endlich ward wie ein Fühl in mir, das, was meine Träumungen in Visionen geben, mit der gigantischen Kraft einer heiligen Überzeugung so meisterhaft klar ausgesprochen zu finden. Das war die seltsame Dämmerstunde, deren ich gestern wieder gedenken mußte.

Sehen Sie, gnädigste Frau, durch diese ahnen Vergißheit, durch die schmeichelnde Kraft Ihrer Worte empfängt mein Werk in meinem Gesicht eine Weihe, eine Sanktion. Wir war wie einem, dem große Träume in Erfüllung gehn mit ihrem Guten und Bösen; denn Ihr Essay verhält sich zu meinen Gedanken wie Träumen zur Wirklichkeit wie ein Wunsch zur Erfüllung.

Rainer Maria Rilke (1875–1926) to Lou Andreas-Salomé
13 May 1897

While staying with a friend in Munich in spring 1897, Lou Andreas-Salomé received a stream of anonymous, admiring letters and poems. On 12 May the young poet, René Maria Rilke, turned up in person. Writing to her the following day, he explains how reading her essay 'Jesus the Jew' in a periodical had evoked a profound sense of creative kinship. Courted in her twenties by (among many others) Friedrich Nietzsche, Lou was unhappily married to a charismatic but unreliable and violent Orientalist, Friedrich Carl Andreas. She and Rilke took off for the Alpine village of Wolfratshausen, becoming lovers and, for the next three years, inseparable companions. The older Andreas-Salomé was confidante, mother-figure and mentor to Rilke, helping him to weather fragile health and vertiginous mood swings, to which she was also prone herself. She persuaded René to change his first name to the 'fine German name' Rainer. They broke up in 1901, when Rilke proposed to the artist Clara Westhoff.

....

Most gracious lady,

Yesterday was not the first twilight hour I have spent with you. There is another in my memory, one that made me want to look into your eyes. It was winter, and all the thoughts and aspirations that the spring wind scatters into a thousand faraway places were crowded into my narrow study and my quiet work. Then suddenly a gift arrived from Dr Conrad: the April 1896 issue of *Neue Deutsche Rundschau*. A letter from Dr Conrad referred me to an essay in it titled 'Jesus the Jew'. Why? [...] he thought I might find this sage treatment interesting. He was wrong. It was not interest that drew me deeper and deeper into this revelation [...] it was like a great rejoicing to me to find expressed in such supremely clear words [...] what my *Visions* present in dreamlike epics. That was the mysterious twilight hour I could not but be reminded of yesterday.

You see, gracious lady, through this unsparing severity, through the uncompromising strength of your words, I felt that my own work was receiving a blessing, a sanction [...] for your essay was to my poems as reality is to dream, as fulfilment is to a desire.

Can you imagine, then, the feelings with which I looked forward to yesterday afternoon? And could I have told you all this yesterday as we talked – over a cup of tea, casually, with a few well-chosen, heartfelt words of admiration. But nothing could have been farther from my thoughts. In that twilight hour I was alone with you and alone I had to be with you – now, as my heart was overflowing with thanks for such a blessing.

I always feel: when one person is indebted to another for something very special, that indebtedness should remain a secret between just the two of them [...]

But these are the words of an old, long-harboured gratitude; to be allowed to express them now feels like
    an honour awarded
            to your:
                René Maria Rilke

with a long letter, desiring me soon answer to

& Hunt's messages.   P B Shelley

London, Dec. 16. 1816.

I have spent a day, my beloved, of somewhat
agonising sensations; such as the contemplation of
vice & folly & hard heartedness exceeding all conception
must produce. Leigh Hunt has been with me
all day, & his delicate & tender attentions to me,
his kind speeches of you, have sustained me against
the weight of the horror of this event.

The children I have not yet got. I have seen
Lory Hill who recommends proceeding with the
utmost caution and resoluteness. He seems interested.
I told him that I was under contract of marriage
to you; & he said that in such an event
all pretences to retain the children would cease.
Hunt said very delicately that this would be
soothing intelligence for you.— Yes, my only hope
my darling love, this will be one among the

Percy Bysshe Shelley (1792–1822) to Mary Godwin
15 December 1816

In his writing, Percy Bysshe Shelley was a passionate advocate for female equality. In his life, he fell short of his ideals. During the summer of 1814, as his marriage to Harriet Westbrook fell apart, he ran off with the sixteen-year-old Mary Godwin (see page 109), leaving his wife and daughter (there was a son on the way too). In December 1816 – by which point Shelley was living with Godwin, though entangled with several other women – Westbrook was found in the Serpentine River in Hyde Park, 'far advanced in pregnancy'. She had drowned herself.

Shelley and Westbrook had been estranged for two years, but his response to her death in this letter – oddly cool, eager to lay the blame elsewhere – doesn't do him many favours. Without naming his former wife, he attacks her family, congratulates himself on his treatment of her and seems less concerned by the misery that drove her to suicide than what the event will mean for him. (He hopes to gain custody of the children, but, after much wrangling between his solicitor, Longdill, and the Westbrook family's lawyer, Desse, they would be sent to live with a vicar.)

Yet it's also clear that, in a life shadowed by many deaths (parents, children, in-laws), Shelley was deeply affected by Westbrook's. After her suicide, he suffered bouts of 'gloomy reverie'. When his friends asked him about it, he admitted that it was because he was thinking of her.

I have spent a day, my beloved, of somewhat agonising sensations, such as the contemplation of vice and folly and hard-heartedness, exceeding all conception, must produce [...]

The children I have not yet got. I have seen Longdill, who recommends proceeding with the utmost caution and resoluteness. He seems interested. I told him I was under contract of marriage to you, and he said that, in such an event, all pretence to detain the children would cease. Hunt said very delicately that this would be soothing intelligence to you. Yes, my only hope, my darling love, this will be one among the innumerable benefits which you will have bestowed upon me [...]

It seems that this poor woman – the most innocent of her abhorred and unnatural family – was driven from her father's house, and descended the steps of prostitution until she lived with a groom of the name of Smith; who deserting her, she killed herself. There can be no question that the beastly viper her sister, unable to gain profit from her connection with me, has secured herself the fortune of the old man – who is now dying – by the murder of this poor creature. Everything tends to prove, however, that beyond the mere shock of so hideous a catastrophe having fallen on a human being once so nearly connected with me, there would, in any case, have been little to regret. Hookham, Longdill, every one, does me full justice; hears testimony to the upright spirit and liberality of my conduct to her [...]

Chapter 5

'Everything is going badly'

imal income, but not a single

ails that I couldn't even have d

detachment in my sorrow, a s

wo total chasms in my memor

gh two long years of imprison

have more bonds and that fou

bly in part to anger you, and in

der **When Troubles Come** wh

rows less, but because we ou

bid all contact between you a

the next months. I don't knov

e all or part of what I'm due fo

ttle slips announcing the pub

t should for ever take that pl

very unhuman rooks up over

hing. What do you think? I'll be

emed undiminished, for the a

are still suffering a stinging p

Mon Cher Accello, j'tâcheras
de trouver le temps de vous
écrire cette Semaine. Mais
j'vous suppli d'luvoyer
50 fr. à Jeanne, nuf luvcloppe,
(Jeanne Prosper 17, Rue
Soffroi, Batignall.) Je
lai/v. dormir le priz de
ung lectures, et j' le réserve
pour mon maître d'hotel
à Pary.
   j'ai beaucoup de Chofes
à vous dire. Jpa/possible
aujourd'hui. Jla pow un

Charles Baudelaire (1821–67) to Narcisse Ancelle
May 1864

Charles Baudelaire was in Brussels, hoping to drum up much-needed income by lecturing about French art and literature, and to persuade a Belgian publisher to take three of his books. On 6 May 1864, a few days after his first lecture, on the painter Eugène Delacroix, he wrote to his mother, enclosing a review cutting from *L'Indépendence Belge*. 'They say it was a phenomenal success. But, between ourselves, I believe that everything is going badly … there's terrific avarice and unparalleled slowness in everything, as well as a lot of empty heads! In short, the people are even more stupid here than the French.'

Baudelaire was far from well. Aged forty-three, he seemed much older – a haunted-looking, white-haired poet–critic, very different from the scandalous Parisian roué his audience had been expecting. He was also worried about the health of his former mistress, Jeanne Prosper (or Duval or Lemer), the muse of his most sensual love poetry. It's Jeanne's lustrous dark locks that the poet explores in 'La Chevelure' ('Tresses') – an 'aromatic forest', a 'sea-swell' that transports him into erotic reverie. Baudelaire had broken with Jeanne a few years before this letter, when he discovered that her 'brother', whom he was also supporting financially, was nothing of the sort.

By 1864, the money he'd burned through in early youth, 'keeping' Jeanne in style, had shrunk to a meagre stream that Narcisse Ancelle, the family lawyer who administered Baudelaire's inheritance, controlled with niggling but well-intentioned economy. When Baudelaire needed fresh funds, he usually had to call on Ancelle in person in Neuilly. In this scribbled note, he asks him to send 50 francs – the modest equivalent of his lecture fee – to 'poor Jeanne' without delay. This is the last letter in which he will mention her name.

My dear Ancelle, I shall try to find time to write to you this week. But I beg you to put 50 fr. in an envelope and send them to Jeanne (Jeanne Prosper, 17 rue Soffroi, Batignolles). I am leaving the money from my lectures untouched and I am keeping it for the proprietor of my hotel in Paris.

I have lots of things to tell you. Impossible today. Another article appeared in *L'Indépendence*, but I don't have it at hand.

I think that poor Jeanne is going blind.

I shall write to you more suitably in two or three days. I am frightfully busy.

I am sending you this receipt made out in advance to avoid all contact between you and her.

Charles

241

28. Februar 33

Lieber Gerhard,

ich benutze eine ruhigere Stunde dieser Verstimmung, um Dir wieder einmal ein Blatt zu schicken. Unmittelbarer Anlaß ist der Empfang Deines überaus bemerkenswerten Aufsatzes im Israelitischen Gemeindeblatt, den ich heute früh erst von Fräulein Marx aus Königsberg nebst Deinem Empfehlungsbriefe und der Ankündigung ihres Kommens empfing. Der Tag verging weiterhin unter Arbeiten und Diktat an einem Hörspiel „Lichtenberg", das ich auf Grund eines Vertrages, dessen besserer Teil längst erfüllt ist und mir die Lust auf die Lektüre verleidet hat, nun abliefern muß.

Das bißchen Fassung, das man in meinen Kreisen dem neuen Regime entgegengebracht hat, ist rasch verbraucht und man gibt sich Rechenschaft, daß die Luft kaum mehr zu atmen ist; ein Umstand, der freilich dadurch an Tragweite verliert, daß einem die Kehle zugeschnürt wird. Dies vor allem einmal wirtschaftlich; die Chancen, die von Zeit zu Zeit durch den Rundfunk geboten wurden und die überhaupt meine einzig ernsthaften waren, dürften so gründlich fortfallen, daß selbst der „Lichtenberg", obwohl er in Auftrag gegeben war, einer Aufführung nicht mehr sicher ist. Die Desorganisation der Frankfurter Zeitung schreitet fort. Ihr Feuilletonredakteur ist von seinem Posten entfernt worden, obwohl er gerade kurz vorher durch Erwerb meiner „Berliner Kindheit" zu einem lächerlichen Preis den Beweis einer zumindest kaufmännischen Eignung erbracht hatte. Jetzt scheint dort geistig Simon zu walten. Die Publikation meiner Arbeit aber ruht nun seit mehr als vierzehn Tagen.

Die Geschichten, die als Buch erscheinen zu sehen, sind aussichtslos. Jedermann fühlt, daß sie so vortrefflich ist, daß die Unsterblichkeit sie auch als Manuskript zu sich nehmen wird. Man druckt Bücher, die es nötiger haben. Im übrigen kann ich seit einer Woche das Werk, wenn ich es will, als abgeschlossen ansehen, da mit der Abfassung des letzten Stücks – der Reihenfolge nach des ersten, denn es ist als Anfangsstück ein Pendant zum Schlußstück „Bucklicht Männlein" gewordene – die Zahl von dreißig erreicht ist. Dabei ist das auf Deinen Rat sekretierte nicht gerechnet.

Soweit mich nicht die faszinierende Gedankenwelt Lichtenbergs fesselt, empfängt mich das Problem, das mir die nächsten Monate stellen, von denen ich nicht weiß, wie ich sie in oder außerhalb Deutschlands überstehen kann. Es gibt Orte, an denen ich ein Minimum verdienen und solche, an denen ich von einem Minimum leben kann, aber nicht einen einzigen, auf den diese beiden Bedingungen

Walter Benjamin (1892–1940) to Gershom Scholem
28 February 1933

German-Jewish intellectuals like Walter Benjamin were disoriented by the speed with which populist anti-Semitism, stoked by Nazi propaganda, was translated into official policy after Hitler's appointment as chancellor on 30 January 1933. Prompted by passionate Zionism rather than self-preservation, Benjamin's younger friend and philosophical sparring-partner Gershom (born Gerhard) Scholem had recently emigrated to Jerusalem. The correspondence they began after Scholem's departure continued over the next seven years, as Benjamin left Berlin for Paris, then, with the fall of France in June 1940, sought safety in Spain, crossing the border with a group of refugees on 25 September. Threatened by the fascist Spanish police with immediate deportation back to France, he took his own life with an overdose the same night.

Benjamin writes from his native Berlin, a city he has been celebrating in his memoir *Berlin Childhood around 1900* but which suddenly, urgently feels unsafe. One of the most original and influential thinkers of his time, Benjamin repeatedly failed to gain an academic job. He realizes that, being Jewish, he will lose his main source of income – writing and presenting talks and children's programmes on German radio. As he anticipates, *Lichtenberg* – a commissioned radio play in which moon people investigate life on earth – will not be produced. Despite his fears, Benjamin writes with a certain humour, reporting the good with the bad, including his recent formulation of 'a new theory of language'.

Dear Gerhard,

I'm using a quiet hour of deep depression to send you a page once again [...]

The little composure that people in my circles were able to muster in the face of the new regime was rapidly spent, and one realizes that the air is hardly fit to breathe anymore – a condition which of course loses significance as one is being strangled anyway. This above all economically: the opportunities the radio offered from time to time and which were my only serious prospects will probably vanish so completely that even 'Lichtenberg', though commissioned, is not sure to be produced [...]

When not captivated by the fascinating world of Lichtenberg's thought, I am absorbed by the problems posed by the next months. I don't know how I will be able to make it through them, whether inside or outside Germany. There are places where I could earn a minimal income, and places where I could live on a minimal income, but not a single place where these two conditions coincide. If I report that, despite such circumstances, a new theory of language – encompassing four small, handwritten pages – has resulted, you will not deny me due homage. I have no intention of having those pages published and am even uncertain whether they are fit for a typescript. I will only point out that they were formulated while I was doing research for the first piece of the *Berlin Childhood* [...]

It would be quite nice to hear from you soon [...]

With all the best,

Yours, Walter

as to oppose & tire the hand of the operator, who was forced to change from the right to the left — then, indeed, I thought I must have ex- pired. I attempted no more to open my eyes, — they felt as if hermetti- cally shut, & so firmly closed, that the Eyelids seemed indented into the cheeks. The instrument this second time withdrawn, I concluded the operation over — Oh no! presently the terrible cutting was renewed — & worse than ever, to separate the bottom, the foundation of this dread- ful gland from the parts to which it adhered — Again all description would be baffled — yet again all was not over, — Dr Larry rested but his own hand; & — Oh Heaven! — I then felt the knife rackling against the breast bone — scraping it! — This performed, while I yet remained in utterly speechless torture, I heard the voice of Mr. Larry, (all others guarded a dead silence) in a tone nearly tragic, desire every one present to pronounce ~~if he thought the question complete, or~~ if any thing more remained to be done; or if he thought the operation complete. the general voice was Yes, — but the finger of Mr. Dubois — which I literally ~~felt~~ elevated over the wound, though, I saw nothing, & though he touched nothing, so indiscribably sensitive was the spot — pointed to some further requisition — & again began the scraping! — and, after this, Dr Moreau thought he discerned a peccant attom — and still, & still, M. Dubois demanded attom after attom — My dearest Esther, not for days, not for weeks, but for months I could not speak of this terrible business without nearly again going through it! I could not think of it with impu- nity! I was sick, I was disordered by a single question — even now, 9 months after it is over, I have a head ache from going on with the account! & this memorable account, which I began 3 months ago, at least, I dare not ~~read~~ ~~nor~~ revise, nor read, the recollection is still so painful.

Frances Burney (1752–1840) to Esther Burney
22 March–June 1812

Frances (Fanny) Burney wrote her novel-in-letters, *Evelina*, when she was in her twenties. It was a literary sensation, gaining her the friendship of Samuel Johnson (see page 53) and providing a model for later British women novelists, including Jane Austen (see page 43). By 1811, Burney, now in her fifties, was living in Paris with her French officer husband, Alexandre D'Arblay. She'd been troubled by a breast lump, tried to ignore it, but was finally persuaded to consult a surgeon. In September she underwent a mastectomy. Against the odds, the agonizing operation, performed without anaesthetic, was successful. Burney was cured.

Aware that her English family, from whom she was isolated by the Napoleonic Wars, will have heard garbled reports of her illness, even death, Burney writes her sister Esther a twelve-page letter giving a detailed account of her illness and surgery. Apart from the Napoleonic medical setting, it feels timeless in its emotional honesty.

When all was ready [...] I rang for my Maid & Nurses, – but before I could speak to them, my room, without previous message, was entered by 7 Men in black [...] M. Dubois ordered a Bed stead into the middle of the room [...] I stood suspended, for a moment, whether I should not abruptly escape – I looked at the door, the windows – I felt desperate – but it was only for a moment, my reason then took the command [...] I mounted, therefore, unbidden, the Bed stead – & M. Dubois [...] spread a cambric handkerchief upon my face [...] but when, Bright through the cambric, I saw the glitter of polished Steel – I closed my Eyes [...] Yet – when the dreadful steel was plunged into the breast – cutting through veins – arteries – flesh – nerves – I needed no injunctions not to restrain my cries.

I began a scream that lasted uninterruptedly during the whole time of the incision – & I almost marvel that it rings not in my Ears still! so excruciating was the agony. When the wound was made, & the instrument was withdrawn, the pain seemed undiminished, for the air that suddenly rushed into those delicate parts felt like a mass of minute but sharp & forked poniards, that were tearing the edges of the wound [...] again I felt the instrument – describing a curve – cutting against the grain [...] The instrument this second time withdrawn, I concluded the operation over – Oh no! presently the terrible cutting was renewed – & worse than ever, to separate the bottom, the foundation of this dreadful gland from the parts to which it adhered – Again all description would be baffled – yet again all was not over [...] Oh Heaven! – I then felt the Knife rackling against the breast bone – scraping it! [...]

Twice, I believe, I fainted; at least, I have two total chasms in my memory of this transaction, that impede my tying together what passed [...]

God bless my dearest Esther – I fear this is all written confusedly, but I cannot read it – & I can write it no more [...]

Muy Poderoso S.̃

Miguel de cerbantes saauedra digo q̃ V. A. le a ℥eℭ℥
m℥ de vna Comisson Para cobrar dos q̃ˢⁱ y quinientas
y tantas mil m̃rˢ q̃ se deuien a su Mg̃. de fincas del ex℥
Reyno de granada Para lo qual a dado fianças de qua
tro mil ducados vistas y admitidas Por V. A. y con
todo esto el Contador Enrrique de Ãraij me pide mas
fianças a cumplim̃ a la dicha cobrança. A V. supp
atento q̃ no deue mas fianças y q̃ soy baste̊ante
quatro mil ducados y ser yo hombre conocido de tra
to y Casado eneste lugar. V. A. le mande se
Contente y me despache luego que en ello Receuire
mrℭ. & ꝰ.

Miguel de cerbantes
saauedra

Miguel de Cervantes (1547–1616) to a nobleman
20 August 1594

In 1594 Miguel de Cervantes was settled back in Spain after the extraordinary adventures of his youth. In the 1570s, he had served as a soldier in the Infanteria de Marina, the Spanish seaborne troops responsible for curbing Ottoman power in the Mediterranean. Wounded in the naval battle of Lepanto in 1571, he had lost the use of his left arm ('for the glory of my right hand,' he would later joke). In September 1575, in sight of the Spanish coast, he'd been captured by pirates and imprisoned in Algiers. After four unsuccessful breakout attempts, he was eventually ransomed in 1580.

Cervantes published his first book, *La Galatea*, a collection of pastoral tales, in 1585. It was not a success. Unable to earn money from writing, he relied on his contacts and service record to find official employment. In the 1580s, he worked in military procurement for the Spanish Armada. Arriving in Madrid in June 1594, he turned to a friend, Don Agustín de Cetina, who did him the dubious favour of recommending him as a tax collector.

A condition of the job was that Cervantes should personally cover any shortfall in his expected takings. His guarantor, Francisco Suárez Gasco, was so unreliable (suspected of poisoning his wife, he was also close to bankruptcy) that Cervantes had to provide additional bonds. Writing to a grandee in the royal administration, he argues that he deserves to be trusted. The following day – as indicated by the notes on the back of the letter – Cervantes and his wife had to sign away their 'persons and goods, present and future', should he fail to hit his targets. In the event, Cervantes's spell as a tax collector ended in imprisonment in 1597. It would be another nine years before the first part of *Don Quixote* finally brought him fame and fortune.

....

Most Powerful Lord

I, Miguel de Cervantes Saavedra, state that Your Highness has granted him a commission to collect two million and five hundred or so thousand *maravedís* which are owed to his Majesty from properties in the Kingdom of Granada. In order to do this, he has given bonds of four thousand ducats, seen and accepted by Your Highness. And with in spite of all this, the receiver Enrique de Araiz is asking me for more surety to carry out the said [tax] collection. Bearing in mind that I do not have more bonds and that four thousand ducats are sufficient, and that I am a man who is well known, of good credit and married in this town, I beg Your Highness to order him to be content and for you to dispatch me herewith, for in this way I will receive great favour.

Miguel de Cervantes Saavedra

[on reverse, in a different hand]

The receiver Enrique de Araiz should inform
in Madrid, 21 August of the year 1594
that the commission be dispatched with the bonds that he has given, and that he and his wife be bound by this.

As I Took y freedome to say to you so I can not but Repeat to yo Lordp: I am at a Loss how to behave my Self and y Goodness and Bounty of y Queen, Her Majtie Buys my Small Services so much too Dear and leaves me so much in y Dark as to my Own Merit That I am Strangely at a Stand what to Say

I have Inclos'd My humble Acknowlegem to Her Majtie: and Perticularly to my Ld Treasurer but when I am writing to you sr Pardon me to alter my Stile, I am Impatient to kno' what in my Small Service pleases and Engages, Pardon me sr Tis a Necessary Enquiry for a Man in y Dark that I may Direct my Conduct and Push that Little Little Merit to a proper Extent

Give me leav sr as at first to Say I can not but Think ~~and~~ Tho' Her Majtie is Good, and My Ld Treasurer kind, yet my wheel within all These wheels must be yo Self, and There I fix my Thankfullness as I have of a Long Time my hope — as God has Thus Mov'd you to Relieve a Distrest family, Tis my Sincere Petition to him, that he would Once Put it into my hand to render you Some Such Signall Service, as might at least Express my Sence of it, and Encourage all Men of Power to Oblige and Espouse Greatefull and Sincere Minds

Your farther Enquiry Into y Misfortunes and afflicting Circum: stances That attend ^and Suppress me fills me wth Some Surprize, what Provi: dence has Reserv'd for me he Only knows, But Sure The Gulph is too

10
                                                          Large

Daniel Defoe (1660–1731) to Robert Harley
May 1704

By the time he was forty, Daniel Defoe had been in more than his fair share of scrapes. His fortunes, as an energetic but not always prudent participant in London's nascent mercantile culture, had followed a pattern of boom and bust. In the late 1680s, he had interests in ships, wine, tobacco, spirits, oysters and cloth, and owned a brick factory. By 1693, he was in prison, having run up debts of £17,000 (about £700,000 today). Ever wily, Defoe bargained his way out. But his writing would cause bigger problems. In 1703 he was charged with sedition following the publication of *The Shortest Way with the Dissenters* (1702), an attack on religious intolerance in Queen Anne's England. Pilloried three times (Alexander Pope described him standing 'unabashed on high'), he then spent six months in Newgate Prison, until Robert Harley, the Tory speaker of the House of Commons, helped to secure his release.

The following year, Defoe writes to Harley, free but unhappy. His brick business has collapsed, his reputation with creditors is in tatters and his 'large and Promiseing family' (he had eight children) is living precariously. He is effusively grateful to Harvey, but he is also on the lookout for opportunities. Harley accepted his offer of any 'Small Service' that might prove useful, employing him as a propagandist and spy. Defoe excelled at both, and was frequently dispatched to Scotland in the run-up to the 1707 Act of Union. In 1704, he also launched the *Review*, a twice-weekly paper entirely written by Defoe, which marked the beginnings of serious political journalism in Britain.

Amid the espionage, trade and writing, which never stopped landing him in trouble, Defoe found time to produce several literary works that would become classics. *Robinson Crusoe* (1719) was an instant success, though its attitudes towards empire – of which Defoe was a vocal proponent – sit uneasily today. In 1722 he published a book that, nearly three centuries later, became one of the definitive texts of 2020: *A Journal of the Plague Year*.

....

[...] I have Enclos'd My humble Acknowledgement to Her Maj[es]tie and Perticularly to my L[or]d Treasurer but when I am writeing to you Sir Pardon me to alter my Stile. I am Impatient to kno' what in my Small Service pleases and Engages. Pardon me Sir Tis a Necessary Enquiry for a Man in the Dark [...]

Your farther Enquiry Into the Missfortunes and afflicting Circumstances that attend and Suppress me fills me with Some Surprise. What Providence has Reserv'd for me he Only knows, but Sure The Gulph is too Large for me to Get ashore again [...]

All my prospects were built on a Manufacture I had Erected in Essex [...] I Employ'd a hundred Poor Familys at work and it began to Pay me Very well. I Generally Made Six hundred pound profit per Annum.

I began to live, Took a Good House, bought me Coach and horses a Second Time [...]

But I was Ruin'd The shortest way and Now Sir had Not your Favour and her Majties Bounty Assisted it must ha' been One of the worst Sorts of Ruine [...]

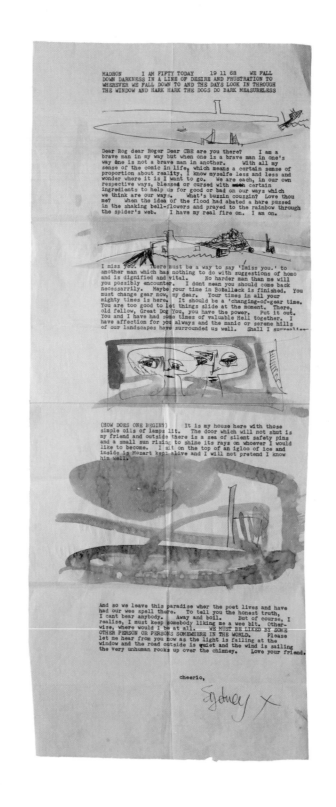

MADRON   I AM FIFTY TODAY   19 11 68   WE FALL
DOWN DARKNESS IN A LINE OF DESIRE AND FRUSTRATION TO
WHEREVER WE FALL DOWN TO AND THE DAYS LOOK IN THROUGH
THE WINDOW AND HARK HARK THE DOGS DO BARK MEASURELESS

Dear Rog dear Roger Dear CBE are you there?   I am a
brave man in my way but when one is a brave man in one's
way one is not a brave man in another.   With all my
sense of the comic in life, which means a certain sense of
proportion about reality, I know myself a less and less and
wonder where it is I want to go.   We are each, in our own
respective ways, blessed or cursed with such certain
ingredients to help us for good or bad on our ways which
we think are our ways.   what's buzzin couzzin? Love thou
me?   When the idea of the flood had abated a hare pussed
in the shaking bell-flowers and prayed to the rainbow through
the spider's web.   I have my real fire on. I am on.

I miss you.   There must be a way to say 'I miss you.' to
another man which has nothing to do with suggestions of homo
and is dignified and vital.   No harder man than me will
you possibly encounter.   I dont mean you should come back
necessarrily.   Maybe your time in Botallack is finished. You
must change gear now, my dear.   Your times in all your
mighty times is here.   It should be a 'changing-of-gear time.
You are too good to let things slide at the moment.   There,
old fellow, Great Dog You, you have the power.   Put it out.
You and I have had some times of valuable Hell together. I
have affection for you always and the manic or serene hills
of our landscapes have surrounded us well.   Shall I surrealise-

(HOW DOES ONE BEGIN?)   It is my house here with those
simple oils of lamps lit.   The door which will not shut is
my friend and outside there is a sea of silent safety pins
and a small sun rising to shine its rays on whoever I would
like to become.   I sit on the top of an igloo of ice and
inside is Mozart kept alive and I will not pretend I know
him well.

And so we leave this paradise wher the poet lives and have
had our wee spell there.   To tell you the honest truth,
I cant bear anybody.   Away and boil.   But of course, I
realise, I must keep somebody liking me a wee bit. Other-
wise, where would I be at all.   WE MUST BE LIKED BY SOME
OTHER PERSON OR PERSONS SOMEWHERE IN THE WORLD.   Please
let me hear from you now as the light is failing at the
window and the road outside is quiet and the wind is sailing
the very unhuman rooks up over the chimney.   Love your friend.

cheerio,

Sydney x

W.S. Graham (1918–86) to Roger Hilton
19 November 1968

The poet W.S. (Sydney) Graham and artist Roger Hilton forged a friendship based
on compulsive intellectual sparring, untamed humour and copious quantities of booze.
In the 1960s both were living in Cornwall, where Graham had moved from his native
Scotland twenty years earlier, surviving in a series of spartan cottages on thin pickings
from poetry and manual labour. His dogged creative integrity and the exacting music of
his verse made him a legend in Cornwall's postwar bohemian scene, where Hilton, a
Londoner who'd settled in the mining village of Botallack, was notorious for his
uncompromising art and satirical tongue. In autumn 1968, after a worsening spiral of
addiction (including imprisonment for drink-driving), Hilton spent several weeks in the
Priory Clinic, London, in an unsuccessful attempt to get 'dealcohoalled'.

Sorely missing Hilton's company, Graham wrote often, trying to cheer his friend
up while sharing his own troubles. He illustrated this letter with watercolours of the
landscape around Hilton's studio-home, ending with an evocative word-picture of the
Cornish winter, the sea-wind 'sailing the very unhuman rooks up over the chimney'.

MADRON I AM FIFTY TODAY 19 11 68 WE ALL FALL DOWN DARKNESS IN A LINE OF DESIRE
AND FRUSTRATION TO WHEREVER WE FALL DOWN TO AND THE DAYS LOOK IN THROUGH
THE WINDOW AND HARK HARK THE DOGS DO BARK MEASURELESS

Dear Rog dear Roger Dear CBE are you there? I am a brave man in my way but when one is a
brave man in one's way one is not a brave man in another. With all my sense of the comic in life,
which means a certain sense of proportion about reality, I know myself less and less and wonder
where it is I want to go. We are each, in our own respective ways, blessed or cursed with certain
ingredients to help us for good or bad on our ways which we think are our ways. What's buzzin
couzzin? Love thou me? When the flood had abated a hare pussed in the shaking bell-flowers
and prayed to the rainbow through the spider's web. I have my real fire on. I am on.

I miss you. There must be a way to say 'I miss you' to another man which has nothing to do
with suggestions of homo and is dignified and vital. No harder man than me will you possibly
encounter. I don't mean you should come back necessarily. Maybe your time at Botallack is
finished [...] Shall I surrealise?

(HOW DOES ONE BEGIN?) It is my house here with those simple oils of lit lamps. The door
which will not shut is my friend and outside there is a sea of silent safety pins and a small sun
rising [...]

Please let me hear from you now as the light is failing at the window and the road outside is
quiet and the wind is sailing the very unhuman rooks up over the chimney. Love your friend.

cheerio, Sydney X

Paris den 18 Sept. 1837.

Ich glaube, lieber Kaedes, daß Ihnen die Nachricht von der glücklichen Herstellung meiner Augen Vergnügen machen wird. Dr. Sichel hat mich von der Gefahr meiner Erblindung genesen; nur leiden die Augen noch an steten Schmerzen, welches aber zur Schwäche ist.

Ich habe Herren Wanner ersucht mir die Briefe, die er etwa für mich erhielt, unter der Adresse: H. H. cité Bergère N. 3 nach Paris zu schicken; für den Fall daß er diese Adresse verloren hätte, bitte ich solche ihm in Erinnerung zu bringen, und ihn zu grüßen, bitte ich Sie freundlich.

Der gelehrte ausländische Trapel hat wieder in der Abendzeitung einen Artikel geschrieben, worin er mich von oben bis unten éclaboussirt; auch Ihrer gedenkt er und sagt daß Börne zwey Adjutanten gehabt, Herrn Kollof u Venedey, welche beiden sich auch mit Schriftstellerey befassten. Das Wort befassten ist mit besonderen großen Buchstaben gedruckt. —

Leben Sie wohl und lassen Sie mich bald viel Gutes von Ihnen hören. Ihr ganz ergeben
H. Heine

Heinrich Heine (1797–1856) to Jakob Venedey
18 September 1837

Like many of his German contemporaries, who grew up during the Napoleonic occupation, Heinrich Heine looked forward to the emergence of an egalitarian democracy in his own country after years of war. This failed to materialize, and in 1830 he emigrated to France. The lyric poetry Heine published in his twenties had, by then, established his reputation and would secure his lasting fame through song settings by Franz Schubert, Felix Mendelssohn and many other composers. In Paris, cushioned by family money, he turned out pieces on travel and politics for the German press and consorted with other liberal émigrés like Ludwig Börne and Jakob Venedey, a journalist who had been arrested for sedition in 1832, escaped from prison and fled to France.

Heine somehow managed to combine his roles as great man of European letters and supporter of radical young firebrands like Venedey, whom he helped financially when the French authorities kicked him out in 1835. This letter is a mixture of expat literary gossip, mentioning the journalists August Traxel and Édouard Kolloff and the recently deceased Börne, and an update on the series of health crises that had beset Heine since the mysterious paralysis of his left hand five years previously. Just recently, in early September 1837, he had experienced a sudden loss of sight in his right eye and blurry vision in his left. After treatment, including bloodletting with leeches, by the eminent ophthalmologist Julius Sichel – another member of the German intellectual community in Paris – his sight has miraculously improved, as he reports to Venedey.

Heine's instinct that Sichel had cured him only 'for the time being' was right. In December, his eye problems returned. Over the following years, they recurred repeatedly, accompanied by other, increasingly debilitating symptoms – facial palsy, depression, loss of sensation in his limbs. By 1848, he was confined to bed, his 'mattress grave'. Even when he had to lift his eyelids with his fingers, however, he went on writing. On the basis of descriptions in his letters, various diagnoses have been proposed. The most likely is multiple sclerosis, a condition that was clinically recognized only after Heine's death.

I believe, dearest Venedey, that you will pleased to hear of the felicitous restoration of my eyes. Dr Sichel has allowed me to see clearly again for the time being; but the pupils are still suffering a stinging pain, which is the only drawback.

I have bidden Herr Wanner to forward any letters he might have received for me to H.H. cité Bergère 3, Paris. I kindly ask you to remind him, should he have lost this address, and also pass on my greetings.

In the evening paper, the learned and upright Traxel wrote another article which besmirches me from top to bottom; he also mentions you and says that Börne has two assistants – Messrs Kolloff and Venedey, both of whom are also involved in writing. The word 'involved' is printed in especially large letters. Farewell, and let me hear a lot of cheerful things from you soon [...]

Liebster Vater,

Du hast mich letzthin einmal gefragt, warum ich behaupte, ich hätte Furcht vor Dir. Ich wußte Dir, wie gewöhnlich, nichts zu antworten, zum Teil eben aus der Furcht, die ich vor Dir habe, zum Teil deshalb, weil zur Begründung dieser Furcht zu viele Einzelheiten gehören, als daß ich sie im Reden halbwegs zusammenhalten könnte. Und wenn ich hier versuche Dir schriftlich zu antworten, so wird es doch nur sehr unvollständig sein, weil auch im Schreiben die Furcht und ihre Folgen mich Dir gegenüber behindern und weil die Größe des Stoffs über mein Gedächtnis und meinen Verstand weit hinausgeht.

Dir hat sich die Sache immer sehr einfach dargestellt, wenigstens soweit Du vor mir und, ohne Auswahl, vor vielen andern davon gesprochen hast. Es schien Dir etwa so zu sein: Du hast

Franz Kafka (1883–1924) to Hermann Kafka
1919

This is the first page of an epic letter that Franz Kafka addressed to his father. Composed as a confessional act of self-analysis as much as explanation, it was handed to his mother but never delivered. Kafka frames the failures of the patriarchal Hermann and his disappointing son within the 'prison' of family life: if the prisoner escapes, 'he cannot rebuild, and if he rebuilds, he cannot escape'. Noting his father's 'aversion to my writing', he realizes that his fiction has been 'an intentionally long and drawn-out leave-taking from you'. As Kafka may almost have foreseen, this letter became a classic text of father–son relations.

Dearest Father,

Recently you asked me why I maintain that I'm afraid of you. And, as usual, I didn't know how to answer, in part because of my fear of you; and in part because my fear rests on so many details that I couldn't even have discussed half of it. And if I attempt to give you an answer in writing, it will still be far from complete: because I'm still hindered by my fear, and all that flows from it; and because there is far too much for my mind to remember and consider.

You have always put the matter extremely simply [...] It appears thus to you perhaps: you have worked hard all your life, and for the sake of your children, above all for me, you have sacrificed everything; and I have lived the high life, with complete freedom to study what I wanted, and with no cares about food – and so for you, no cares at all – and for this you have never demanded gratitude [...] but you expect some recognition, some sign of sympathy; instead of which I have always crawled away from you, to my room, to books, to mad friends, to extreme ideas [...] And if you were to sum up your judgment it would come to this: you have not accused me of being evil or indecent (except possibly with regard to the last woman I wanted to marry) but cold, remote, ungrateful. And more than this: it is all my fault; I am *guilty* [...] and, by the same token, you are innocent – except that you have been too good to me [...]

There is just a single incident I can remember from these early years [...] Once I whimpered long in the night for water: not from thirst, but probably in part to anger you, and in part to entertain myself. After threats had failed to help, you took me out of my bed, carried me to the courtyard balcony and left me there alone in my shirt for a little while outside the closed door. I won't say that you were wrong; perhaps that was the only way to get some peace in the night; but I will say that it characterized your education methods and their effects on me [...]

Chalet Beau Site.   Les Siablerets   (Vaud)
                                        Suisse

4 Feby 1928
                Dear Mason
                        Many thanks for your letter,
which came on here — Rather gloomy! Poor old Rabelais,
after all these years! It's too damned stupid.

                        I'm going over my novel here —
the typescript — and I'm going to try to expurgate
and substitute sufficiently to produce a properish
public version for Alf Knopf, presumably, to publish
But I want to publish the unmutilated version
myself in Florence — 1000 copies in all — half for England
I shall send out no review copies. I shall make no
advertisement — just circulate a few little slips
announcing the publication. Then, perhaps, if I
post direct from Florence to all private individuals
before I send any copies to England, so that there
can be no talk beforehand — perhaps that would be
safest. I'm terribly afraid a crate might arouse suspicion.

D.H. Lawrence (1885–1930) to Harold Mason
4 February 1928

'Poor old Rabelais, after all these years!' An edition of the sixteenth-century French satirist's work – still considered obscene in 1928 – had been seized by American customs officers. Writing from Switzerland to the bookseller Harold Mason in Philadelphia, D.H. Lawrence was concerned that his own new novel, *Lady Chatterley's Lover*, would suffer a similar fate. Centring on the love affair between Constance Chatterley and her disabled husband's gamekeeper, Mellors, it contained explicit sex scenes and 'one-syllable Anglo-Saxon words'. For Lawrence, this taboo-breaking was essential in the cause of writing honestly – and beautifully – about sex. But he couldn't afford for the book to be banned. As he explains to Mason, he's editing the typescript to produce an expurgated edition for general sale, while hoping that Mason can organize the covert distribution of a small unexpurgated edition in America. Mason supplied private addresses for mailing twenty-five copies. Not a single one got through; the copy posted to Mason himself was 'arrested' and placed under lock and key in a jail.

Lawrence refers in passing to his health – he was in the late stages of a struggle with tuberculosis. In 1932, two years after Lawrence's death, the American publisher Alfred A. Knopf finally brought out an expurgated edition of *Lady Chatterley's Lover*.

Dear Mason

Many thanks for your letter, which came on here – Rather gloomy! Poor old Rabelais, after all these years! It's too darned stupid.

I'm going over my novel here – the typescript – and I'm going to try to expurgate and substitute sufficiently to produce a properish public version for Alf Knopf, presumably, to publish. But I want to publish the unmutilated version myself in Florence – 1000 copies in all – half for England. I shall send out *no* review copies. I shall make *no* advertisement – just circulate a few little slips announcing the publication. Then, perhaps, if I post direct from Florence to all private individuals before I send any copies to England, so that there can be no talk beforehand – perhaps that would be safest. I'm terribly afraid a crate might arouse suspicion, and the whole thing be lost. We might crate 50 copies to you – or more even, you needn't look on them as *ordered*: perhaps to the other bookshops you mention too. But I daren't crate the whole damn thing. What do you think? I'll be glad if you'll help me. But I'll send a set of proofs. – Write to the Villa Mirenda, we shall be back there in early March, I suppose. We are here for the time in the snow to see if it'll do my chest any good. I think it does [...]

I shall send the MS to the printer as soon as I get it revised – but I don't want to bring out the unexpurgated edition long before the public one – perhaps I'll have to wait till June.

All good wishes – and don't be impatient with me.

D.H. Lawrence

Cher Raynaldo

Marcel Proust (1871–1922) to Reynaldo Hahn
October 1914

The Venezuelan-French composer Reynaldo Hahn was a nineteen-year-old musical prodigy when he met Marcel Proust, an ambitious young writer who had yet to publish his first book. They had a brief affair, followed by a lifelong friendship. When war broke out in 1914, Hahn, although over conscription age, volunteered for the army. For Proust, he helped to obtain medical exemption on the grounds of asthma.

In this letter, written on return from an autumn break in his old seaside haunt of Cabourg, Proust, still agonizing about the possibility of call-up, grieves for the death of his sometime chauffeur, secretary and lover, Alfred Agostinelli, who was training as a pilot when his plane crashed at Antibes in May. Under his famously obsessive self-scrutiny, Proust's grief seems alternately to fade and intensify. He might write about these feelings sometime, he suggests, through his character Charles Swann, a central figure in his great multi-volume novel À la recherche du temps perdu (In Search of Lost Time). But 'I've no need to do this,' he sighs. For years now, he feels as if he has been reliving a life he's already lived in his fiction.

....

Dear Reynaldo

Heartfelt thanks for your letter [...]

My dear little one you're so kind to have thought that Cabourg would be painful to me because of Agostinelli. I must confess to my shame that it wasn't as bad as I expected and that, rather, this trip marked the first stage of detachment in my sorrow, a stage after which I'm glad to say that once back home I am again suffering as I did at first [...]

I loved Alfred so much. It's not enough to say that I loved him. I adored him. And I don't know why I'm writing this in the past tense because I still love him. But in spite of everything, in feelings of grief, there's both something involuntary and a sense of obligation that defines the involuntary and determines its duration. While this sense of obligation doesn't apply to Alfred who treated me very badly, I grieve for him as I can't help grieving, I don't feel drawn to him by duty in the way that I am connected to you, even if I owed you a thousand times less, if I loved you a thousand times less [...]

It's not because others have died that sorrow grows less, but because we ourselves die. And one needs enormous vitality to retain and keep whole and alive the 'I' of a few weeks ago. Your friend hasn't forgotten it, poor Alfred. But he has died with it, and its heir, the 'I' of today, loves Alfred but has known him only through what the former 'I' tells him. It's a second-hand tenderness. Please say nothing of all this to anyone [...] If I ever want to give form to such things it will be through the pseudonym of Swann. Besides, I've no need to do this. It's a long time since life offered me anything but events that I've already described [...]

Saint
Maurice
Seine

Asile National de
Vincennes, ~~fall~~ Galerie
Brugand, chambre 5, lit n°
13. — (public admis jeudi Dimanche et
fêtes de suite, ~~Juillet~~ 1887
à 4 heures.) 1er Août

Mon cher Kahn, Tellement bousculé
par affres de toutes sortes ces mois ci qu'il m'a
été comme impossible de répondre à l'envoi
de vos Palais nomades comme il fallait.
Les mêmes ~~motifs~~ excuses existent toujours
plutôt se fondant, mais il finit par me
tarder de vous envoyer mes meilleures
et très sincères félicitations sur ce volume
qui datera. J'adore beaucoup de vos
pièces et non des moins hardies dans l'
envoyage. faire foutre des rimes mi-
nutieuses et les compteries par trop sur
les doigts. Cela dit, je n'en reste pas
moins pour les règles très élastiques
mais pour les règles quand même, —
mais pourquoi comme d'ailleurs, m'en
fâcherais-je contre vous. Ce qui est
beau et bon est beau et bon parceque
et quoique. Voilà je pense une for-
mule à n'embêter personne et ce serait la
mienne si j'en avais. Et puis, dans
ces palais, que de subtilités de langue
et d'heureux raccourcis et d'amusantes
redondances! Bravo — et bis et ter
et ... indésinenter, comme dit le
divin Rimbaud.

Il paraît que vous avez vu
dans la rue Brouchet (on a dit Trouchet)
une vieille affiche à la mais avec un
nom dedans, qu'on réclame au dit pour
des besognes. Je suppose bien que vous

Paul Verlaine (1844–96) to Gustave Kahn
August 1887

Bedridden with leg sores, Paul Verlaine writes to Gustave Kahn, a younger poet, editor and leading spirit in the Symbolist movement. Verlaine has been in hospital for months and isn't sure of the date (he changes July to August). Kahn's first poetry collection, *Palais nomades* (*Nomadic Palaces*), came out in June, so Verlaine's congratulations are – as he confesses – rather late, coming from an admired friend and fellow writer.

Kahn claimed to have invented *vers libre*, or free verse, which follows the rhythm of the spoken phrase, rather than the classic rules of French prosody, and would become the medium of many twentieth-century poets. Verlaine launches into high but garbled praise – he claims to 'love' many poems, especially the iconoclastic ones, and enthuses vaguely about Kahn's 'delectable subtleties of language'. He then invokes 'the divine Rimbaud' (see page 209), quoting the kinds of gnomic comments he'd make in the margins of manuscripts (*indesinenter* is Latin for 'ceaselessly'). In 1886, Kahn's new journal, *La Vogue*, published Rimbaud's collection *Les Illuminations*, with an introduction by Verlaine.

Verlaine is in a bad way. Homeless after the breakup of his marriage, which followed the scandal of his relationship with Rimbaud, then his imprisonment for shooting his lover, he is also suffering from diabetes, syphilis and the effects of drug and alcohol addiction. He has, in fact, already sent congratulations to Kahn via his co-editor, Édouard Dujardin. Which suggests that the main prompt for this letter may be the last subject he broaches: money. Kahn and Dujardin still owe him for work they published last year. No doubt they're pleased to have France's greatest living poet on board – but when are they going to pay him?

My dear Kahn, So unsettled by matters of all kinds these past months that I wasn't able to reply as promptly as I should have done to your *Palais nomades* [...] I love many of your pieces, and not those that set out least boldly to say 'Get stuffed!' to fussy rhyming and metrical bean-counting. That said, on balance I'm in favour of very flexible rules, but rules all the same – but why, like some others, am I getting impatient with you? That which is beautiful and good is beautiful and good because and although. Here I think is a formula with which no one would disagree and which would be mine if I had one. And then, in these *Palais*, what delectable subtleties of language in delightful elisions and curious redundancies. Bravo – and *bis* and *ter* and ... *indesinenter* as the divine Rimbaud says [...]

A delicate matter, or rather very straightforward. Can you pay me all or part of what I'm due for my work in *La Vogue* and for *Les Illuminations*? If yes, O do it without delay! Dujardin owes me for the poems because he had them from [Théodore de] Banville who is very punctual in these matters. I think that he who is in charge of the publication really could extract from his till the few sous he owes me, and without delay [...]

H. M. Prison.
Reading.

Dear Bosie,

After long and fruitless waiting I have determined to write to you myself, as much for your sake as for mine, as I would not like to think that I had passed through two long years of imprisonment without ever having received a single line from you, or any news or message even, except such as gave me pain.

Our ill-fated and most lamentable friendship has ended in ruin and public infamy for me, yet the memory of our ancient affection is often with me, and the thought that loathing, bitterness and contempt should for ever take that place in my heart once held by love is very sad to me: and you yourself will, I think, feel in your heart that to write to me as I lie in the loneliness of prison-life is better than to publish my letters without my permission or to dedicate poems to me unasked, though the world will know nothing of whatever words of grief or passion, of remorse or indifference you may choose to send as your answer or your appeal.

I have no doubt that in this letter in which I have to write of your life and of mine, of the past and of the future, of sweet things changed to bitterness and of bitter things that may be turned into joy, there will be much that will wound your vanity to the quick. If it prove so, read the letter over and over again till it kills your vanity. If you find in it something of which you feel that you are unjustly accused, remember that one should be thankful that there is any fault of which one can be unjustly accused. If there be in it one single passage that brings tears to your eyes, weep as we weep in prison where the day no less than the night is set apart for tears. It is the only thing that can save you. If you go complaining to your mother, as you did with reference to the scorn of you I displayed in my letter to Robbie, so that she may flatter and soothe you back into self-complacency or conceit, you will be completely lost. If you find one false excuse for yourself, you will soon find a hundred, and be just what you were before. Do you still say, as you said to Robbie in your answer, that I "attribute unworthy motives" to you? Ah! you had no motives in life. You had appetites merely. A motive is an intellectual aim. That you were "very young" when our friendship began? Your defect was not that you knew so little about life, but that you knew so much. The morning dawn of boyhood with its delicate bloom, its clear pure light, its joy of innocence and expectation you had left far behind. With very swift and running feet you had passed from Romance to Realism. The gutter and the things that live in it had begun to fascinate you. That was the origin of the trouble in which you sought my aid, and I, so unwisely according to

Oscar Wilde (1854–1900) to Lord Alfred Douglas
December 1896–March 1897

In February 1895, Oscar Wilde, flush from the success of his new play, *The Importance of Being Earnest*, arrived at his club to find a card waiting for him. It had been left by the Marquess of Queensberry, the combative father of Wilde's not-so-secret lover Lord Alfred 'Bosie' Douglas, who accused him of being a 'somdomite'. Encouraged by Bosie, who loathed his father, Wilde sued for libel. But when Queensberry's defence team produced evidence of Wilde's gay double life, the case collapsed. Wilde was arrested, tried and convicted for 'gross public indecency', and sentenced to two years' imprisonment with hard labour.

Towards the end of his time in Reading Gaol, ill, malnourished and harrowed by the brutality of the Victorian penal system, Wilde was allowed access to ink, a pen and one sheet of paper each day. Between December 1896 and March 1897, he wrote a 50,000-word letter, now known as *De Profundis* ('from the depths'), addressed to Bosie. On his release, he gave the letter to his friend Robert Ross, who typed up two copies and sent one to Bosie (who may or may not have read it).

De Profundis is both a beautiful love letter and a merciless character assassination. Wilde accuses Bosie of exploiting him, distracting him from his art, separating him from his family, bankrupting him and ultimately betraying him. He picks over old arguments and reels off examples of Bosie's vapidity and greed, which are all the more stinging for their epigrammatic precision ('Your interests were merely in your meals and moods'). Is it fair? Not entirely. Bosie, though capable of extreme self-absorption and fecklessness, had petitioned for Wilde's release while he was in prison and campaigned for social reform. But *De Profundis* is also an intensely humane piece of writing – tender, vulnerable, full of emotional insight.

Wilde left prison destitute, a shadow of his former self. He and Bosie were reconciled, moving to Naples until the money ran out, before going their separate ways. In the autumn of 1900, Wilde collapsed in a Paris street after undergoing surgery for chronic middle-ear disease. He died on 30 November at the Hôtel d'Alsace.

....

Dear Bosie,

After long and fruitless waiting I have determined to write to you myself, as much for your sake as for mine, as I would not like to think that I had passed through two long years of imprisonment without ever having received a single line from you, or any news or message even, except such as gave me pain.

Our ill-fated and most lamentable friendship has ended in ruin and public infamy for me, yet the memory of our ancient affection is often with me, and the thought that loathing, bitterness and contempt should for ever take that place in my heart once held by love is very sad to me: and you yourself will, I think, feel in your heart that to write to me as I lie in the loneliness of prison-life is better than to publish my letters without my permission or to dedicate poems to me unasked [...]

Chapter 6

'Herewith a story'

Literary Business

Chinua Achebe NNMA OFR

P.O. Box 53
Nsukka Anambra State

21 May 1987

John A. Williams
693 Forest Ave,
Teaneck, N.J. 07666

Dear John,

Your letter of Nov 15 1986 accompanied by the typescript
of your novel has just reached me. I began reading the letter
without taking notice of the date until you said the novel would
be published "early next year". Then I thought seven to eight
months away was too good and then saw the date. I checked the
envelope then and saw that your publisher had sent it by surface
mail. What a shame! I should have enjoyed writing a little
promotional sentence for you; not that you needed it but it
would have given me pleasure. I shall wait and read the book.
Congratulations on the new book and on all the other things
you have done since we were last in touch.

There is a chance my wife and I will be at UMass this fall
for a year. If it works out I hope to see you in the course of
our stay.

Sincerely,

Chinua Achebe.

Rec'd June 1, 1987

Chinua Achebe (1930–2013) to John A. Williams
21 May 1987

'Blurbing' – a practice described by George Orwell as 'disgusting tripe' – is a much-maligned but stubbornly persistent part of the publishing process. Some time before publication, proofs of a book are sent to potentially sympathetic writers – the more illustrious the better – in the hope that they will offer a couple of sentences of ringing (or even roundabout) endorsement. When the African-American novelist and academic John A. Williams was looking for a puff for *Jacob's Ladder*, his tale of CIA meddling in West Africa during the 1960s, the Nigerian writer Chinua Achebe was an obvious choice. Achebe had shot to fame with his 1958 debut, *Things Fall Apart*, a searing portrait of Nigeria's colonial subjugation in the nineteenth century, and he remained Africa's reigning literary champ. He and Williams also knew each other from the conference circuit in the US – so he was a safe bet, surely?

But things didn't go according to plan. Williams's book was posted from America to Lagos by surface mail and took six months to arrive, by which point copies of *Jacob's Ladder* were rolling off the printing presses. Achebe courteously expresses his regret, though in truth he may not have been too disappointed by the reprieve. Whatever the case, it's unlikely that a glowing blurb, even from Achebe, would have lifted sales of *Jacob's Ladder*, described in one of its more positive reviews as 'sporadically intriguing'. Later that year, Achebe released a novel of his own – his first since 1966. *Anthills of the Savannah*, about a coup in a fictional West African country, was widely considered his best since *Things Fall Apart* and shortlisted for the Booker Prize.

- -

Dear John,

Your letter of Nov 15 1986 accompanied by the typescript of your novel has just reached me. I began reading the letter without taking notice of the date until you said the novel would be published 'early next year'. Then I thought seven to eight months away was too good and then saw the date. I checked the envelope and saw that your publisher had sent it by surface mail. What a shame! I should have enjoyed writing a little promotional sentence for you; not that you needed it but it would have given me pleasure. I shall wait and read the book. Congratulations on the new book and on all the other things you have done since we were last in touch […]

Sincerely,
Chinua

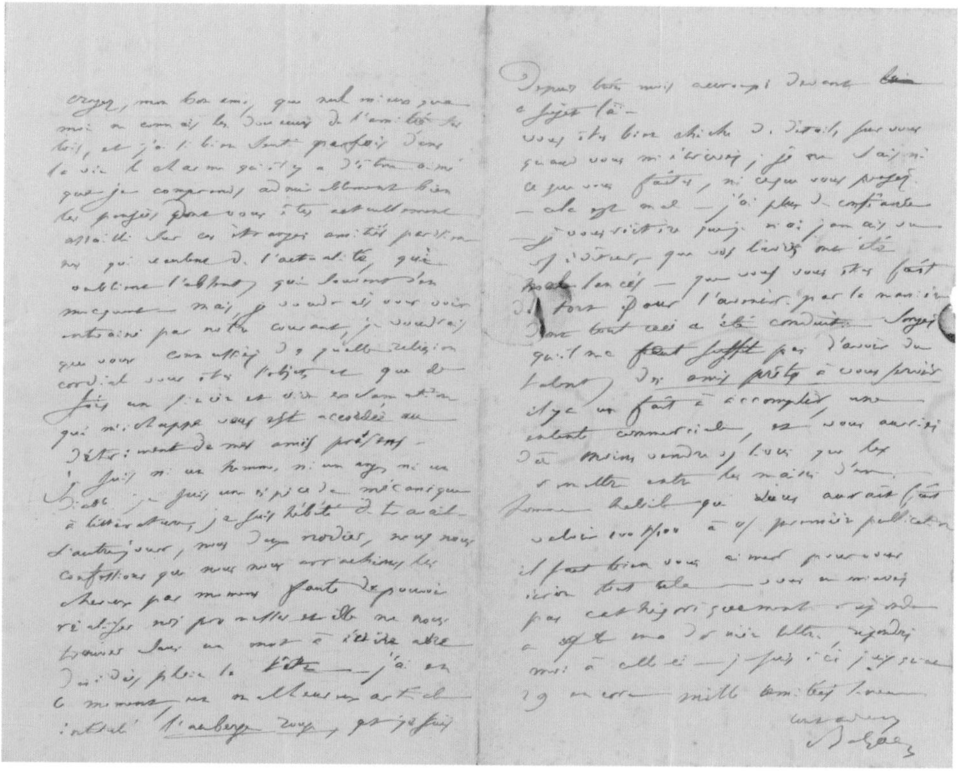

Honoré de Balzac (1799–1850) to Samuel-Henry Berthoud
18 August 1831

As well as persuading his reluctant parents to support his writing ambitions with a modest allowance, the young Balzac threw his energy into a series of loss-making business ventures, including a printing works. He remained friends with a junior typographer there, Samuel-Henry Berthoud, who went on to become a literary editor. In 1830, Balzac, who had so far earned little from his writing, received a contract from the publishers Charles Gosselin and Urbain Canel for his novel *La Peau de chagrin* (*The Skin of Sorrow*). He delivered the manuscript five months late in July 1831, but managed in the meantime to generate interest by publishing single chapters from the book in the journal *Revue de Paris*. *La Peau de chagrin* was an instant success: when the first, two-volume edition of 750 copies looked like selling out within weeks of publication in August, Balzac quickly produced a second, enlarged to three volumes by the addition of twelve 'philosophical tales'.

These are the books he promises to send Berthoud as soon as he can. Though he dramatizes his situation, claiming to be *assassiné* (literally 'assassinated') by his journalistic commitments and 'numb with work', Balzac's portrayal of himself as a 'writing machine' isn't far from the truth. The fantastical story on which he's been working, 'The Red Inn', will appear in the *Revue de Paris* within days.

....

My good Berthoud, consider that it is impossible for me to send you *La Peau de chagrin* for at least eighteen days, such, as you know, are the demands of booksellers. Gosselin has kept the entire first edition for sale – we have two volumes of the reprint and the third won't take long to do – so, you'll have 3 fine handsome and worthy volumes instead of two. – I've been done in by journalism commitments [...] If I haven't written to you, it's because of the vast amount of work I've had to do as a result of the financial needs brought on by my illness and enforced inactivity.

Believe me, my good friend, that no one knows better than I do the delights of friendship, its laws, and I have felt so often in life the charm there is in being loved that I completely understand the thoughts you are prey to at the moment concerning these strange Parisian friendships that exist in the here-and-now, that forget the absent one and often make fun of him. But I would like to see you taking part in our life here, I would like you to be aware of the religious warmth of feeling of which you are the object [...] I'm neither man nor angel nor devil. I am a sort of writing machine, I am numb with work ... Right now I have a wretched piece titled *The Red Inn*, and I've been slaving at that for three months [...]

June 24   107 The Chase
                                               London SW4 ONR

Bill Buford
Granta
King's College
Cambridge
CB2 IST

Dear Bill,

Thank you for GRANT, which looks perfectly splendid. Congratulations.

Herewith a story, COUSINS, which ought to be about 3,500 words.
It is another wolf-~~child~~ child story - of course, you may not be
aware of this obsession of mine; I have an obsession with wolf-
children, and this story is by no means the last of it. Actually,
it is really about nature and culture, but don't want to cross the
t's and dot the i's. *(Well, not too much.)* Obviously, it is meant to read plain and clumsy.
I can punctuate perfectly ~~adaq~~ adequately when I want to. Anyway,
I hope it's okay.

Glad you liked the Updike review. ~~Ru~~ Does he, and Roth, et al,
realise how sexist ~~huxixixxSomebodyxshould xxipxsixHxixxix~~ they are?
It beats me.

In haste, in order to catch the post - but I'm supposed to be going
to the States, next year, myself, so would like a word or two
before I go -

yours,

Angela

PS.

Angela Carter (1940–92) to Bill Buford
24 June 1980

'I have an obsession with wolf-children,' Angela Carter tells Bill Buford, editor of the recently resuscitated literary magazine *Granta*, who has commissioned a story from her. Wolves had featured prominently in Carter's potent, provocative 1979 collection, *The Bloody Chamber*, which reworked traditional fairy tales from a feminist perspective, mixing gothic horror, sexual transgression, stylized violence and postmodern irony. In one story, based on 'Little Red Riding Hood', the tables are turned and the protagonist cuts off a werewolf's paw; in another, a young woman ends up in bed with a 'tender wolf'.

Carter had no time for what she called 'bourgeois realism', in particular the so-called Hampstead novel, associated with British writers such as Margaret Drabble, which typically involved the moral quandaries and sleeping arrangements of middle-class bohemians. So when Buford, an American who had his own reservations about the state of fiction in his adoptive country, decided to put together an edition of *Granta* called 'The End of the English Novel', it made sense to include something from her. The story Carter offers him is indeed a long way from Hampstead: a boy living in a village in the shadow of a mountain discovers that his cousin is being raised by wolves. He brings her back to his grandmother's house, where she wreaks havoc. But Carter saw short stories as 'an argument stated in fictional terms', and there's more going on than meets the eye: the simple folk tale is a means of exploring bigger themes of 'nature and culture'.

Carter trained as a journalist after leaving school and maintained a sideline as a punchy, irreverent essayist and reviewer. It appears that her latest casualty is John Updike, high priest of libidinal, bourgeois realism in America. The future of the novel may not lie in the States either – but Carter is still planning a visit next year.

....

Dear Bill,

Thank you for GRANT, which looks perfectly splendid. Congratulations.

Herewith a story, COUSINS, which ought to be about 3,500 words. It is another wolf-child story. Of course, you may not be aware of this obsession of mine; I have an obsession with wolf-children, and this story is by no means the last of it. Actually, it is really about nature and culture, but don't want to cross the t's and dot the i's. (Well, not too much.) Obviously, it is *meant* to read plain and clumsy. I can punctuate perfectly adequately when I want to. Anyway, I hope it's okay.

Glad you liked the Updike review. Does he, and Roth, et al, realise how sexist they are? It beats me.

In haste, in order to catch the post – but I'm supposed to be going to the States, next year, myself, so would like a word or two before I go –

yours,
Angela

STATION:
SANDLING JUNCTION,
S.E.R.

PENT FARM,
STANFORD, NEAR HYTHE,
KENT.

18th Oct 1905

My dear long suffering
Douglas.

You much have
thought me a
conscienceless brute.
Alas! I have been
an overworked one.
I may safely add
that I haven't had
more than 3 weeks
of decent health

Joseph Conrad (1857–1924) to Norman Douglas
18 October 1905

Joseph Conrad and Norman Douglas met on the island of Capri, where Conrad and his wife Jessie and son spent the early months of 1905. Conrad wanted to escape the English winter so that Jessie could recover from a knee operation while he wrote. It was, he told the novelist H.G. Wells, 'a mad extravagant' trip. They were short of money, Conrad was depressed about his work, and Jessie found travelling excruciating.

Once installed on Capri, after a journey fraught with costly mishaps, Conrad toyed with writing a popular travel guide. He was beset by domestic distractions, however, complaining of having to 'lay down my pen ten times in the course of a day'. He had insomnia and caught flu. Meeting Douglas, with whom he could talk books and grumble about his health, was a high point of his stay.

The recently divorced, cash-strapped Douglas was planning to hack a living as a writer. Capri was cheap, and a safer haven for a gay man than England. When Conrad returned, he took with him some of Douglas's manuscripts, promising to do his best to get them published (*Siren Land: A Celebration of Life in Southern Italy* eventually came out in 1911). Writing six months after his return to England, Conrad confesses temporary failure. He suggests that he and Douglas (to whose name he adds an s, perhaps a friendly reference to Douglas's misspelled birth certificate) are in the same boat, in a society that demands 'subserviency', not intelligence, from its writers.

My dear long suffering Douglass.

You must have thought me a conscienceless brute. Alas! I have been an overworked one. I may safely add that I haven't had more than 3 weeks of decent health in the whole time since I left Capri [...]

I am afraid you are bitterly disappointed at the slowness in placing your articles. My dear Douglass believe me that all that could be done has been done and is being done. The first campaign failed but I am going to open the second when we go to London for a week end Nov [...] I don't see what good it would do you to get the stuff back. I have talked of it in many places – and if suddenly anybody were to ask for it I would not like to have to say I hadn't got it [...]

Don't forget my dear fellow that your point of view in general is the unpopular one. It is intellectual and uncompromising. This does not make things easier. People don't want intelligence. It worries them – and they demand from their writers as much subserviency as from their footmen if not rather more.

I trust you are not angry with me. I have had a deucedly hard time of it lately. I am just just keeping my head above water.

Good bye for the present. I'll write again soon. Kindest regards from my wife. Always yours

J[ose]ph Conrad.

Dorchester: 18.1.92

My dear Gosse:

Have you any idea of
the writer of the review of Tess
in the Saturday? I ask because
what he has done has never
before come within my experience;
although, as you know, I have
been attacked pretty much,
first & last - in years gone
by. By a rearrangement of
words in my preface he makes
me say something quite different
from what I do say: he suppresses

Thomas Hardy (1840–1928) to Edmund Gosse
18 January 1892

When Thomas Hardy's novel *Tess of the d'Urbervilles* was published in January 1892, it received very mixed reviews. Some critics hailed it as a masterpiece of social realism. Others panned it for its perceived moral depravity and even – as in a piece in the *Saturday Review* that particularly nettled Hardy – its bad grammar.

Tess is a coming-of-age story set against a background of rural poverty in mid-nineteenth-century Dorset, which Hardy knew from his own childhood. An intelligent young woman without education or prospects, Tess is seduced by her first employer (some readers were outraged that Hardy refused to make her either a chaste saint or a fallen woman), then courted by a young idealist who spurns her when he discovers her past. Finally, after again becoming her seducer's mistress, she murders him. Hardy subtitled the book *A Pure Woman*.

The *Saturday Review*'s hatchet job was, like much reviewing at this time, anonymous. Hardy hopes that Edmund Gosse – who knows everyone in literary London – can tell him who wrote it, so that he can 'shake his hand at the Savile', the gentlemen's club to which Hardy, Gosse and many other writers belong. Rich, successful, he still can't stand his work being misinterpreted. Why shouldn't the eighteen-year-old Tess be both naive and physically well-developed? How can a blatant misprint be exploited to make him seem incompetent? As new editions of *Tess* appeared, Hardy went on revising the text for twenty years.

My dear Gosse:

Have you any idea of the writer of the review of Tess in the Saturday? I ask because what he has done has never before come within my experience; although, as you know, I have been attacked pretty much, first & last, in years gone by. By a rearrangement of words in my preface he makes me say something quite different from what I do say: he suppresses half the title of the story, these being the words without which the aim & purpose of the novel cannot be understood. Then an obvious misprint of 'road' for 'load' in a sentence he professes to quote, is made to appear bad grammar by changing the adjoining word into one not in the original. As the same phrase 'the summit of the load' occurs again in the next paragraph but one, the reader of the book can see that the first is a misprint – which reveals the *animus* of the critic. Again he reverses the statements in the book that the heroine's mother lets her go into temptation with tears, doubts, sighs &c, & says it is with *sang froid*, like 'the vilest of her sex'. Also an assertion in the book to the effect that the heroine looked more developed & marriageable than she was, is made to mean something indecent which I never thought of.

But I won't bore you with any more of it. Only I should like to know who my gentleman is – to shake his hand at the Savile.

Yours sincerely
T. Hardy.

Dresden den 23ᵈᵉ Januar 1874. —

Kære herr Grieg!

Jeg henvender disse linjer til Dem i anledning af en plan, som jeg agter at iværksætte, og i hvilken jeg vil forespørge om De skulde ville være deltager.

Sagen er følgende. "Peer Gynt", — hvoraf nu et bredje oplag snart skal udkomme, — agter jeg at indrette til opførelse på scenen. Vil De komponere den dertil fornødne musik? Jeg skal i korthed antyde for Dem, hvorledes jeg tænker at indrette stykket.

Første akt bibeholdes helt, kun med nogle forkortninger i dialogen. Peer Gynts monolog side 23, 24 og 25 ønsker jeg behandlet enten melodramatisk eller delvis som recitativ. Scenen i bryllupsgården, side 28, må der ved hjælp af ballet gøres meget mere ud af, end der står i bogen.

Henrik Ibsen (1828–1906) to Edvard Grieg
23 January 1874

'I don't think the play's for acting,' was Henrik Ibsen's initial verdict on *Peer Gynt*, a five-act verse drama he published in Copenhagen in November 1867. Following the adventures of the Norwegian folk hero Per Gynt (whom Ibsen believed to have been a historical figure), it ranges from the mountains of Norway to the Egyptian desert and involves more than fifty characters in a series of loosely connected episodes, some dreamlike, others more realistic.

Six years later, as he finally embarked on preparing *Peer Gynt* for the stage, Ibsen approached the young composer Edvard Grieg to 'enhance' the play with incidental music. He wrote from Dresden, where he'd been living since 1868. Much of this time had been spent writing *Emperor and Galilean*, a now little-known drama set in ancient Rome, which Ibsen was almost alone in regarding as his masterpiece. Though reputedly unmusical himself, he would have been aware of Grieg's reputation as an up-and-coming composer in an appropriately nationalist Romantic idiom. Grieg had recently produced settings for twenty-five Norwegian folksongs and his first music for the stage, for a production of *Sigurd Jorsalfar* ('Sigurd the Crusader', a medieval Norwegian king) in Christiana (now Oslo).

Grieg must have felt flattered to be approached by the leading dramatist of the time. Under the impression – understandable from Ibsen's brisk description of his 'project' – that only a few pieces of music would be needed, he accepted the invitation. But *Peer Gynt* turned out to be a far bigger undertaking than planned. Grieg worked continuously on the score from June 1874 to July 1875, producing some forty pieces. More than ten years later, he revisited his music for *Peer Gynt*, recasting selected highlights in the form of two orchestral suites. Movements from these suites, like 'In the Hall of the Mountain King', with its hummable *alla marcia* vigour, and the yearning Nordic air of 'Solveig's Song', have become perennially popular classics.

Peer Gynt was Ibsen's last verse drama. He is better known today for plays such as *The Doll's House* and *Hedda Gabler*, in which he pioneered modern domestic realist theatre. It's Grieg who is more strongly associated with the folkloric landscape – the trolls, exotic wanderings and mythopoeic self-realizations – that Ibsen dreamed up for *Peer Gynt*.

Dear Mr Grieg!

I write to you concerning a project that I intend to undertake, in which I would like to ask you to take part.

The situation is as follows. I intend to adapt 'Peer Gynt' – a third edition of which will soon be published – for the stage. Would you compose the music required for this? I must explain briefly to you how I'm thinking of enhancing the work.

The first act will be completely retained, with just some cuts to the dialogue. I would like Peer Gynt's monologue on pages 23, 24 and 25 to be treated either melodramatically or as a partial recitative. The wedding scene dance, page 28, should be treated according to the book [...]

Dear Marlon

I'm praying that you'll buy ON THE ROAD and make a movie
of it. Dont worry about structure, I know how to compress and
re-arrange the plot a bit to give perfectly acceptable movie-type
structure: making it into one all-inclusive trip instead of the
several voyages coast-to-coast in the book, one vast round trip
from New York to Denver to Frisco to Mexico to New Orleans to New York
again. I visualize the beautiful shots could be made with the camera
on the front seat of the car showing the road (day and night) unwinding
into the windshield, as Sal and Dean yak. I wanted you to play the
part because Dean (as you know) is no dopey hotrodder but a real
intelligent (in fact Jesuit) Irishman. You play Dean and I'll play
Sal (Warner Bros. mentioned I play Sal) and I'll show you how Dean
acts in real life, you couldnt possibly imagine it without seeing a
good imitation. Fact, we can go visit him in Frisco, or have him
come down to L.A. still a real frantic cat but nowadays settled
down whth his final wife saying the Lord's Prayer with his kiddies
at night...as you'll seen when you read the play BEAT GENERATION.
All I want out of this is to be able to establish myself and my
mother a trust fund for life, so I can really go roaming around the
world writing about Japan, India, France etc. ...I want to be free
to write what comes out of my head & free to feed my buddies when
they're hungry & not worry about my mother.

Incidentally, my next novel is THE SUBTERRANEANS coming
out in N.Y. next March and is about a love affair between a white
guy and a colored girl and very hep story. Some of the characters
in it you knew in the Village (Stanley Gould? etc.) It easily could
be turned into a play, easier than ON THE ROAD.

What I wanta do is re-do the theater and the cinema in
America, give it a spontaneous dash, remove pre-conceptions of
"situation" and let people rave on as they do in real life. That's
what the play is: no plot in particular, no "meaning" in particular,
just the way people are. Everything I write I do in the spirit
where I imagine myself an Angel returned to the earth seeing it with
sad eyes as it is. I know you approve of these ideas, & incidentally
the new Frank Sinatra show is based on "spontaneous" too, which is
the only way to come on anyway, whether in show business or life.
The French movies of the 30's are still far superior to ours because
the French really let their actors come on and the writers didnt
quibble with some preconceived notion of how intelligent the movie
audience is, the talked soul from soul and everybody understood at once.
I want to make great French Movies in America, finally, when I'm rich
...American Theater & Cinema at present is an outmoded Dinosaur
that aint mutated along with the best in American Literature.

If you really want to go ahead, make arrangements to
see me in New York when next you come, or if you're going to Florida
here I am, but what we should do is talk about this because I
prophesy that it's going to be the beginning of something real
great. I'm bored nowadays and I'm looking around for something to do
in the void, anyway——writing novels is getting too easy, same with
plays, I wrote the play in 24 hours.

Come on now, Marlon, put up your dukes and write!

Sincerely, later,   Jack Kerouac

Jack Kerouac (1922–69) to Marlon Brando
1957

It's 1957 and Jack Kerouac is buzzing from the success of *On the Road*, his Beat Generation buddy story. Everyone in Hollywood, it seems, wants to adapt the book for the big screen – but Kerouac has other ideas. He writes to Marlon Brando – hot property after his turn in *On the Waterfront* – and asks if he will buy the rights. He envisages Brando as Dean Moriarty, the wayward, self-destructive dreamer based on Kerouac's friend Neal Cassady. For someone who's only just hit his stride as a novelist, Kerouac is remarkably confident about his film-making capabilities. He will play Sal Paradise, the autobiographical protagonist, he tells Brando. And no need to worry about the script – he's got that covered too. 'What I wanta do is re-do the theater and the cinema in America,' he modestly explains.

What did Brando make of this chutzpah, this jabbering novelist telling him his own business? He kept the letter – but never replied.

Dear Marlon

I'm praying that you'll buy ON THE ROAD and make a movie of it. Don't worry about structure, I know how to compress and re-arrange the plot a bit to give perfectly acceptable movie-type structure: making it into one all-inclusive trip instead of the several voyages coast-to-coast in the book, one vast round trip from New York to Denver to Frisco to Mexico to New Orleans to New York again. I visualize the beautiful shots could be made with the camera on the front seat of the car showing the road (day and night) unwinding into the windshield, as Sal and Dean yak. I wanted you to play the part because Dean (as you know) is no dopey hotrodder but a real intelligent (in fact Jesuit) Irishman. You play Dean and I'll play Sal (Warner Bros. mentioned I play Sal) [...]

What I wanta do is re-do the theater and the cinema in America, give it a spontaneous dash, remove pre-conceptions of 'situation' and let people rave on as they do in real life. That's what the play is: no plot in particular, no 'meaning' in particular, just the way people are. Everything I write I do in the spirit where I imagine myself an Angel returned to the earth seeing it with sad eyes as it is. I know you approve of these ideas [...]

If you really want to go ahead, make arrangements to see me in New York when next you come, or if you're going to Florida here I am, but what we should do is *talk* about this because I prophesy that it's going to be the beginning of something real great. I'm bored nowadays and I'm looking around for something to do in the void, anyway – writing novels is getting too easy, same with plays, I wrote the play in 24 hours.

Come on now, Marlon, put up your dukes and write!

Sincerely, later, Jack Kerouac

Pittsfield, July 17th

My Dear Hawthorne: —   This name of
"Hawthorne" seems to be ubiquitous. I have
been on something of a tour lately, and it has
saluted me vocally & typographically in all sorts of
places & in all sorts of ways. — I was at the
solitary Crusoeish island of Naushon (one of the Elizabeth
group) and there, on a stately piazza, I saw it gilded
on the back of a very new book, and in the hands of a
clergyman. — I went to visit a gentleman in
Brooklyne, and as we were sitting at our wine, in
came the lady of the house, holding a beaming volume
in her hand, from the city — "My Dear," to her
husband, "I have bought you Hawthorne's new book."
I entered the cars at Boston for this place. In came
a lively boy "Hawthorne's new book!" — In good
time I arrived home. Said my lady-wife "there is
Mr Hawthorne's new book, come by mail" And this
morning, lo! on my table a little note, subscribed
Hawthorne again, — Well, the Hawthorne is a
sweet flower; may it flourish in every hedge.

            I am sorry, but I can not
at present come to see you at Concord as you

Herman Melville (1819–91) to Nathaniel Hawthorne
17 July 1852

'This name of "*Hawthorne*" seems to be ubiquitous,' Herman Melville reports in an ebullient letter to Nathaniel Hawthorne, whose third novel, *The Blithedale Romance*, has just been published. The two writers had become close after meeting on a hike in 1850 – a coup for Melville, who had declared several months earlier in an anonymous review that Hawthorne's work had 'dropped germanous seeds into my soul'. Soon after, he uprooted his entire family from New York and moved to Pittsfield, Massachusetts, to be closer to his new friend.

By 1852, it wasn't Hawthorne who needed a boost. His reputation was on the rise, while Melville's was in freefall. Melville had found fame early with *Typee* (1846), based on his adventures in Polynesia, but *Moby-Dick* (1851), dedicated to Hawthorne, had been a flop – and his latest, *Pierre*, had been reviewed under the headline 'HERMAN MELVILLE CRAZY'. He talks cheerfully about his recent travels, but it sounds like he's at a loose end. Five years later, he stopped writing fiction.

They were an odd pair. Hawthorne, born into a venerable New England family, was brooding and reticent, while Melville, the son of a New York merchant, was brash and impulsive. But it was clearly an intense relationship. On Melville's side, there appeared to be more than just a desire for friendship, which may have been too much for Hawthorne. In 1854, he left the Berkshires, meeting Melville only once more.

My dear Hawthorne: – This name of '*Hawthorne*' seems to be ubiquitous. I have been on something of a tour lately, and it has saluted me vocally & typographically in all sorts of places [...] I was at the solitary Crusoeish island of Naushon (one of the Elisabeth group) and there, on a stately piazza, I saw it gilded on the back of a very new book, and in the hands of a clergyman. – I went to visit a gentleman in Brooklyne, and as we were sitting at our wine, in came the lady of the house, holding a beaming volume in her hand, from the city – 'My Dear,' to her husband, 'I have brought you *Hawthorne*'s new book.' [...] Well, the Hawthorne is a sweet flower; may it flourish in every hedge [...]

I am but just returned from a two weeks' absence; and for the last three months & more I have been an utter idler and a savage – out of doors all the time. So, the hour has come for me to sit down again [...]

As I am only just home, I have not yet got far into the book but enough to see that you have most admirably employed materials which are richer than I had fancied them. Especially at this day, the volume is welcome, as an antidote to the mooniness of some dreamers – who are merely dreamers – Yet who the devel aint a dreamer? [...]

of Indianapolis who published
"When Knighthood was in
Flower" — what name is he?
Bowen Merrill? Something —
such a name. Perhaps I
may have chance to publish
them in London, may be not
I cannot tell yet.
I made many a nice, young,
lovely, kind friend among
literary genius (attention!)
— W.B. Yeats or Lawrence
Binyon, Moore and Bridges.
They are so good, they invite
me almost every day. They
are jolly companions. Their
hair are not long, I tell you.
151 Brixton Road   good luck and
S.W.   strong health.
24th   yone

Dear Leonie,

Yes, my new book will
be out in fortnight at the latest.
All the proofs were corrected, and
the cover was done. Hurrah,
book — London book!
Oh, no, I shall not destroy
your most interesting letters
ever I received. I will keep
it as long as I live. As
to the "Letters"? I wish you
will try with some other
magazine once more.
And if no one did'nt want
them? And then you will
try them for publication as
book. Book-publishers I
mean. Doubleday, perhaps for
instance. Or the publisher

Yone Noguchi (1875–1947) to Léonie Gilmour
24 February 1903

Elated by his first taste of literary success in London and the glittering roll-call of his new friends, the Japanese poet and novelist Yonejirō (known as Yone) Noguchi writes to his editor and English teacher in New York, Léonie Gilmour. Born in Tsushima, Noguchi studied literature at Keio University in Tokyo, then sailed for San Francisco at the age of eighteen. He worked on an émigré Japanese political newspaper and met American literati, like the poet Joaquin Miller, whose example fired his ambition to become a professional author. By 1901, he was living in New York, writing his first novel, *The American Diary of a Japanese Girl*, for which he employed Gilmour to edit and, quite possibly, collaborate on the text. Interest in all things Japanese, from architecture to poetry, had been running high in Europe and America for some time, but Noguchi was the first modern Japanese writer to make a reputation in the West.

Arriving in London in December 1902, he wasted no time. In January he self-published a poetry collection, *From the Eastern Sea*, sending fifty copies to leading British writers and critics. Their enthusiastic response took even Noguchi by surprise. In April an enlarged edition, 'Dedicated to the Spirits of Fuji Mountain', came out. This is the '*London book*!' he announces to Gilmour. Oscar Wilde's 1882 American tour had left the impression that all British poets were long-haired fops; Noguchi delightedly reports that this isn't true of W.B. Yeats, Laurence Binyon and the other '*geniuses*' who have become his 'jolly companions'. He encourages Gilmour to keep pushing her own work out for publication, but is noncommittal about his ability to help ('may be not').

On his return to America in the autumn, Noguchi and Gilmour became lovers and were secretly married, though their vows were apparently vague. In early 1904, when they were already drifting apart, Gilmour discovered she was pregnant. Their son, Isamu, born that November, would become a famous modernist sculptor.

Dear Leonie,

Yes, my new book will be out in a fortnight at the latest. All the proofs were corrected, and the cover was done. Hurrah, book – *London book*!

Oh, no, I shall not destroy your most interesting letter ever I received. I will keep it as long as I live. As to the 'Letters'? I wish you will try with some other magazine once more.

And if no one didn't want them? And then you will try them for publication as book. Book-publishers I mean. Doubleday pays for instance. Or the publisher of Indianapolis who published 'When Knighthood was in Flower' – what name was he? Bowen Merrill? Something – such a name. Perhaps I will have chance to publish them in London, may be not. Cannot tell yet.

I made many a nice, young, lovely, kind friend among literary *geniuses* (attention!) – W.B. Yeats & Laurence Binyon, Moore and Bridges. They are so good, they invite me almost everyday. They are jolly companions. Their hair is not long, I tell you.

Good luck and strong health.

Yone

Dear Shed,

Lest I should have made some mistake in the
hurry I transcribe the whole alteration.

Instead of the whole stanza commencing "Wondering
at the stillness broken &c – substitute this

Startled at the stillness broken by reply so aptly spoken,
"Doubtless", said I, "what it utters is its only stock and store
Caught from some unhappy master whom unmerciful Disaster
Followed fast and followed faster till his songs one burden bore –
Till the dirges of his Hope the melancholy burden bore,
            'Nevermore – ah, nevermore!'"

At the close of the stanza preceding this, instead of
"Quoth the raven Nevermore", substitute "Then the
bird said 'Nevermore'".

                Truly yours
                    Poe

Edgar Allan Poe (1809–49) to John Augustus Shea
3 February 1845

The early 1840s were a grim time for Edgar Allan Poe. His wife Virginia (or 'Sissy') – a cousin, whom he'd married when she was thirteen – was showing the first signs of tuberculosis. After several lucrative jobs in journalism, he had fallen out with his employers and was scraping a living writing announcements for the *New York Evening Mirror*. He was drinking too much, again.

Then, in January 1845, he published a poem in the *Mirror*, about a grieving lover tormented by a talking raven. Beguilingly sinister, and with a distinctive, eerily insistent rhythm, the poem was extraordinarily popular. In less than a month, 'The Raven' had been reprinted ten times by other outlets, and Poe found himself accosted by cawing strangers as he walked down the street.

Before one of these syndications, this time in the *New-York Daily Tribune*, Poe writes to his editor, John Augustus Shea, suggesting a couple of changes. They are small but shrewd amendments, tightening the language, quickening the pace and, in their incremental way, ramping up the sense of dread. Poe had published many poems and short stories before 'The Raven' appeared, but he was best known for his combative literary criticism, which earned him the nickname 'Tomahawk Man'. He had strong views about why poems succeeded or failed, with a particular hatred of 'didactic' verse, which valued the message over the means of expression. And, in 'The Raven', he practised what he preached. While the poem could hardly be described as subtle, it does, in T.S. Eliot's phrase, 'communicate before it is understood'.

Dear Shea,

Lest I should have made some mistake in the hurry I transcribe the whole alteration.
    Instead of the whole stanza commencing 'Wondering at the stillness broken &c – substitute this.

> Startled at the stillness broken by reply so aptly spoken,
> 'Doubtless', said I, 'what it utters is its only stock and store
> Caught from some unhappy master whom unmerciful Disaster
> Followed fast and followed faster till his songs one burden bore –
> Till the dirges of his Hope the melancholy burden bore,
>   'Nevermore – ah, nevermore!'

At the close of the stanza *preceding* this, instead of 'Quoth the raven Nevermore', substitute Then the bird said 'Nevermore'.

Truly yours,
Poe

56 Euston Square – N.W.
4 February.

Dear Mr Macmillan

Thank you very much. Here
is my little story on trial.

Will you think me too eccentric
for returning – but with cordial
sense of your liberal kindness –
your cheque (herein) for 15/
& begging you to favour me by
substituting for it one for that
precise £5.9.0 which is all
that I have earned? I have
more than enough for my
wedding present, & like to feel
that in the future an odd

Christina Rossetti (1830–94) to Alexander Macmillan
4 February 1874

Money and manuscripts. On the face of it, Christina Rossetti's letter to her publisher, Alexander Macmillan, is part of the routine traffic in a long-term business relationship. But author–publisher dealings are fraught with ambivalence. Who really wields the power? The writer without whose work there would be no bestsellers, or the publisher who controls the writer's access to her readers? Can business and friendship really mix? Beneath its brisk practicality, Rossetti's letter reveals her sensitivity to these nuances.

In Victorian Britain, few middle-class women had independent business dealings, and very few indeed were professional writers. Rossetti and Macmillan have been corresponding since he published her first, successful book, *Goblin Market and Other Poems*, in 1862, but her opening remains formal – no first-name terms. She is returning his cheque because it's too generous: she wants Macmillan's money to represent real earnings not patriarchal largesse, however kindly meant.

Rossetti writes from the house in Euston Square that she shares with her mother and sister. She has rejected three marriage proposals, but independence comes with a sense of isolation from wider literary and social life. Her health is poor, her freedom limited and Macmillan's cheque would have been useful. Yet, she writes, she has enough for a wedding present for her brother William Michael, an art critic, and Lucy Madox Brown, sister of one of the Pre-Raphaelite comrades of her artist brother, Dante Gabriel.

The new story she encloses is probably one of the children's fantasy tales in *Speaking Likenesses*, which Macmillan will publish in December for the increasingly lucrative 'Christmas Books' market. There's also been some discussion about reissuing *Goblin Market* – a strange poem ostensibly for children, but today often interpreted in psychosexual terms – as a two-volume set with Rossetti's second collection, *The Prince's Progress* (1866). Like any shrewd publisher, Macmillan wants to tempt buyers with the promise of exclusive new material. Rossetti demurs: 'The fire has died out, it seems; & I know of no bellows potent to revive dead coals.' Characteristically straight-talking (she has been called 'the most naked of poets'), she opts for the plain truth, rather than trying to spin things to her advantage.

....

Dear Mr Macmillan

Thank you very much. Here is my little story on trial.

Will you think me too eccentric for returning – but with cordial sense of your liberal kindness – your cheque (herein) for 15£, & begging you to favour me by substituting for it one for that precise £5. 9s. 0d which is all that I have earned? I have more than enough for my wedding present, & like to feel that in the future an odd sovereign or two may now & then drop in.

The possibility of your thinking proper some day to reprint my 2 vols in one, is really gratifying to me as you may suppose, but as to the additional matter, I fear there will be little indeed to offer you. The fire has died out, it seems; & I know of no bellows potent to revive dead coals. I wish I did.

Very truly yours

Christina G. Rossetti.

may be over in Quinn
may ... the risk. I would
I dare say do ... not ...
... off ... some American
resentment, things I ...
the ... house, view of
myself completely, (I do
not mean the German plot
which is, or you know, a
... in somebody's ...)
... their English ... a
... ... (as I think
... not is) to ... his
affairs in Ireland.
Yrs ...
WB Yeats

Ballinamantane House
Gort
July 15   Co Galway
My dear Ezra: I send you
"The Phases ... the moon"
... should go with "The
Double Vision "; you ...
to use this? without ...
"The Double Vision " is too
obscure. Read my symbols
... picture — allowing your
mind to ... beyond the words
and ... the symbol ...
this symbol seems, to me things
as beautiful. After all one
art is not it chief ..., life
... an accident in ones search
for reality or rather perhaps

William Butler Yeats (1865–1939) to Ezra Pound
15 July 1918

Enclosed with this letter, W.B. Yeats sends poems that he hopes Ezra Pound will publish in the literary magazine he's editing, *The Little Review*. Yeats's thinking and poetry are becoming increasingly mystical. He senses that, without some explanation, Pound may find his new work incomprehensible. 'Read my symbol with patience,' he advises, 'allowing your mind to go beyond the words to the symbol itself.' Pound's impatience with mysticism relates to his conviction that modern poetry should reject overtly poetic language in favour of concrete imagery. This was the basis for the Imagist movement he founded in 1912 and for his own magnum opus, *The Cantos*, on which he has been working since 1915.

When Pound arrived in Britain from the United States in 1908, Yeats was his poetic hero. Between 1913 and 1916 he spent several winters living with him as his secretary, encouraging the older poet to write in a more modern, Imagist manner – with noticeable effect. By 1918, however, Yeats was deeply immersed in working out a private belief system, based on the phases of the moon. In 'The Double Vision of Michael Robartes', the eponymous figure from Irish legend recounts how 'the mind's eye/Has called up the cold spirits that are born/When the old moon is vanished from the sky/And the new still hides her horn'. The 'Gregory' is an elegy to Robert Gregory (son of Yeats's close friend and patron Lady Gregory), who had been killed on active service in the Royal Air Force in January. This letter is addressed from Ballinamanton, near her country mansion, Coole Park, in County Galway.

Pound was an inspired and vigilant editor with unrivalled connections in the literary avant-garde. Alongside 'In Memory of Robert Gregory', the September 1918 issue of *The Little Review* contained four poems by his fellow American T.S. Eliot and Chapter 6 of James Joyce's experimental novel-in-progress, *Ulysses* (see page 55).

My dear Ezra: I send you 'The Phases of the Moon' which should go with 'The Double Vision' if you want to use this? Without it 'The Double Vision' is too obscure. Read my symbol with patience – allowing your mind to go beyond the words to the symbol itself – as this symbol seems to me strange and beautiful. After all ones art is not its chief end, life's but an accident in ones search for reality or rather perhaps ones method of search. I am now at the 30th page of my prose dialogues expounding this symbol & there will be 3 dialogues of some 40 pages each, full of my sort of violence and passion. The mere mathematic discord or concord between different phases needs many pages [...]

Now about this cable, what I must know is whether 'Gregory' is going out in the Little Review in September or to know it in sufficient time for me to secure my English copyright [...]

Y[ou]rs s[incerel]y

WB Yeats

Chapter 7

'Like an old war horse'

Voice of Experience

Issy-les-Moulineaux
24. 1. 65

Dear Harold

Forgive my not having written
before now to tell you how nice,
(phew!) I am by the (Hemezoving;
it seems to me the best "venture"
you've seen the Cantables - perhaps
the best of all - best meaning
of course nothing else, but you
know what I mean. The part
of the fader is tremendous and should
play like a bomb. I wish Pat could
do it. Wish I could tell you better
how I feel about it and how glad
I am. But too tired and stupid
and have been waiting too long to
be kinder, before writing, to write,
all longer. So just - chapeau.
and may it run to be nice.

Affectionately
Sam

Samuel Beckett (1906–89) to Harold Pinter
27 January 1965

Samuel Beckett and Harold Pinter began corresponding in August 1960, when Beckett wrote to thank the younger playwright for sending the script of *The Caretaker*. Opening at the Arts Theatre in London in April, in a production directed by Beckett's friend Donald McWhinnie, it made Pinter's reputation. The play's central character is a destitute man, Mac Davies, who is invited by two brothers to act as a caretaker in their seedy flat. With his hand-me-down shoes and hazy grasp of the events leading up to his present situation, Davies has an obvious kinship with the two existentialist tramps in Beckett's *Waiting for Godot*, who while away their time in a desolate arena waiting for something to happen that will give their lives meaning. To critics and audiences, Pinter seemed like Beckett's natural successor – only more focused on the material textures and social relationships of the 1960s. The two finally met in January 1961, when Pinter was in Paris for the French production of *The Caretaker* (*Le Gardien*).

In January 1965, Beckett wrote to the actor Patrick Magee, for whom he had written the one-man play *Krapp's Last Tape*, saying how 'impressed' he was by Pinter's new play, *The Homecoming*. He responded especially to the lines Pinter gave his roughcut *paterfamilias*, Max. 'It's about the most beautiful part he has written,' he told Magee. 'Pity you can't do Max.' Peter Hall was directing the Royal Shakespeare Company in the first production of *The Homecoming*, but Magee was already engaged to play the Marquis de Sade for RSC.

Writing a couple of days later to Pinter, Beckett reiterates his praise for the part of Max, predicting that it will 'play like a bomb', and salutes his achievement – '*chapeau!*' ('hats off!'). He excuses himself for not saying so sooner and not sounding more lively, being 'too tired and stupid' to 'tell you better how I feel about it'. Beckett and Pinter both had a reputation for subverting clichés and putting an indefinably ironic spin on plain, familiar words. There's a sense of shared humour, and a refusal to let bland words stand, in Beckett's wanting and not wanting to pronounce *The Homecoming* 'the best you have done' – 'best meaning of course nothing here, but you know what I mean'.

Dear Harold

Forgive my not having written before now to tell you how impressed I am by the *Homecoming*. It seems to me the best you have done since the *Caretaker* & perhaps the best of all – best meaning of course nothing here, but you know what I mean. The part of the father is tremendous and should play like a bomb. I wish Pat could do it. Wish I could tell you better how I feel about it and how glad I am. But too tired and stupid and have been waiting too long to be less so, before writing, to wait any longer. So just – chapeau! and may it soon to be seen.

Affectionately
Sam

Nov 25- 1878.

Dear Friend,
            It seems a long time
that I have not exchanged a word
with you — not since Daniel Deronda
retired into silence — A sort of crisis
has come in my life — the greater
of a century allowed in copy right
to a book has expired & in renewing
the same, we are led to prepare a
new Edition ^of Uncle Toms Cabin. As introductory
a history of the work its causes
& results is given and a bibliographic
account of the various translations
and editions has been prepared
by Mr Bullen of the British
Museum. I send you herewith
a copy of the new Edition

I am quite sure that tho "at this
era of my life tho I am saddened
by feeling that scarce one of the
brave men who were with me are here now
in the first of the struggle —
& almost every one in England

Harriet Beecher Stowe (1811–96) to George Eliot
25 November 1878

The story goes that when Harriet Beecher Stowe, author of the wildly successful anti-slavery novel *Uncle Tom's Cabin* (1852), met Abraham Lincoln in 1863, at the height of the American Civil War, the president identified her as the woman who had started the conflict. Whether or not Lincoln really said this, the tale reflects Beecher's standing, and not just in her own country. She was the first American to write an international bestseller.

Across the Atlantic, George Eliot (see page 79) was living a quieter life. But she was still the most famous woman novelist in Britain, celebrated for giving depth and dignity to ordinary lives in novels such as *Middlemarch* (1871–2), and notorious for 'living in sin' with the philosopher George Henry Lewes. She regarded *Uncle Tom's Cabin* as a work of 'rare genius', but it was Stowe who reached out to her, in 1869, with a letter praising the moral seriousness of her writing. Over the following decade, the pair kept up a warm, candid correspondence. They had their differences: Stowe was Christian with spiritualist tendencies, Eliot a staunch humanist. But they supported each other's work, and when Eliot was writing *Daniel Deronda* (1876), which explored the injustices faced by British Jews, she sought Stowe's advice. The lull in their correspondence that Stowe ascribes to her own 'crisis' may also relate to Lewis's fragile state of health: he died a few days after this letter arrived.

Stowe refers to Eliot's great last novel in this letter, in which she also encloses a new edition of *Uncle Tom's Cabin* (protections for authors in the nineteenth century left much to be desired, with copyright lasting just twenty-eight years). She reflects on what has changed since the novel first appeared. Slavery has been abolished and now, she notes later in the letter, there are even schools for African-American children that 'would be an honour to any city'. Yet things remain 'far from desirable or perfect': America is still a segregated society. The struggle continues.

....

Dear Friend

It seems a long time that I have not exchanged a word with you – not since Daniel Deronda retired into silence – A sort of crisis has come in my life – the quarter of a century allowed in copy right to a book has expired & in reviewing the same, we are led to prepare a new edition of Uncle Tom's Cabin. As introductory a history of the work its causes & results is given and a bibliographic account of its various translations and editions has been prepared by Mr Bullen of the British Museum. I send you herewith a copy [...]

I am quite sure that tho at this era of my life [...] I am saddened by feeling that scarce one of the brave men who were with me in the first of the struggle are here now – & almost every one in England who at that time met & welcomed me are gone, – yet I should be sure of sympathy in a heart like yours in the joy & thankfulness in which to day I remember that slavery is no more – the whole structure of wrong and cruelty – melted, dissolved and gone [...]

Anton Chekhov (1860–1904) to Alexander Amfiteatrov
13 April 1904

Chekhov's last play, *The Cherry Orchard*, opened at the Moscow Art Theatre in January 1904. He was living at his villa in the Black Sea resort of Yalta, where the climate was kinder to his tubercular lungs. A letter from a writer friend, Alexander Amfiteatrov, enclosing reviews of the play, reminds Chekhov of their shared past as contributors to the humorous magazine *Alarm Clock*, and an old team photo with its editor, A.D. Kurepin. Exiled in 1902 for satirizing the Russian imperial family, Amfiteatrov has returned to report on the Russo-Japanese War. Chekhov, a qualified doctor, announces his intention – once he is better – to serve on the front, on the far eastern border of the Russian Empire.

With its enthusiastic suggestions for meeting up in Yalta or Moscow, and reflections on what he's been reading (he has particularly enjoyed a two-part story, 'Blacksoil', by Ivan Bunin, whom he knows Amfiteatrov admires), Chekhov's letter gives no hint that he is terminally ill. A few weeks later, he travelled with his wife, Olga, to the German spa town of Badenweiler. 'Things are going well with me,' he told his sister on 26 June. 'My health gets better all the time.' On 2 July – in Olga's account – his doctor prescribed a glass of champagne, which Chekhov drank, 'lay down peacefully on his left side, and presently was silent for ever'.

....

I bow low to you for your kind letter and the two reviews [of *The Cherry Orchard*] which I read (I shan't hide it) twice with great pleasure. Those two reviews of yours wafted upon me a breath of the past, something long forgotten, as if you were a fellow-villager of mine; and there sprang to life in my memory that jubilee picture in the *Alarm Clock*, where you and I stand near Kurepin and Kicheyev and Passek, who has a telephone receiver in his ear [...]

When you come to Yalta, let me know the same evening over the telephone without fail. Do give me that pleasure. I repeat, I want very, very much to see you – remember that; but if you leave Petersburg after May 1st and stop in Moscow for a day or two, we will arrange a meeting at a restaurant in Moscow.

I write little at present, but I read very much. I read *Rus*, to which I am a subscriber. Today I read the *Collection*, published by the Association for Learning, with Gorki's 'Man', which reminded me very much of a sermon by a beardless young priest pronouncing broad vowels in a bass voice. I also read the superb story by Bunin, 'Blacksoil'. It really is an excellent story; there are passages simply amazing in it, and I commend it to your attention.

If I am well enough I will go to the Far East in July or August, not as a correspondent but as a doctor. It seems to me that a doctor will see more than a correspondent can [...]

Wir wollen,ob die Welt nun bald
vollends untergehe oder nicht,uns
an dem wenigen Guten freuen,das un-
zerstörbar ist.Mozart,Goethe,Giotto,
und auch der Heiland,der hl. Franz etc etc
etc,das alles ist genau so lang am
Leben,als noch ein Menschenherz in
ihnen zu leben und ihre Schwingungen
mitzuschwingenfähig ist.Solang ich
lebe und einen Takt Bach oder Haydn
oder Mozart vor mich hin summen oder
mich an Hölderlinverse erinnern kann,
solang sind Mozart und Hölderlin
noch nicht erloschen.Und dass es so et-
was wie Freundschaft und Treue gibt,
und hie und da Sonnenschein,und ein
Engadin,und Blumen,das ist ja auch sehr
gut.Lieber Freund,ich grüsse Euch alle
von Herzen und mit vielen guten Wün-
schen, auch von Ninon.   Ihr H Hesse

14.5.1931

Lieber Freund Englert

Heut ist Himmelfahrtstag,und Ihr
lieber Brief trifft mich wahrhaftig
immer noch in Zürich,aber heut ist
der letzte Tag,Ninon ist jetzt endlich mit ihren Vorhängen,Lampen,Ta-
peten und Kochhäfen hier fertig ge-
worden,und morgen Mittag fahren wir
endlich ins Tessin.Da steht uns eine
unruhige Zeit bevor.Einziehen können
wir vor Juli nicht,und Ninon muss sch
schon vorher aus ihrer jetzigen Wohn-
ung heraus,und dann kommt der Umzug
etc. Hoffentlich geht es mir dann
besser als grade jetzt,ich habe mit
den Augen böse Wochen hinter mir,und

Hermann Hesse (1877–1962) to Joseph Englert
14 May 1931

Hermann Hesse's books are full of travel. In his 1922 novel *Siddhartha* – a bible of the questing 1960s counterculture – the eponymous hero wanders through ancient India in search of enlightenment. As a young man, Hesse himself had a taste for adventure, spending three months in the Far East in 1911. But the following year, he moved with his family from Germany to Switzerland, in protest against the rising nationalism in his home country. And after that, as he tells his friend Joseph Englert, he barely left.

Englert was an engineer with unusual interests. Once a disciple of Rudolf Steiner, he had turned to astrology – and Hesse had turned to him for a horoscope when, in the wake of the First World War, he was going through a personal crisis. Feeling alienated from European society, Hesse had left his wife and children in Bern and moved to the village of Montagnola. Englert lived nearby, and is thought to have been the inspiration for the Armenian astrologer in Hesse's 1919 novella, *Klingsor's Last Summer*, about a debauched, dying painter.

By 1931, Hesse's life is calmer. He is happily married to Ninon, his third (and final) wife, and they divide their time between Zurich and the Swiss countryside, with scenes of which he often illustrates his letters. His latest novel, *Narcissus and Goldmund* (1930), has been widely praised. Yet there is also a sense of detachment: his 'curiosity' about the world, he tells Englert, is long gone. Given subsequent events in Germany, this attitude has been criticized. But, in his quiet way, Hesse resisted Nazi ideology, helping exiled writers like Thomas Mann and promoting the work of banned Jewish writers, including Franz Kafka (see page 141). The Second World War challenged his belief, expressed here, in the humanizing power of art – but his dedication to it saw him win the Nobel Prize in Literature in 1946.

....

My dear friend Englert,

[...] We're still in Zurich, where your kind letter reached me. It's definitely our last day here; Ninon has finally got all the curtains, lamps, carpets, and cooking equipment together, and we're leaving tomorrow [...]

I'm almost envious of your wonderful journey through Italy by car, even though I'm no longer all that curious and haven't travelled 'for fun' since the war. Just imagine: I haven't been in Italy since 1914 [...] I used to visit Italy nearly every year [...] Then the war broke out, and when it ended, I found out that I not only couldn't afford to travel but had lost much of my previous curiosity about countries and people, along with my belief in a better future. So I'm not very surprised when you say that a new world war is in the offing [...]

Regardless of whether the world is about to be destroyed or not, we want to go on enjoying those few great indestructible things in life: Mozart, Goethe, also the Saviour, St Francis [...] They will live as long as there is a human heart who comes alive through them and can dance to their rhythm [...]

Adress telegrams
To "Socialist Westrand-London.

10 Adelphi Terrace,

London, W.C.2.

Dear Madam,

I have read several fragments of Ulysses in its serial
form. It is a revolting record of a disgusting phase of civilisation; but it is a truthful one; and I should like to put a
cordon round Dublin; round up every male person in it between the
ages of 15 and 30; force them to read it; and ask them whether on
reflection they could see anything amusing in all that fouled
mouthed, foul minded derision and obscenity. To you, possibly, it
may appeal as art: you are probably (you see I don't know you)
a young barbarian beglamoured by the excitements and enthusiasms
that art stirs up in passionate material; but to me it is all
hideously real: I have walked those streets and know those shops
and have heard and taken part in those conversations. I escaped
from them to England at the age of twenty; and forty years later
have learnt from the books of Mr. Joyce that Dublin is still what
it was, and young men are still drivelling in slackjawed blackguardism just as they were in 1870. It is, however, some consolation to find that at last somebody has felt deeply enough about
it to face the horror of writing it all down and using his literary genius to force people to face it. In Ireland they try to make
a cat cleanly by rubbing its nose in its own filth. Mr. Joyce
has tried the same treatment on the human subject subject. I hope
it may prove successful.

I am aware that there are other qualities and other
passages in Ulysses; but they do not call for any special comment
from me.

I must add, as the prospectus implies an invitation
to purchase, that I am an elderly Irish gentleman, and that if
you imagine that any Irishman, much less an elderly one, would
pay 150 francs for a book, you little know my countrymen.

Faithfully,

G. Bernard Shaw.

Miss Sylvia Beach,
8, Rue Dupuytren,
Paris (6)

George Bernard Shaw (1856–1950) to Sylvia Beach
11 June 1921

James Joyce published *Ulysses* in 1922, but the world had known about the book well before then. From 1919, it was serialized in *The Little Review* in America, where the 'Nausicaa' episode – in which Leopold Bloom, Joyce's protagonist, masturbates on a beach – ultimately resulted in an obscenity charge. Publishers had reason to be wary. Finally, however, Joyce found someone willing to take the risk: Sylvia Beach, an American in Paris, who owned the Shakespeare and Company bookshop. In 1921, she sent out a 'prospectus' to influential figures in the literary world, offering limited editions. One recipient was George Bernard Shaw, who had risen from humble beginnings in Dublin to become one of Britain's best-loved dramatists with plays such as *Man and Superman* (1903) and *Pygmalion* (1913), social comedies with a philosophical edge.

Beach thought Shaw, as a senior Irishman-in-exile, would be sympathetic. Joyce was doubtful and proposed a bet: if Shaw said yes, he would buy Beach a silk handkerchief; if Shaw said no, she would buy him a box of Voltigeurs, his favourite cigars. Shaw said no. In his reply, at once tetchy and impish, he explains that Joyce's unsparing descriptions of Dublin life, which he had read in the book's serializations, are all too familiar to him, and he doesn't want to be reminded. There's no doubting Joyce's 'genius', he admits, but his subject matter is 'revolting'.

Joyce was delighted with the letter, making several copies for himself and friends – and claiming his cigars.

....

Dear Madam,

I have read several fragments of Ulysses in its serial form. It is a revolting record of a disgusting phase of civilisation; but it is a truthful one; and I should like to put a cordon round Dublin; round up every male person in it between the ages of 15 and 30; force them to read it; and ask them whether on reflection they could see anything amusing in all that fouled mouthed, foul minded derision and obscenity. To you, possibly, it may appeal as art [...] but to me it is all hideously real: I have walked those streets and know those shops and have heard and taken part in those conversations. I escaped them to England at the age of twenty; and forty years later have learnt from the books of Mr Joyce that Dublin is still what it was, and young men are still drivelling in slackjawed blackguardism just as they were in 1870. It is, however, some consolation to find that at last somebody has felt deeply enough about it to face the horror of writing it all down and using his literary genius to force people to face it [...]

I must add, as the prospectus implies an invitation to purchase, that I am an elderly Irish gentleman, and that if you imagine that any Irishman, much less an elderly one, would pay 150 francs for a book, you little know my countrymen.

Faithfully,
G. Bernard Shaw.

Farrar Straus & Giroux
19 Union Square West
New York, NY 10003

2 March 1988

Dear Hilda Reach,

I was very touched by your letter. It was
good of you to write me and share with
me your love and admiration for Thomas
Mann. So you were his secretary for
nine years, the last nine years of his
stay in the United States: —— you are probably
the closest living witness to that period, in
the middle of which I paid that awkward,
unforgettable visit I recount in "Pilgrimage."

You'll be interested to know that I've received
many, many letters since "Pilgrimage" came
out in The New Yorker in late December, from
people all over the United States whom I
don't know, who aren't writers, who live
(most of them) in small towns, telling me
about their bookish childhoods and
adolescences and how much, in particular,
Thomas Mann meant to them. This deluge
of letters — more than I usually receive for
something I publish — has given me
great pleasure, because it is about
beautiful feelings, chivalrous feelings,
that people today often don't feel free
to share.

Again, thank you for writing me and my
best wishes for your ⎯⎯ project of writing
your recollections of your Thomas Mann.
Cordially, Susan Sontag

S. Sontag

FARRAR, STRAUS & GIROUX, INC. *Book Publishers*

HILL & WANG   OCTAGON BOOKS

19 Union Square West, New York, New York 10003

Susan Sontag

VIA AIR MAIL

Hilda Reach
502 Euclid Street
Santa Monica, California
                    90402

ETATS-UNIS

Susan Sontag (1933–2004) to Hilda Reach
2 March 1988

In December 1987, Susan Sontag, America's star intellectual, published a long essay in *The New Yorker* about an event in her adolescence. 'Over the years,' she wrote, 'I have kept it a secret, as if it were something shameful.' In 'Pilgrimage', Sontag told how, as a precocious and forgivably pretentious teenager in late 1940s California, she had become obsessed with *The Magic Mountain*, Thomas Mann's sprawling novel of ideas set in a Swiss tuberculosis sanitorium. After reading it once, and then all 750 pages again aloud, she pressed it on her friend and fellow high-culture connoisseur Merrill Rodin. Then, to her horror, Rodin phoned Thomas Mann – who was living just down the road in Pacific Palisades, one of many artists who had fled totalitarianism in Europe for the improbable haven of the West Coast – and arranged to go for tea.

In her essay, Sontag described their awkward hour and a half with the German Nobel laureate, who 'had the stature of an oracle in Roosevelt's *bien pensant* America'. She was funny about his mannerisms ('He sat very erectly and seemed to be very, very old. He was in fact seventy-two') and honest about the frustrations of the meeting – that she wasn't able to be herself with her hero, and that he appeared to have been playing the part of mid-European sage, coming out with solemn pronouncements like: 'Both the heights and the depths of the German soul are reflected in its music.'

Sontag's recollections of Mann struck a chord with a surprising number of readers, and she was flooded with letters. One came from Hilda Reach, a German-Jewish immigrant who had been Mann's secretary for his last nine years in America, during which time the young Sontag paid her visit.

....

Dear Hilda Reach,

I was very touched by your letter. It was good of you to write me and share with me your love and admiration for Thomas Mann. So you were his secretary for nine years, the last nine years of his stay in the United States: – you are probably the closest living witness to that period, in the middle of which I paid that awkward, unforgettable visit I recount in 'Pilgrimage'.

You'll be interested to know that I've received many, many letters since 'Pilgrimage' came out in the *New Yorker*, in late December, letters from people all over the United States whom I don't know, who aren't writers, who live (most of them) in small towns, telling me about their bookish childhoods and adolescences and how much, in particular, Thomas Mann meant to *them*. This deluge of letters [...] has given me great pleasure, because it is about beautiful feelings, chivalrous feelings, that people today often don't feel free to share.

Again, thank you for writing me and my best wishes for your project of writing your recollections of your Thomas Mann.

Cordially, Susan Sontag

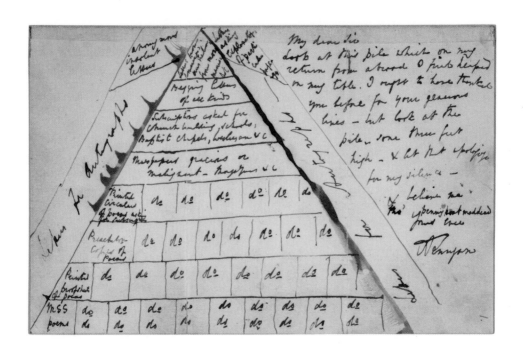

Alfred Tennyson (1809–92) to William Cox Bennett
22 October 1864

Returning from a family holiday in Brittany and Normandy in September 1864, Alfred Tennyson discovered 'a whole monticule of letters and poems on my drawing room table'. For all his jokey complaints about his postbag, he can't have been surprised. Following his appointment as poet laureate on William Wordsworth's death in 1850, Tennyson became the great public bard of the Victorian age. He looked and acted the part, striking all who met him with his craggy air of Romantic genius.

Tennyson set about clearing his desk, writing within days to acknowledge a royalty payment from his American publisher, James Thomas Fields, and reply to an enquiry from the German publisher Bernhard von Tauchnitz. It took another month to get round to thanking the journalist William Cox Bennett for his 'generous lines' – perhaps an appreciation of Tennyson's new narrative poem, *Enoch Arden*, published in August. By this time, Tennyson must have made inroads into the letter mountain 'three feet high', but he wanted to sweeten his apology to Bennett by making him smile.

He drew a pyramid resembling an archaeological diagram and labelled each level. At the apex are 'Letters from America, Australia, from Monomaniacs &c', then 'Begging letters of all kinds', 'Subscriptions asked for church building, schools, Baptist chapels, Wesleyan &c', 'Newspapers gracious or malignant – Magazines &c', 'Printed circulars of poems asking for subscriptions', 'Presentation copies of poems', 'Printed proofsheets of poems' and finally 'MSS poems', with the inner 'bricks' of the pyramid marked 'do' (ditto). There's an outer layer, starting with 'Anonymous insolent letters' and 'Letters asking explanation of particular passages', then on each side, 'Letters for Autographs'.

The photographer Julia Margaret Cameron – another Isle of Wight neighbour – reported that Tennyson believed that 'every vice of the world was connected with the passion for autographs and anecdotes and records, – that the desiring anecdotes and acquaintance with the lives of great men was treating them like pigs to be ripped open for the public'. Friends observed his refusal to embrace celebrity. Walking with the artist and writer Edward Lear one day, Tennyson insisted on returning 'by muddy paths (over our shoes)' to avoid being recognized by villagers. Yet the same day he wrote to Bennett, he had a visit from the photographer J.J.E. Mayall, for whom he posed with face upturned in poetic reverie, wild hair swept back – a photo that became the most widely reproduced image of Tennyson.

My dear Sir

Look at this pile which on my return from abroad I find dumped on my table. I ought to have thanked you for your generous lines – but look at this pile, some three feet high, & let that apologize for my silence –

 believe me
 tho' penny post maddened
 Yours ever
 A Tennyson

À Octave Mirbeau

Cher confrère,
Ce n'est qu'avant hier que j'ai
reçu votre lettre.
Je crois que chaque nationa-
lité emploie différents moyens
pour exprimer dans l'art
l'idéal commun à toute
l'humanité et c'est à cause
de cela que nous éprouvons
une jouissance particulière
à voir notre idéal exprimé
d'une manière nouvelle
et inattendue pour nous.
L'art français m'a donné
jadis ce sentiment de dé-
couverte ~~que~~
quand j'ai lu pour la première

fois les œuvres de Rousseau, de
Vigni, de Stendhal, de V. Hugo
et surtout de Rousseau.
Je crois que c'est au même
sentiment qu'il faut attribuer
la trop grande importance
que vous attachez aux écrits
de Dostoïewsky et surtout
aux miens.
Dans tous les cas je vous
remercie pour votre lettre
et votre dédicace qui m'a
fait plaisir.
S'il est vrai, comme disent
les journaux, que vous avez
écrit un drame du temps
de la grande révolution
je me promets une grande
jouissance de le lire.
                    Léon Tolstoy.
12 octobre 1903

Leo Tolstoy (1828–1910) to Octave Mirbeau
12 October 1903

By his seventies, Leo Tolstoy had become a uniquely Russian institution – both a literary giant and an opinionated Christian sage, the restless yet grandfatherly conscience of the nation. Advocating a simple life, expressed in vegetarianism and wearing peasant clothes, he had taken to disparaging the novels he'd written as a younger man. No matter that many readers considered *War and Peace* and *Anna Karenina* the greatest novels ever written, in any language – Tolstoy turned instead to producing moral parables and essays, like 'Work, Death, and Sickness' and 'To the Orthodox Clergy', both published in 1903.

Tolstoy replies to a letter from the influential French critic and popular novelist Octave Mirbeau, addressing him as a *confrère* or brother writer. In fluent though ponderous French (the language spoken in Russian aristocratic households in his youth), he recalls the 'profound pleasure' he experienced when he first recognized his own ideals reflected in the works of French writers. This sort of pleasure, he suggests, can make us overestimate foreign literature, hence 'the too great importance' ascribed to his own and Dostoevsky's novels in France.

Mirbeau was having a good year. His play *Les Affaires sont les affaires* (*Business Is Business*) had premièred in Paris that April. Satirizing the nouveau-riche plutocracy of the Belle Époque in the predatory figure of the press baron Isidore Lechat, it became an international hit. In May, he inscribed a copy of the script to Tolstoy, posting it with a letter in which he showered the Russian master with hyperbolic praise. But Mirbeau's long-term project, a French historical novel to rival *War and Peace*, was going nowhere (the first three chapters were eventually posthumously published). This may be the 'play' that Tolstoy has seen mentioned in the press. He is evidently still interested in what his literary contemporaries are up to, though the rather remote tone of his response to Mirbeau's blandishments is that of a player who has determinedly hung up his boots.

....

Dear *confrère*,

I only received your letter the day before yesterday.

I observe that each nationality employs different means to express in art the ideal that is shared by all humanity and that as a result we experience a particular profound pleasure in seeing our ideal expressed in a new and unexpected manner. French art once gave me this feeling of discovery when I read for the first time the works of Alfred de Vigny, Stendhal, V. Hugo and above all Rousseau. I think this same feeling must be responsible for the exaggerated importance ascribed to the writings of Dostoevsky and above all my own.

In any event, I thank you for your letter, and for your dedication, which pleased me greatly.

If it true, as the newspapers report, that you have written a play about the time of the great revolution, I look forward to the great delight of reading it.

Léon Tolstoy

William Wordsworth (1770–1850) to John Wilson
7 June 1802

After an itinerant decade, William Wordsworth was recently settled in Grasmere, in the Lake District, when in June 1802 he received a fan letter. The author was John Wilson, a precocious Scottish student and fledgling poet, who spoke rapturously of *Lyrical Ballads*, which Wordsworth had published with Samuel Taylor Coleridge in 1798. Rejecting the 'artifice' of eighteenth-century poetry in favour of 'the very language of men', *Lyrical Ballads* served as a manifesto for the Romantic movement. Wilson told Wordsworth that his poems had 'made an impression on my mind that nothing will ever efface'. There was just one he had doubts about, 'The Idiot Boy', dealing with the relationship between a mother and her disabled son. For Wilson, it had 'nothing in it to excite interest'. The feelings it described were 'natural', but 'they do not please'. The young upstart didn't expect his hero to reply.

In fact, Wordsworth responded at length, in a letter that is both generous and, in places, decidedly prickly. Defending his poem, he reiterates a point made in the preface to *Lyrical Ballads* – that poetry shouldn't simply exist to please the educated classes. And he makes clear that he regards poets as teachers, widening their readers' range of sympathy.

Wordsworth and Wilson stayed in touch. Several years later, after academic glory at Magdalen College, Oxford, Wilson moved to the Lake District, where he became close friends with the Wordsworth family, as well as Coleridge and Thomas de Quincey.

[...] You begin what you say upon the 'Idiot Boy', with this observation, that nothing is a fit subject for poetry which does not please [...] Does not please whom? Some have little knowledge of natural imagery of any kind, and, of course, little relish for it [...] some cannot bear to see delicate and refined feelings ascribed to men in low conditions in society, because their vanity and self-love tell them that these belong only to themselves [...] others are disgusted with the naked language of some of the most interesting passions of men [...] I return then to [the] question, please whom? or what? I answer, human nature as it has been [and ever] will be. But, where are we to find the best measure of this? I answer, [from with] in; by stripping our own hearts naked, and by looking out of ourselves to [wards men] who lead the simplest lives [...]

People in our rank in life are perpetually falling into one sad mistake, namely, that of supposing that human nature and the persons they associate with, are one and the same thing. Whom do we generally associate with? Gentlemen, persons of fortune, professional men, ladies, persons who can afford to buy, or can easily procure books of half-a-guinea price [...] These persons are, it is true, a part of human nature, but we err lamentably if we suppose them to be fair representatives of the vast mass of human existence [...]

Médan, 24 juin 95

Mon cher Léon, j'achève les "Kamtchatka," sous mes arbres, et je veux vous remercier du très bonnes heures que votre livre vient de me faire passer. Vous savez que ce que j'aime en vous, c'est la belle fougue, la passion, l'outrance même; et il y a là, dans la satire, une gaieté féroce qui m'a ravi. Peut-être tous les niais et les gâtés que vous flagellez ne méritaient-ils pas une si verte volée. Mais cela, le commencement surtout, est amusant au possible.

Vous êtes en train de vous faire une jolie collection d'enne-

Émile Zola (1840–1902) to Léon Daudet
24 June 1895

Émile Zola's summer reading in 1895 included *Les 'Kamtchatka': moeurs contemporaines* ('The "Kamtchatkas": Modern Manners'), a collection of satirical vignettes published by Léon Daudet, the twenty-six-year-old journalist son of his novelist friend Alphonse Daudet. Léon clearly valued Zola's opinion – he was, after all, the most successful novelist in France. Writing to thank him for the book, Zola sounds as if he's genuinely enjoyed it. It's an encouraging letter to a younger writer, with a gentle note of critical caution: don't too get too carried away by your lively satirical gifts, the master of naturalist fiction seems to be saying.

Zola describes reading *Les 'Kamtchatka'* 'under my trees', in the garden of his country mansion in the village of Médan, north-west of Paris. He'd bought the house after sales from *L'Assommoir* (*The Drinking Den*, 1877) made him rich. This novel of working-class life in Paris was the seventh in his twenty-novel series, the Rougon-Macquart, charting the fortunes of successive generations of two families in nineteenth-century France. The last of the series, *Le Docteur Pascal* (*Doctor Pascal*), came out in 1893. His letter has a retrospective tone, as if the 'extravagance' of Daudet's satire has made Zola, the 'old war horse', recall more passionately engaged times in his own writing life.

Zola's most famous battle against injustice was, however, still to come. The life sentence handed down to Captain Alfred Dreyfus in January 1895, on charges of spying for the Germans, had aroused little controversy until, in August 1896, evidence of a cover-up emerged. The innocent but Jewish Dreyfus had been the victim of institutionalized anti-Semitism in the French military. A rigged retrial took place, at which his conviction was upheld. In January 1898, Zola published 'J'Accuse…!', an open letter excoriating the government for anti-Semitism and acting unlawfully. In February, Zola was tried for criminal libel and fled to England to avoid imprisonment, returning to France the following year, when the Supreme Court ordered a retrial for Dreyfus. Léon Daudet, a deep-dyed anti-Semite for whom Dreyfus was 'a wreck from the ghetto', turned the 'wild gaiety' of his satire against anyone, including Zola, who stood up for truth in the Dreyfus case or questioned the actions of the state.

....

My dear Léon, I've finished 'Kamtchatka' under my trees, and I thank you for the very enjoyable hours your book has given me. You know what I like about you, it's the fine impulsiveness, the passion, extravagance even. And there is, in the satire, a wild gaiety that very much appealed to me. Maybe all the fools and losers that you lay into don't deserve such a lively thrashing. But all of that – especially the beginning – couldn't be funnier. You're on the way to making yourself a fine collection of enemies. They'll keep you warm in your old age. That reminds me a bit of my glory days, and I sometimes trembled, reading you, like an old war horse who hears the bugle.

Yours with best wishes,
Émile Zola

Chapter 8

'That's all'

ect upon my own decline, I w

I've had a very light wooden

ry shawl; she loved it so. But

er amusement, to excite curio

prefer to end my life at the ri

this long night! I, who am mo

t let my brass pig be lost. I sh

rite **Leave Taking** of these wo

e remembered after my death

me. This is not a good method

e review is Hemlock to a suck

t people to see, and if there i

the world, – though I by no m

d can promise me a safe del

feel bound to fulfil a final ob

se them to pay my taxes. The

I think you ought to marry ag

n beneath the earth. I hope y

340

Ra.d. April & 6.o.th 1821

Dear Murray —

I sent you by last post a short packet — which will not do for publication (I suspect) being as the Apprentices say — "damned low!" — I put off also for a week or two sending the Italian Scrawl which will form a Note to it. — the reason is that letters being opened I wish to "bide a wee". —

Well — have you published the Trag.? and does the letter take? —

Is it true — what Shelley writes me that poor John Keats died at Rome of the Quarterly Review? I am very sorry for it — though I think he took the wrong line as a poet — and was spoilt by Cockneyfying and Suburbing — and versifying Tooke's Pantheon and Lempriere's Dictionary. — —

Lord Byron (1788–1824) to John Murray
26 April 1821

In the weeks after John Keats (see page 113) died in Rome in February 1821, a rumour went the rounds in literary circles that he'd been killed by a hatchet job in the *The Quarterly Review*. The aristocratic *homme fatal* Lord Byron had never had much time for Keats, the sickly son of a stable manager. As poets, they were poles apart. Byron, an admirer of the urbane verse of the eighteenth century, dismissed Keats's work as 'mental masturbation – he is always frigging his imagination'. Keats, meanwhile, thought Byron's fame was due more to looks than talent. 'You see what it is to be six foot tall and a Lord,' he sighed, after seeing his rival praised in print.

Byron was living in Ravenna, north-east Italy, having moved there in 1819 to be with the nineteen-year-old Countess Teresa Guiccioli. Besides drinking, shooting and supporting the revolutionary Carbonari, he was enjoying one of his most productive periods, which resulted in *The Prophecy of Dante* and three cantos of *Don Juan*, as well as the poetic dramas *Marino Faliero*, *Sardanapalus*, *The Two Foscari* and *Cain*. In this letter to his publisher, John Murray, he refers to the notorious review of Keats's narrative poem *Endymion* by John Wilson Croker, which had appeared in 1818. Croker sneered that Keats must have written under a pseudonym, since 'we almost doubt that any man in his senses would put his real name to such a rhapsody'. Byron wonders whether his friend Shelley (see page 123) is right – that it was this review, rather than tuberculosis, that caused Keats's death. He recalls his own rough treatment at the hands of the critic Francis Jeffrey. But he can't resist contrasting Keats's sensitivity with his own raffish insouciance, knocking back 'three bottles of claret' as an antidote to hurt pride. If he feels a twinge of guilt over his own disparagement of Keats ('sorry' is changed to 'very sorry'), it doesn't last long. His characterization of Keats's work as *Lemprière's Classical Dictionary* in verse has the ring of a well-worn dinner-party quip.

Dear Moray. –

[...] Is it true what Shelley writes me that poor John Keats died at Rome of the Quarterly Review? I am very sorry for it – though I think he took the wrong line as a poet, and was spoilt by Cockneyfying, and Suburbing, and versifying Tooke's Pantheon and Lempriere's Dictionary.

I know by experience that a savage review is Hemlock to a suckling author – and the one on me [...] knocked me down – but I got up again. – Instead of bursting a blood-vessel – I drank three bottles of claret – and began an answer – finding that there was nothing in the Article for which I could lawfully knock Jeffrey on the head in an honourable way. – However I would not be the person who wrote the homicidal article – for all the honour & glory in the world, – though I by no means approve of that School of Scribbling – which it treats upon [...]

Всем

В том, что умираю не вините никого и по-
жалуйста не сплетничайте. По-
койник этого ужасно не
любил.

Мама сестры и товарищи
простите — это не способ (дру-
гим не советую) но у
меня выходов нет.

Лиля — люби меня.

Товарищ правительство,
моя семья это Лиля
Брик, мама, сестры и
Вероника Витольдовна По-
лонская.
Если ты устроишь

Vladimir Mayakovsky (1893–1930) to 'All of you'
12 April 1930

Imprisoned at the age of sixteen for revolutionary activism, Vladimir Mayakovsky began writing poetry. Later at Moscow Art School, he co-founded an experimental literary group that in 1912 produced *A Slap in the Face of Public Taste*, the Russian Futurist manifesto. Mayakovsky became the movement's bad-boy star: strikingly tall, conspicuous in his trademark home-made yellow shirt, he toured Russia, performing his explosive, confrontational verse. In 1915, he fell in love with Lily Brik, whose husband, Osip, infatuated with Mayakovsky, published several collections of his poetry. When the Bolshevik Revolution came in 1917, Mayakovsky pledged his support.

Producing a stream of poems, plays and scripts for films in which he also acted, Mayakovsky became the most audible literary voice of the new Soviet state. He edited the journal of the Left Art Front and gave barnstorming recitals at the Bolshoi Theatre and Red Hall in Moscow. Under Stalin's leadership in the 1920s, however, experimental literature increasingly attracted official censure. Mayakovsky was condemned for being too obscure. At a reading in April 1930, a student audience heckled him.

Though his sexual relationship with Lily Brik was over, she remained his soulmate. He was now, however, involved with a young actress, Veronika Polonskya, whose refusal to divorce her husband led to violent rows. Leaving Mayakovsky's Moscow flat after the last of these, on 14 April 1930, Polonskaya reportedly heard a loud bang and returned to find her lover shot through the heart. The exact circumstances of his death remained ambiguous. Neighbours spoke of hearing two shots, the fatal bullet did not match Mayakovsky's pistol – there was talk of assassination. His suicide note, written two days earlier, is a puzzling mixture of solicitude for his family, ambiguous irony ('Comrade Government'), concern for settling his tax bill and a poem whose opening lines – 'Love boat/has crashed against the daily grind' – are reprised from earlier poems.

....

To All of You:

Don't blame anyone for my death, and please, don't gossip about it. The deceased hated gossip.

Mama, sisters, comrades, forgive me. This is not a good method (I don't recommend it to others), but for me there is no other way out.

Lily, love me.

Comrade Government, my family consists of Lily Brik, mama, sisters and Veronika Polonskaya.

If you can, provide a decent life for them. Thank you [...]

Love boat/has crashed against the daily grind/I don't owe life a thing/and there is no point/in counting over/mutual hurts,/harms/and slights.

Best of luck to all of you!

Vladimir Mayakovsky

4/12/30 [...]

In the desk drawer I have 2,000 roubles. Use them to pay my taxes. The rest can be obtained from the State Publishing House.

LETTER LEFT WITH KAY TO BE OPENED AFTER HER DEATH)

September 9, 1919

My darling Boy

I am leaving this letter with Mr. Kay just in case I should pop off suddenly and not have the opportunity or the chance of talking over these things.

If I were you I'd sell off all the furniture and go off on a long sea voyage on a cargo boat, say. Don't stay in London. Cut right away to some lovely place.

Any money I make is yours, of course. I expect there will be enough to bury me. I don't want to be creamated and I don't want a tombstone or anything like that. If it's possible to choose a quiet place, please do. You know how I hate noise.

Should any of my friend care for one of my books to remember me by- use your discretion.

All my MS. I simply leave to you.

I think you had better leave the disposal of all my clothes to L.M.

Give the wooly lamb to Brett, please, and also my black fox fur.

I should like Anne to have my flowery shawl; she loved it so. But that is as you think.

Jeanne must have the greenstone.

Lawrence the little golden bowl back again.

Give Pa all that remains of Chummie.

Perhaps I shall have something Chaddie would like by then. I have nothing now- except perhaps my chinese skirt.

See that Rib has an honorable old age and don't let my

Katherine Mansfield (1888–1923) to John Middleton Murry
9 September 1919

Katherine Mansfield began a relationship with the writer and editor John Middleton Murry in 1911, the year she published her first short story collection, *In a German Pension*. Though she left him twice in the next two years, Murry would be one of the more stable features in Mansfield's emotional landscape: they married in 1918. After moving to Britain from her native New Zealand, Mansfield had established herself in London's progressive literary circles, where friends included Virginia Woolf and D.H. Lawrence (see pages 65 and 143). In 1917 she was diagnosed with tuberculosis, for which the standard prescription was still – as in Keats's or Chekhov's time – to decamp to somewhere with a reliably mild autumn and winter climate.

In September 1919, Murry, Mansfield and her college friend Ida Baker (aka Lesley Morris or LM) set off for San Remo in Italy. Spooked by Mansfield's symptoms, the hotel manager turned them away, so they rented a villa nearby. Mansfield and Baker planned to stay six months, while Murry – newly appointed editor of the *Atheneum*, a leading literary journal – returned to London. Shortly before they set off, fearing she might not come home, Mansfield had typed out her will in the form of a letter for Murry to open after her death. 'One knows how easy it is to die,' she told him, after an alarmingly cold turn in the weather. 'The barriers that are up for everybody else are down for you and you've only to slip through.'

....

My darling Boy

I am leaving this letter with Mr Kay just in case I should pop off suddenly and not have the opportunity or the chance of talking over these things.

If I were you I'd sell off all the furniture and go off on a long sea voyage on a cargo boat, say. Don't stay in London. Cut right away to some lovely place.

Any money I make is yours, of course. I expect there will be enough to bury me. I don't want to be creamated and I don't want a tombstone or anything like that. If it's possible to choose a quiet place, please do. You know how I hate noise [...]

All my MS. I simply leave to you.

I think you had better leave the disposal of all my clothes to LM.

Give the wooly lamb to Brett, please, and also my black fox fur.

I should like Anne to have my flowery shawl; she loved it so. But that is as you think.

Jeanne must have the greenstone.

Lawrence the little golden bowl back again [...]

See that Rib has an honourable old age and don't let my brass pig be lost. I should like Vera to have it.

That's all. But don't let anybody *mourn* me. It can't be helped. I think you ought to marry again and have children. If you do give your little girl the pearl ring.

Yours forever

Wig

K. Mansfield Murry. (for safety's sake.

Marseille le 10 Juillet 1891

Ma chère Sœur

J'ai bien reçu tes lettres des 4 et 8 juillet. Je suis heureux que
ma situation soit enfin déclarée nette. Je vous inclus
le certificat de mon amputation, signé du Directeur de l'hôpital
de Marseille, car il paraît qu'il n'est pas permis aux
médecins de signer de tels certificats à des pensionnaires.
Gardez donc cette pièce, pour moi je n'en aurai besoin que
dans le cas de mon retour. Ne la perdez pas, joignez-la
à la réponse de l'intendance) Quant au livret, je l'ai en effet
perdu dans mes voyages. Quand je pourrai circuler je verrai
si je dois prendre mon congé ici ou ailleurs. Mais si c'est à
Marseille, je crois qu'il me faudrait en mains la réponse
autographe de l'intendance. Il vaut donc mieux que j'aie
en main cette déclaration, envoyez-moi la. Avec cela personne
ne m'approchera. Je garde aussi le certificat de l'hôpital et
avec ces deux pièces je pourrai obtenir mon congé ici.

Je suis toujours levé, mais je ne vais pas bien. Jusqu'ici
je n'ai encore appris à marcher qu'avec des béquilles et encore
il m'est impossible de monter ou descendre une seule marche.
Dans ce cas on est obligé de me descendre ou monter à bras le corps.
Je me suis fait faire une jambe en bois très légère, vernie et
rembourrée, fort bien faite (prix 50 f.) Je l'ai mise il y
a quelques jours et ai essayé de me traîner en me soulevant
encore sur des béquilles, mais je me suis enflammé le
moignon et ai laissé l'instrument maudit de côté.
Je ne pourrai guère m'en servir avant 15 ou 20 jours,
et encore avec des béquilles pendant au moins un mois,
et pas plus d'une heure ou deux par jour. Le seul
avantage est d'avoir 3 points d'appui au lieu de deux.

Arthur Rimbaud (1854–91) to Isabelle Rimbaud
10 July 1891

Into the years between fifteen, when he left his hometown in north-east France for Paris, and twenty-one, when he wrote his last poem, Rimbaud packed a lifetime's sensation and achievement. He fought for the short-lived Paris Commune of 1871 and had a notorious affair with the older poet Paul Verlaine (see page 147), shuttling between Paris, Brussels and London. All the while he was writing poems and prose – 'Le Bateau ivre' ('Drunken Boat'), *Une Saison en enfer* (*A Season in Hell*) and dozens of lyrics – that excited the literary world with their precocious command of a startlingly modern idiom.

Then he stopped writing, except for letters, and began an itinerant life, enlisting in the Dutch Colonial Army, joining a circus and eventually becoming an arms dealer in the Middle East. In Aden in early 1891, Rimbaud developed agonizing synovitis in his right knee. Returning to France, he had his leg amputated in Marseille. Here he gives his sister Isabelle a graphic description of his stop-start recovery, including a sketch of the 'light wooden leg' he has had made, and looks forward to coming home – which he did in July. In August, Rimbaud was back in hospital, where his condition deteriorated. He died on 10 November, aged thirty-seven.

My dear sister,

I have received your letters of 4 and 8 July safely [...]

I'm still out of bed, but I'm not well. So far I still haven't learnt to walk except with crutches, and still find it impossible to go up or down a single step. In which event they're obliged to lift me up or down bodily. I've had a very light wooden leg made, varnished and stuffed, very well made (price 50 francs). I put it on a few days ago and tried to haul myself about on the crutches, but the stump became inflamed and I put the accursed instrument aside [...]

I'm beginning to go on crutches again therefore. What tedium, what weariness, what sadness when I think of all my old journeys, and how active I was only five months ago! Where are the trips through the highlands, the rides on horseback, the excursions, the deserts, the rivers and the seas? [...] For I'm beginning to realize that crutches, wooden legs and mechanical legs are so many bad jokes [...] And I who'd just decided to come back to France this summer to get married! Farewell marriage, farewell family, farewell future! My life is over, I'm no longer anything but an immobile tree-stump [...]

I'd very much like to come home to you, because it's cool there, but I don't fancy there's too much ground there suitable for my acrobatic exercises. And then I'm afraid that it may go from cool to cold [...] My room is paid for until the end of July; I'll think about it and *see what I'm able to do* in the interim [...]

Write to me.

Fond regards.

RIMBAUD

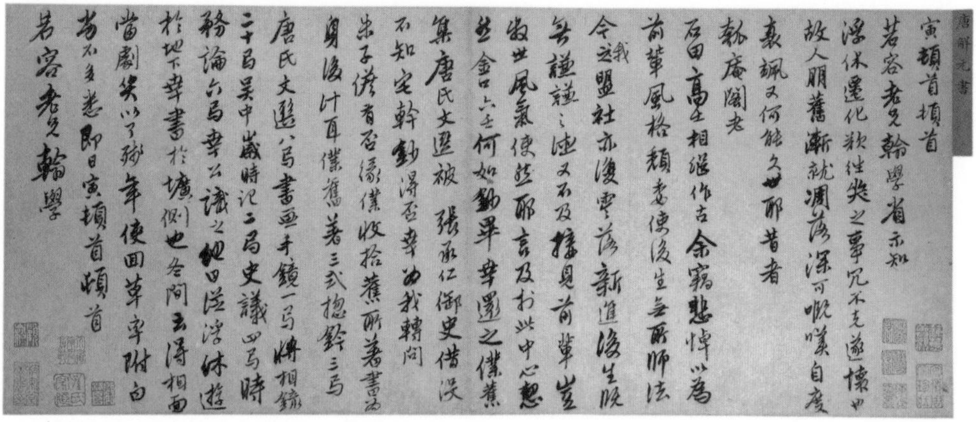

寅頓首頓首

若容老先生翰學省示知

浮休遷化歎惟類之哀兄不克遽懷也

故人凋落舊就凋落深可嘅嘆自愛

衰颯又何能久也耶昔者

勅庵閣老

石田高士相繼作古余竊悲悼以為

前輩風格類意使後生無所師法

今遂盟社亦復寥落新進後生既

無謹謹之遊又不及�前輩豈

俗世風氣使然耶言及此出中心懇

絲金石壬何如勤罪辜罔之僕焉

集唐氏文選被張承仁御史借沒

不知定幹勤得歪耷此我轉問

朱子傍者容鎰僕收拾蕉而著書法

身後汁百僕焉著三武擬鋟三與

二十昌吳中藏時汜工局史議四寫時

務論六昌辜公議之細日漾洋林遊

於坦下辜書於壙例也各閩玉浮相面

當劇笑以殘年使回草卒附白

為知多悲即日寅頓首頓首

若容老先生翰學

Tang Yin (1470–1524) to Xu Shangde
1520s

The Chinese poet Tang Yin, known as one of the 'Four Literary Masters of Wuzhong', was celebrated equally for his calligraphy and painting. Over the centuries, his life story also provided material for a series of wacky fictional retellings – he was said, for example, to have had himself sold into slavery in order to pursue a slave girl with whom he'd fallen in love. In this letter, confessing to his friend Xu Shangde that he is in 'a bad mood', Tang Yin sounds like – or acts – the typical, timeless grumpy old man. He reflects gloomily on the deaths of contemporaries, the uselessness of the younger generation and 'this degenerate age'. He's also considering his legacy, trying to get his literary oeuvre into shape before he disappears 'to roam beneath this earth'. Tang Yin's range as a writer was evidently broad, embracing art, regional culture, biography and current affairs. The note of anxiety in his appeal to Xu Shangde turned out to be warranted, however: few of the works he proudly lists survive.

[...] From your letter I learn that Fuxiu has passed away [...] How deeply lamentable it is that friends of old gradually dwindle, one by one. As I reflect upon my own decline, I wonder how much longer I can remain in this world.

Formerly Wu Kuan, who was an old hand at court, and the lofty gentleman Shen Zhou passed away one after the other. Inaudibly, I mourned in sorrow, wondering whether the high character of the senior generation had not passed away too, leaving the men of younger generation with nothing to emulate. Now our group is also at a low ebb. These latter-day successors, upstarts just freshly arrived, have neither the virtue of self-deprecation nor the chance of becoming acquainted with the seniors. Might it not be the result of the prevailing spirit of this degenerate age? [...]

I am getting together my past writings so that I might be remembered after my death. I hope that all my writings: the three volumes of the *Sanshi zongqian*, eight volumes of *Tang's Anthology*, one volume of the *Mirror of Painting and Calligraphy*, twenty volumes of *Biographies of Generals and Ministers*, two volumes of the *Annual Festivals of the Wu Region*, two volumes of *Historical Discussions*, and the six volumes of *Discussions of Current Affairs* will be remembered by you. Someday, when I have followed Fuxiu to roam beneath the earth, I hope you will write of these works on my tombstone. If we should get to meet this winter, we ought to close out the year in merry laughter.

I write this letter in haste to send back with your messenger. I shall not relate anything further since I am in such a bad mood. On the same day.

Yin.

158   Aug. 30. 1797.

I have no doubt of seeing the animal
to day; but must wait for Mrs Blenkinsop
to guess at the hour — I have sent for
her — Pray send me the news paper —
I wish I had a novel, or some
book of sheer amusement, to
excite curiosity, and while away
the time — Have you any thing of the kind?

159   Aug. 30. 1797.

Mrs Blenkensop tells me that Every thing
is in a fair way, and that there is no fear
of the events being put off till another day —
Still, at present, she thinks, I shall
not immediately be freed from my load —
I am very well — Call before dinner time unless
you receive another message from me —

160   Three o'clock.   Aug. 30. 1797

Mrs Blenkinsop tells me that I am in the
most natural state, and can promise me a safe
delivery — But that I must have a little patience

4

Mary Wollstonecraft (1759–97) to William Godwin
30 August 1797

Mary Wollstonecraft and William Godwin were two of the great radical thinkers of the eighteenth century, but their marriage, on 29 March 1797, came as a surprise. For a start, they hadn't originally liked each other much, parting 'mutually displeased' (in Godwin's phrase) after their first meeting in 1791. And both were sceptical about the institution of marriage itself. Wollstonecraft, author of *A Vindication of the Rights of Woman*, had scandalized polite society with her affairs, about which she was emphatically unapologetic ('Independence I have long considered as the grand blessing of life'). Godwin, one of the era's most prominent political philosophers and an early proponent of anarchism, had railed against 'the evil of marriage', arguing that it should be abolished. But when Wollstonecraft became pregnant, they decided that it might be a necessary evil, as they wanted the baby to be legitimate.

In any case, marriage didn't stop them doing things their way. In late spring, they moved to Somers Town, in north-west London, but lived twenty doors apart, and much of their communication was by letter. Their correspondence reflected a true marriage of equals – generous, supportive and frank. They were described as 'the most extraordinary married pair in existence', an intellectual power couple of the Enlightenment.

By late August, Wollstonecraft's pregnancy was at full term. She wrote these three notes, her last to Godwin, as she went into labour ('I have no doubt of seeing the animal today'). Her expectation of a lengthy first stage ('I wish I had a novel') was initially confirmed by the midwife. But within hours, she had given birth to a daughter. Wollstonecraft contracted a postpartum infection, dying of septicaemia eleven days later, aged thirty-eight. Her daughter would become Mary Shelley (see page 109), author of *Frankenstein* – the story of a strange birth gone wrong.

1

I have no doubt of seeing the animal to day; but must wait for Mrs Blenkinsop to guess at the hour – I have sent for her – Pray send me the newspaper – I wish I had a novel, or some book of sheer amusement, to excite curiosity, and while away the time – Have you any thing of the kind?

2

Mrs Blenkinsop tells me that Every thing is in a fair way, and that there is no fear of the event being put off till another day – still, at present, she thinks, I shall not immediately be freed from my load – I am very well – call before dinner-time, unless you receive another message from me –

3

Mrs Blenkinsop tells me that I am in the most natural state, and can promise me a safe delivery – But that I must have a little Patience

Declaração

Ehe ich aus freiem Willen und mit klaren Sinnen aus dem Leben scheide, drängt es mich eine letzte Pflicht zu erfüllen: diesem wundervollen Lande Brasilien innig zu danken, das mir und meiner Arbeit so gute und gastliche Rast gegeben. Mit jedem Tage habe ich dies Land mehr lieben gelernt und nirgends hätte ich mir mein Leben lieber vom Grunde aus neu aufgebaut, nachdem die Welt meiner eigenen Sprache für mich untergegangen ist und meine geistige Heimat Europa sich selber vernichtet.

Aber nach dem sechzigsten Jahre bedürfte es besonderer Kräfte um noch einmal völlig neu zu beginnen. Und die meinen sind durch die langen Jahre heimatlosen Wanderns erschöpft. So halte ich es für besser, rechtzeitig und in aufrechter Haltung ein Leben abzuschließen, dem geistige Arbeit immer die lauterste Freude und persönliche Freiheit das höchste Gut dieser Erde gewesen.

Ich grüsse alle meine Freunde! Mögen sie die Morgenröte noch sehen nach der langen Nacht! Ich, allzu Ungeduldiger, gehe ihnen voraus.

Stefan Zweig

Petropolis 22. II 1942

Stefan Zweig (1881–1942) to 'All my friends'
22 February 1942

On 23 February 1942, police officers in Petrópolis, south-east Brazil, discovered the bodies of the Austrian-Jewish writer Stefan Zweig and his wife, Lotte, lying hand-in-hand in their rented house. They also found a suicide letter signed by Zweig, which one of the officers pocketed. Thirty years later, now retired, he was persuaded to sell it to a German-Jewish businessman, Fritz Weil, who donated Zweig's letter to the National Library of Israel.

After publishing his first work of fiction at the age of nineteen, Zweig had become one of the most prolific and commercially successful writers in Europe, author of a string of bestselling novellas and biographies and several stage plays. Widely translated, stories such as *Letter from an Unknown Woman* and *Moonbeam Alley* sold well in North and South America as well as Europe. Even before the Nazi annexation of Austria, however, systematic anti-Semitic persecution was underway in Vienna. In 1934, Zweig had a visit from the police, who searched his apartment. Days later, he and his first wife, Friderika, left for London.

In 1938, the Zweigs divorced, and Stefan moved to Bath, where he married his secretary, Lotte Altmann. The lightning Nazi invasion of Poland the following year convinced him that only on the other side of the Atlantic would they be safe. In 1940, they sailed for New York, moving on in August 1941 to Brazil, where Zweig received a celebrity welcome. He had always seen himself as a 'citizen of the world', but after a year in Petrópolis he was clearly struggling with the prospect of indefinite exile as well as sheer exhaustion. It's possible that, in his decision 'to end my life at the right time' with an overdose of sleeping pills, he did not expect Lotte to join him (his note speaks in the first-person singular). The previous day she had finished typing up his autobiography, *The World of Yesterday*, and posted the manuscript to the publishers. When their bodies were discovered, hers was still warm.

Declaration

Before I leave my life of my own free will and with a clear mind, I feel bound to fulfil a final obligation – to give heartfelt thanks to this wonderful land of Brazil [...] Every day I learned to love this country more, and I would not have asked to rebuild my life in any other place after the world of my own language sank and was lost to me, and my spiritual homeland, Europe, destroyed itself.

But to start everything anew after a man's 60th year requires special powers, and my own power has been expended after years of wandering homeless. I thus prefer to end my life at the right time, upright, as a man for whom cultural work has always been his purest happiness and personal freedom – the most precious possessions on this earth.

I send greetings to all my friends! May they live to see the dawn after this long night! I, who am most impatient, go before them.

Stefan Zweig

20 MARTIN ROAD
CENTENNIAL PARK
SYDNEY, 2021

9. iv. 77

Dr G. Chandler
National Library of Australia
Canberra.

Dear Dr Chandler,

P23/3/978 of Folio 3 25th March. Thank you for your
I can't let you have my "papers"
because I don't keep any. My mss are
destroyed as soon as our books are printed
I put very little into notebooks, don't
keep my friends' letters as I urge
them not to keep mine, and anything
unfinished when I die is to be
burnt. The final versions of my
books are what I want people to
see, and if there is anything of importance in me, it will be in
those.

Yours sincerely,

Patrick White

Patrick White (1912–90) to George Chandler
9 April 1977

How much do we need to know about a writer's life? Nothing at all, according to the novelist Patrick White, in this letter to Dr George Chandler, director-general of the National Library of Australia. Despite his growing literary reputation during the 1960s, White had succeeded in keeping a relatively low profile. But then, in 1973, he won the Nobel Prize in Literature (the only Australian to do so). Journalists wanted interviews and, eventually, librarians wanted papers. White sent them on their way. The books, he insisted, were all that mattered.

Yet the curiosity was understandable. White's best-known work – and the one that had swayed the Nobel panel – was *The Vivisector* (1970), an unruly, unsparing novel all about the life of an artist. It follows Hurtle Duffield, a painter and weapons-grade egomaniac, and explores the terrible toll that his creative endeavours take on his personal relationships. One dissenting Nobel judge was reluctant to endorse the book, fearing it gave the impression that being an artist was fundamentally incompatible with being a decent human being.

Did White have anything to hide? Not much, it seems. He did little to conceal his homosexuality – an openness that would have been unusual in Australia at the time – and lived quietly in the Sydney suburbs with his partner, Manoly Lascaris, whom he'd met in Alexandria in 1941. (He was serving in the RAF, Lascaris in the Greek army.) But while he could be generous – he used his Nobel money to set up a writers' fund – he also had a talent for falling out with people, abruptly and often spitefully. He once cut off an old friend after she criticized his cooking. And he burnt years' worth of correspondence with another – a gesture presumably intended to hurt, rather than make a formalist point. Years later, his letter to Dr Chandler still feels like a little rebuke to those of us who rummage around in the private affairs of writers – though, in the event, White left a mountain of papers behind.

Dear Dr Chandler,

Thank you for your P23/3/978 of 25th March.

I can't let you have any of my 'papers' because I don't keep any. My mss are destroyed as soon as the books are printed, I put very little into notebooks, don't keep my friends' letters as I urge them not to keep mine, and anything unfinished when I die is to be burnt. The final revisions of my books are what I want people to see, and if there is anything of importance in me, it will be in those.

Yours sincerely,

Patrick White

Timeline

Index

Credits

The publishers thank the following for permission to reproduce the letters in this book. Every effort has been made to provide correct attributions. Any inadvertent errors or omissions will be corrected in subsequent editions.

About the authors

Michael Bird is a writer and art historian. His books include *Artists' Letters: Leonardo da Vinci to David Hockney* (White Lion Publishing, 2019), *Studio Voices: Art and Life in 20th-century Britain* and *The St Ives Artists: A Biography of Place and Time*. He is Royal Literary Fund Fellow at the University of Exeter.

Orlando Bird is a journalist. He works at the *Telegraph*, where he is deputy editor on the Letters desk and writes about books and travel. His work has also appeared in the *Financial Times* and *Literary Review*. He lives in London.

Acknowledgments

We would like to thank Sander Berg, Trevor Dadson, Alison Elgar, Carmen Fracchia, Christopher Howse, Rebecca Jeffery, Annina Lehmann, Felicity Mara, Eleanor Robertson, Masami Walton, Daniela Winter, staff at the London Library and Penryn Campus library, and Fergus the cat. It has been a great pleasure to work again with the team at Frances Lincoln – a big thankyou to our editors Nicki Davis and Michael Brunström and picture researcher Sophie Basilevitch.

Brimming with creative inspiration, how-to projects and useful information to enrich your everyday life, Quarto Knows is a favourite destination for those pursuing their interests and passions. Visit our site and dig deeper with our books into your area of interest: Quarto Creates, Quarto Cooks, Quarto Homes, Quarto Lives, Quarto Drives, Quarto Explores, Quarto Gifts, or Quarto Kids.

First published in 2021 by Frances Lincoln,
an imprint of The Quarto Group.
The Old Brewery, 6 Blundell Street
London, N7 9BH,
United Kingdom
T (0)20 7700 6700 F (0)20 7700 8066
www.QuartoKnows.com

Introduction and commentaries © 2021 Michael Bird & Orlando Bird
Illustrations and translations © as listed on pages 222–3

A catalogue record for this book is available from the British Library.

ISBN 978-0-7112-4875-5

10 9 8 7 6 5 4 3 2 1

Typeset in New Caledonia and Akkurat
Design by Paileen Currie

Printed in China